The Psych 101 Series

James C. Kaufman, PhD, Series Editor
Department of Educational Psychology
University of Connecticut

Christopher J. Ferguson, PhD, is a clinical psychologist and department chair of psychology at Stetson University in DeLand, Florida. He has done extensive research on the effects of media in realms ranging from video game and television violence to body image to advertising. He has also examined how methodological issues, researcher expectancies, questionable researcher practices, and societal pressures and incentives can create false positives in media psychology. Clinically, he has done extensive work with criminal justice populations including juvenile offenders, adult inmates, and child protective services.

In addition to his academic work, Chris is the author of a mystery novel, *Suicide Kings*, which follows a young woman in Renaissance Florence investigating her mother's death. He has also published a number of short stories, mainly in speculative fiction. He lives near Orlando with his wife and young son.

Website: www.ChristopherJFerguson.com
Twitter: CJFerguson1111
Facebook: https://www.facebook.com/SuicideKingsFerguson

Media
Psychology

Christopher J. Ferguson, PhD

SPRINGER PUBLISHING COMPANY
NEW YORK

Springer Publishing Company, LLC
11 West 42nd Street
New York, NY 10036
www.springerpub.com

Acquisitions Editor: Nancy S. Hale
Composition: Amnet

ISBN: 978-0-8261-9673-6
e-book ISBN: 978-0-8261-9674-3

15 16 17 18 19 / 5 4 3 2 1

The author and the publisher of this Work have made every effort to use sources believed
to be reliable to provide information that is accurate and compatible with the standards
generally accepted at the time of publication. The author and publisher shall not be li-
able for any special, consequential, or exemplary damages resulting, in whole or in part,
from the readers' use of, or reliance on, the information contained in this book. The
publisher has no responsibility for the persistence or accuracy of URLs for external or
third-party Internet websites referred to in this publication and does not guarantee that
any content on such websites is, or will remain, accurate or appropriate.

Library of Congress Cataloging-in-Publication Data

Ferguson, Christopher J.
  Media psychology 101 / Christopher J. Ferguson, PhD.
     pages cm
  Includes bibliographical references.
  ISBN 978-0-8261-9673-6 (print : alk. paper) — ISBN 978-0-8261-9674-3 (e-book)
  1. Mass media—Influence. 2. Mass media—Psychological aspects. I. Title.
  P94.F38 2015
  302.2301'9—dc23
                                                                    2015016538

Printed in the United States of America by Gasch Printing.

This book is dedicated to my father, Edwin, and my son, Roman, my Saturday afternoon movie buddies. And, as ever, to my wife, Diana, for her ongoing support without which I would never get anything done.

Contents

contents

Preface

verybody knows that media does or doesn't (pick one) have a profound influence on our lives and behavior. It's common sense! Except what is common sense to one person is absolute rubbish to the next. There are probably few areas of modern social science that are as fiercely and rancorously debated as is media psychology. Beginning with the Payne Fund studies of the 1930s, nearly a century of social science research has failed to definitively bring us to any conclusions. Are there any?

Media certainly is an important part of our lives. Our use of media exploded through the 20th and into the 21st centuries, such that media ranging from books to computers to cell phones are an integral part of most of our lives. Further, the line between entertainment media and industry media has become increasingly blurred. But do media profoundly shape us? Or does media merely reflect our own lives (sometimes in ways that are less than flattering)? Despite considerable hyperbole and politicking, the answers are often subtle and individualized. Or, put another way, it's often hard to give people the answer they want to hear if we are sticking close to the data.

This book concerns itself with the research on how media influences people, how people influence media, and how society even influences the way we try to answer questions about how media influences people. In addressing many of the questions about how the media influences us, the answers may surprise you. You may not like some of them. But I hope you will enjoy joining me on this exploration of this ubiquitous force in most of our lives.

Media
Psychology

Society and Media
Through History

n August 2013, entertainer and former child star Miley
Cyrus generated controversy by "twerking" at the MTV
Video Music Awards (VMAs). Twerking, if you didn't know,
is a suggestive dance move that involves considerable
wiggling of the buttocks. Personally, the outcome generally
appears more silly than erotic, but it's certainly designed to
offend those with gentler sensibilities. It's perhaps not surprising, then, that Cyrus's efforts, which included suggestive dancing
with singer Robin Thicke, raised both news headlines and
hackles. The Parents Television Council (PTC), an antimedia
advocacy group that has been involved in numerous disputes
over television content, including Janet Jackson's 2004 "wardrobe malfunction" at the Super Bowl, promptly criticized the
performance in a press release. All this criticism was, of course,
a wonderful way to draw attention and viewership to the performance, presumably the opposite of the stated intention of

those very same critics. Being a fan of neither the VMAs nor Miley Cyrus, I would not have seen the clip other than to find out what all the fuss was over. Some began to speculate that both Cyrus and the PTC calculated how to profit over the controversy, speculation that was fueled by the observation that Miley Cyrus's father, Billy Ray Cyrus, sat on the PTC's advisory board.

The Miley Cyrus twerking incident was hardly the end of the world, but it highlights the issues of concern to media psychology. Was Cyrus's behavior in some way harmful to society? Would young girls, for instance, be encouraged to sexualize themselves in imitation of Miley Cyrus? Some people observed that Cyrus received much more criticism than Robin Thicke, the male performer in the act. Is there sexism at play in how men and women are judged for their sexuality? Why do certain media events elicit such intense emotional reactions from audiences? (The Janet Jackson "wardrobe malfunction," in which her pierced nipple was visible for approximately half a second on network television, is another such example.) How do those emotional reactions shape the rhetoric of politicians and, indeed, scientists themselves? Can the social science of media effects be separated from the politics and cultural wars that so often surround media? Our personal and societal interaction with media is complex, difficult to disentangle, and often infused with great controversy. And that's part of what makes it fun!

WHAT IS MEDIA PSYCHOLOGY?

As is often the case with psychological disciplines, there is no single, agreed-upon definition of media psychology. Division 46 (2014), the Division of Media Psychology and Technology of the American Psychological Association, offers this definition: "Media Psychology applies the science of psychology, from cognitive psychology and neuroscience to clinical practice, to research, analyze and develop mediated experiences using technology with the goal of benefiting society." The division emphasizes that "media" does not necessarily imply "mass media." Bernard Luskin (2013) wrote that media psychology involves not only research into media effects, but working with media producers, developing media using psychological principles, providing education on media, and appearing in media to educate. Pamela Rutledge (2010) outlined media psychology under the following points (quoting directly):

1. Media technologies are everywhere.
2. People of all ages use media technologies a lot.
3. Young people use them the most.
4. Older people worry about younger people.
5. Technology is not going away.
6. We all worry if this is good or bad or somewhere in-between.
7. Psychology is the study of people of all ages.

Rutledge summed up her observations: "Media psychology is using #7 to answer #6 because of #1 through #5."

Media psychology has a unique challenge. Unlike studying, say, the bacteria that live in the gut of an earthworm, or whether we process words more with the left hemisphere of our brain or the right, media is an integral and often disputed part of our culture. That is to say there have been perennial struggles over the content of media and what is acceptable. Liberal elements among media producers typically try to push the envelope of what is acceptable, while more conservative elements of society push back, often with expressed worry over media effects. The case of Janet Jackson's 2004 wardrobe malfunction, mentioned earlier, is an excellent example. During the halftime performance of the 2004 Super Bowl, televised nationally, singer Justin Timberlake pulled away part of Janet Jackson's jacket to reveal (for about half a second) her exposed breast. Whether this "wardrobe malfunction" was accidental or calculated has itself been the subject of intense speculation. The brief incident elicited a firestorm

3

of both criticism and corresponding incredulity over the intensity of that criticism (so much fuss, after all, being made of a half-second of breast). The Federal Communications Commission, receiving most of those complaints, ultimately fined CBS hundreds of thousands of dollars for the incident but, in legal wrangling that lasted until 2011, the fines were ultimately overturned because of vagueness in the FCC's rules.

We might legitimately ask, what influence does brief exposure to a woman's breast have on the minds of developing children who happened to be watching the Super Bowl? But it can be challenging to remain objective when there is so much emotional and social pressure and politics in play over a media-content issue. Indeed, as we see in the next section, the history of media and society has often involved considerable push and pull between social forces advocating greater liberalization or restriction of media content.

MEDIA THROUGH HISTORY

Modern concerns about media content are nothing new. Wherever there have been efforts to entertain through media, there have been critics concerned about the deleterious effect of such efforts on youth. No one really knows when Homo sapiens began to attempt to entertain each other through some form of early media. Dance, music, and storytelling may have emerged soon after the emergence of symbolic thought and language, although such expressions don't leave physical traces in the sense that tools do.

The oldest forms of artistic expression for which we do have records are cave paintings. Such art ranges from simplistic drawings and shapes to more elaborate depictions of hunting, dancing, and religious symbolism. The earliest known cave art is thought to be about 40,000 years old (Pike et al., 2012). This is a rough estimate of course—carbon dating isn't always precise, older paintings may have washed or faded away, and so on. But we can say that modern humans were interested in some form of media at least 40,000 years ago, if not longer. Some of the early paintings appear to even depict sex acts. So as soon as we had cave art, we had cave porn!

As far as books or literature go, one of the earliest literary works is the *Epic of Gilgamesh*, the tale of an early Sumerian king, which is dated at approximately 2000 BCE (Hallo & Simpson, 1971). The *Epic of Gilgamesh* concerns the Sumerian king Gilgamesh, who may have been a half-forgotten historical figure, much as some speculate the Briton King Arthur may have had some historicity, ignoring all the bits about Merlin and magic swords. According to the epic, Gilgamesh is a powerful ruler but also a bit of a jerk who, among a variety of other jerkish behaviors, forces young brides to spend their wedding nights with him rather than with their new husbands. The Sumerian gods aren't exactly the best behaved either but, in this case, take umbrage at Gilgamesh's haughtiness and naughtiness. They send a beast-man, Enkidu, to fight Gilgamesh and humble him. The two heroic figures fight an epic battle (of course, this is an epic) which ends in a draw. This makes them fast friends, and Enkidu becomes a kind of spiritual leader for Gilgamesh, reforming the bad boy into a more responsible king. Together like brothers, they go on to fight all manner of naughty creatures threatening Sumer, end up annoying the Goddess of Love and War, Ishtar, whose advances Gilgamesh rebuffs (Ishtar's lovers had a habit of ending up dead, so who can blame him?), and search for the secrets of immortality.

Like plenty of books, movies, and television, *Gilgamesh* is rife with violence and sex. It is the *Game of Thrones* of its time. *Gilgamesh* is perhaps the best known of the early Sumerian legends that have survived, but themes of heroic adventure, violence, sex, rape, and cruelty are not uncommon among other Sumerian stories (Hallo & Simpson, 1971). Was the sex and violence in this origin story controversial to the Sumerian people? Were there early Sumerian advocates for the equivalent of content labels on *Gilgamesh*? Few records of public discourse exist from this time, and Sumer wasn't exactly the sort of culture that prided itself on public discourse and debate anyway, so we don't know. However, the very popularity and survival of *Gilgamesh* across such a span of time speaks volumes.

Gilgamesh makes it clear that people have always been interested in seeing explicit material in their media, whether sex or violence. Perhaps this is because such material reflects human nature (Kottler, 2011). Because of its explicit nature, however, media has often come into struggle with moral advocates who worry about the influence of media, particularly for groups society has sometimes perceived as impressionable. Currently we worry mainly about the poor, but historically society has sometimes considered the poorer classes, immigrant groups, or even all women as impressionable! Concerns about the harmful and corrupting nature of media on consumers, particularly youth, have been recorded since at least the time of the Greeks and Romans. In some of his writings, Plato appears to have cautioned against the corrupting influence of plays and poetry on youth, although as he often spoke in dialogues, it's possible he was merely repeating common folk wisdom of the day (Griswold, 2003). Plato has the distinction of being the first person to argue that youth can't distinguish fact from fiction (a belief contradicted in more recent research; see Woolley & Van Reet, 2006). His mentor, Socrates, is reported to have been suspicious even of the alphabet (McLuhan & Fiore, 1967) as a source of harm. Imagine a world with no alphabet!

Probably the most dramatic example of brutal mass media would be the Roman gladiatorial games, which featured public executions, fights between men and wild animals, and combats between trained gladiators. The Romans even featured plays in which criminals were killed to make the death scenes more realistic (Coleman, 1990; Wells, 1995). That's taking method acting to an extreme. The games were hugely popular and thought of as one means of placating the vast, poor population of Rome who were otherwise unruly and discontent. Curiously, the Romans seemed to advocate the games using a theoretical approach we would now think of as *routine activities theory* (Cohen & Felson, 1980). Routine activities theory suggests that, whatever the short-term effects of media might be, violent media can nonetheless reduce crime simply by keeping aggressive individuals busy. We discuss some recent research on movie and video game violence regarding routine activities theory when we come to those chapters, but the Romans saw the games as one method to keep the poor citizens of Rome from rioting! Whether this worked or not, early Christian theorists such as Tertullian (200 CE) and Augustine (397 CE), as well as pagan orators (e.g., Seneca, 64 CE), worried that the games would have a negative moral impact on spectators.

With the fall of the Western Roman Empire, these vicious gladiatorial games, already on the decline due to the Christianization of the Roman Empire, became a thing of the past entirely. This didn't end people's prurient interest in media. Western literature, including *Beowulf* (approximately 8th–9th century), Geoffrey of Monmouth's *History of the Kings of England* (1138, featuring the King Arthur legends), Dante's *Inferno* (1302), and the plays of Shakespeare, continued to demonstrate ongoing human interest in subjects related to violence, sex, and everything else naughty. The reemergence of popular plays in the later Middle Ages represents an essential return to the Grecian variant on mass media in the form of public performances of theater. The Roman gladiatorial games were a permanent thing of the past, yet they were replaced by the popular jousting tourneys. These battles weren't meant to be fought to the death (although deaths did happen) but still featured bloody combat between trained warriors. Public outcries regarding jousting in particular came from the Roman Catholic Church (National Jousting Association, 2008), although these concerns appeared to focus on a variety of issues, from the potential for loss of life to their distracting knights from the Crusades. Despite attempts to ban the sport, it remained popular into the 17th century. This same time period also saw the popularity of public executions (which were considered public entertainment) attended by families and at which food vendors often sold their wares.

7

As the Middle Ages slowly moved into the Renaissance, a new source of controversy arose: the Christian Bible. Like many religious texts, the Bible contains a rather considerable amount of gratuitous sex and violence. But this wasn't the controversy in question. Blame Gutenberg: His invention of movable type in 1450 allowed for mass printing, potentially taking the Bible out of the Catholic monasteries that had been faithfully copying it for centuries. Because of religious reformations during this period and dissatisfaction with the Catholic Church in some areas, a market quickly emerged for non-Latin translations of the Bible. Throughout most of Christian history, the Bible was only available in Latin or perhaps Greek, languages that were inaccessible to the average person even if, by some miracle, he or she could read at all. Most people had to take their priest's word for what the Bible said. Translating the Bible into local languages had been banned as early as 1199 by Pope Innocent III in response to several heretical movements. Now a Bible translated into English by William Tyndale in 1524 came under criticism for allegedly mistranslating several words in order to promote anticlericalism (i.e., anti-Roman Catholicism). Tyndale paid the ultimate price for this transgression and was burned at the stake (Daniell, 2004). The Roman Catholic Church worried that these Bibles translated into local languages would promote heresy by convincing people to reject the Church and, instead, seek an individualized relationship with God.

The rise of mass media as we know it today was driven by Gutenberg's invention of the movable type printing press in 1450. The printing press made it possible to mass produce books, making literature cheaper to buy than the hand-printed books of the past. Slowly, and as literacy increased, books were produced more and more often to appeal to the tawdry tastes of the mass media market. By the 16th century, "true crime" books began to appear, gruesomely detailing criminal events as well as the brutal executions of the offenders (Trend, 2007). These books appear to have satisfied both a public attraction to violent depictions as well as providing a sense of justice and warning to would-be offenders.

During the same time period, some complained that popular folk songs presented criminals as heroes (Pearson, 1983).

The prototypical novel emerged in the 17th century. Among the first examples of a popular novel was *Don Quixote* by Cervantes. The book depicted a country gentleman who descends into fantasy, believing he is a medieval knight who goes chasing windmills thinking they are giants. Though certainly popular then as now, *Don Quixote* was met with a certain disdain about the quality and impact of chivalric romance novels (Kirschenbaum, 2007). By the 18th century, we begin to see the introduction of the modern novel (Trend, 2007). This time period also sees a new influx of concerns regarding the impact of literature on reader morality. In 1776, one Joseph Hanway, an English philanthropist, stated that newspapers and other "debasing amusements" were responsible for, as he put it, "the host of thieves which of late years has invaded us" (Cumberbach, 2007). Samuel Richardson's novel *Pamela*, published in 1741, was condemned for its "lewd" content and for assaulting the principles of virtue (Trend, 2007). During the 19th century, many social commentators particularly worried about the impact of novels on women readers who, it was thought, could not adequately distinguish reality from fiction (Kirschenbaum, 2007).

During the 19th century, the potential to sell large quantities of literature to a mass audience that was increasingly literate became obvious. "Dime novels" were the answer: cheap oftentimes lurid works with dubious literary value, at least according to the scions of society. Similarly, "penny dreadfuls," which looked a lot like early comic books, begin to emerge, many of them hinging upon violent or horror themes. *Varney the Vampire* (see Prest, 1847, for an archived copy) was one of the early popular stories, following the exploits of a vampire who found himself to be loathsome. Not surprisingly, given these works' content, social commentators worried about the impact of these penny dreadfuls, particularly on young boys among whom they were popular (Cumberbach, 2007). By this point, we begin to see that one factor that emerges in debates about media is the distinction between "high" and "low" culture, with elements of "low" culture (e.g., dime novels, penny dreadfuls) typically blamed for social problems.

Thus we see that culturally "elite" groups such as politicians and academics, were historically most inclined to see problems with media, particularly "low" culture media (Trend, 2007). Very often, such dialogues implied that society was "better off" or purer before the introduction of some form of "low" culture media, and that this new media has ruined culture or made society less moral.

This is something I refer to as the "Goldilocks Effect": Each generation of elders believes that the generation before them was too conservative on the issue of media, but the generation of youth after them are out of control and without moral limits. In other words, each generation thinks it got media "just right." More on that later, but for now it should be noted, however, that archaeological evidence suggests that violence was rather common in even prehistorical societies devoid of modern media (McCall & Shields, 2008), and we appear to be living now in one of the most peaceful epochs on record (Pinker, 2011).

Such data was probably less clear in the 19th century, however, and, regardless, commentators tended to worry about new trends in media sparking disastrous social downward spirals (Trend, 2007). The commentary tended to worry particularly about non-elite groups, such as low socioeconomic status (SES), working-class children and immigrant groups. These groups, along with women, were seen as particularly vulnerable to media effects. Scientific and medical terms were adopted more and more often by social critics to equate their moral beliefs with scientific reasoning and impart greater immediacy to the potential problems of media. Media regulation and censorship became more than a moral issue, but rather a public health crisis allegedly on par with smoking and lung cancer (e.g., Bushman & Anderson, 2001).

Despite the increasing use of scientific (or pseudoscientific) lingo in cultural debates, true efforts to adopt protoscientific methodology for media effects only began during the early film era. The advent of film dovetailed with other moral issues of the early 20th century, including sexuality, temperance, and immigration, as well as a liberalizing trend in society (Trend, 2007). Thus, anti-media crusades fit into a general pattern of moral crusading for multiple causes in the early 20th century. It has been noted that these moral crusades were rooted in a sense of "inerrancy" vis-à-vis a particular set of beliefs. Some groups held that their moral beliefs were "factual," and those of other groups were wrong (Sherkat & Ellison, 1997).

In the early days of film, filmmakers began to experiment, not surprisingly, with a variety of objectionable material, including violence, sex, and nudity (see, for example, the frontal nudity of Hedy Lamarr in 1933's *Ecstasy*). During the 1930s the first social science efforts to explore the adverse effects of film began. The Payne Fund studies (Blummer, 1933) purported to find a link between movie viewing and delinquency. Arguably, these Payne Fund studies began with the conclusion that films were bad for youth and set about trying to find evidence for that belief (a tendency that often seems to continue into modern social science on media). Setting the stage for debates that would occur over the next century, critics of the Payne Fund studies noted the lack of control groups, difficulties in validly measuring aggression, and sampling problems as limiting their usefulness (Lowery & DeFleur, 1995). Taking a blank-slate approach on child development, the Payne Fund studies provided considerable fuel to the fire of belief that media exposure could harm youth.

Nonetheless, whatever their weaknesses or agenda, the Payne Fund studies were used by the U.S. government to pressure the film industry to self-censor. Prior to the 20th century, little censorship in media existed in the United States. That changed as mass media became more popular, with bannings of some books, such as *Tropic of Cancer*, and efforts to pressure other media industries to clean up their content. Despite the First Amendment, it wasn't entirely clear what the government could and couldn't legislate concerning censorship, particularly when the government declared a pressing public health interest (whether real or not). In an effort to head off looming government censorship, the motion picture industry established the Hays Code in 1930.

11

Graphic depictions of violence, the techniques of murder or other crimes, smuggling and drug trafficking, the use of liquor (unless required by the plot), revenge, safecracking, train robberies, adultery (which was not to be presented as an attractive option), interracial relationships, sexually transmitted diseases, nudity, and even "lustful kissing" were all forbidden or strictly controlled under the Hays Commission.

Despite a considerable self-censorship regime in the movie industry, concerns regarding the impact of media on youth resurfaced in the 1950s. Films such as *Rebel Without a Cause* (1955) seemed to be marketed more and more toward a younger audience and seemed to promote rebelliousness (Trend, 2007). Concern over the insidious effects of media became part of a culture paranoid over communism and other "anti-American" influences.

During the 1950s, comic books took center stage of the controversy. Many comic books of this time were horror or crime focused and included graphic, if cartoonish, depictions of violence and scantily clad women. Naturally, such comic books were a hit with young males. One psychiatrist, Dr. Frederic Wertham, published a book called *Seduction of the Innocent* (1954/1996), which claimed that comic books were a major cause of juvenile crime. During testimony before Congress, Wertham also claimed that comic books promoted homosexuality, as characters such as Batman and Robin were secretly gay. Although Wertham's book was anecdotal rather than based on empirical research, it touched off considerable concern, which ultimately came to the attention of the Senate Subcommittee on Juvenile Delinquency. Rather than risk open censorship, the comic book industry, like the movie industry, volunteered to rigidly self-regulate, a move which doomed many comic books with violent content.

Wertham himself, through the lens of history, has gradually come to represent not so much a righteous battle against corrupting media but overzealous moral crusading. In one recent analysis, Tilley (2012) argued that he manipulated his own data and misrepresented or altered the biographies of adolescents he interviewed to support his thesis that comic books were damaging.

The Rise of Television

The great thing about moral debates on media is, just as people get used to one form of media, something new comes along to push the envelope. By the 1950s and 1960s, this was television. Television ownership became prevalent during the 1950s (although it had been introduced the decade before). With television, the potential for visual mass media to reach audiences increased considerably. Radio had already been popular, and some radio shows included violence, although this was narrated, not viewed directly. Television, like movies, was a visual media foremost; unlike movies, television could be viewed every day, for hours on end, for practically no cost at all. The potential for viewers to greatly increase their diet of mass media was apparent. Shows with violent content, including westerns such as *Bonanza* and *Have Gun, Will Travel* and crime shows such as *Dragnet*, quickly became popular. As the advent of widespread television consumption in the 1950s was followed, in the United States, by a precipitous rise in violent crime a decade and a half later, many commentators were given to wondering whether there might be a causal link between the two (e.g., Bushman & Anderson, 2001; Centerwall, 1989). Yet this rise in violent crime appears to have been fairly unique to the United States, with other countries introducing violent television seeing no similar violent-crime rises. The example of the island of St. Helena provided an interesting opportunity to test the effects of introducing television. St. Helena received television access for the first time in 1995. Aggression in schoolchildren was tracked for the period just before and just after television's introduction (Charlton, Gunter, & Coles, 1998). Rather surprisingly, aggression among school children *decreased* in the 2-year period following the introduction of television. Nonetheless, a more long-term follow-up might produce different results.

Although early television welcomed violent content, sex was different. The introduction of sexuality on television was slow. This can be witnessed in viewing clips of some of the 1950s television classics such as *I Love Lucy*. Lucille Ball and Desi Arnaz were married in real life and played the main married couple in the show. Despite this, when shown in their bedroom, they slept in separate twin beds and dressed in pajamas that looked like snowsuits. Even something as simple as a flush toilet could not be depicted in early television because of perceived audience sensibilities!

Beginning in the 1960s, crime in the United States (which ultimately declined again beginning in the 1990s; see Federal Bureau of Investigation, 1951–2012) began to rise precipitously, giving fuel to concerns linking television to societal violence. Criminologists tend to agree that this rise in violence was due to multiple factors including civil strife and the counterculture movement, the Vietnam War, racial disparities, a downturn in the economy, increased poverty, and increased availability and trade in illicit drugs, among other factors (see Savage, 2008). But the rise in violence in the 1960s appeared to correlate with the introduction of television the decade before. Was it possible that a generation brought up on television had become significantly more violent than previous generations? Thinking so involved ignorance of an entire history of vicious human behavior (Pinker, 2011), but following on the relatively peaceful years of the late 1940s and 1950s, it was tempting to see a correlation.

As such, social science interests in media effects that had rather died off after the Payne Fund studies increased once again. Media effects research particularly saw a lift following the "bobo doll" studies of Albert Bandura (1965). In brief, these studies had children watch adults in filmed sequences engage in a series of aggressive acts against a bobo doll (an inflatable toy doll designed to be boxed or hit). So, for instance, the models would sit on the bobo doll and punch it in the nose or whack it with a mallet. The researchers then irritated the children by showing them a host of toys that they were not allowed to play with before

14

bringing them to the test room with the bobo doll. Children who had seen an adult model aggressive behaviors were more likely to engage in similar behaviors. Although the bobo doll studies are not media violence studies per se, they purport to demonstrate that aggression can be imitated by children.

However, the bobo doll studies have also been demonstrated to have serious limitations (Gauntlett, 2005). First, the effects appear to be small overall and evaporate very quickly. Second, the "aggression" in the study was directed at an object, not another person, and it remains unclear if the studies' results can be generalized to real-life aggression against people. Related to that is the concern that the entire situation is contrived; after all, one might ask, what else are you supposed to do with a bobo doll other than hit it? Third, it is unclear whether the children were necessarily more motivated to engage in aggression in general, as opposed to mimicking *specific* aggressive acts. In other words, overall aggressive behaviors may not have changed much, but the style of the aggressive behaviors might have been altered because of the novel kinds of aggressive behaviors presented. Fourth, it is unclear that the children were necessarily motivated by aggression, as opposed to aggressive play or even the desire to please the adult experimenter. Children are quite used to being given instructions by adults, and they may arguably have simply viewed the models (who were adults) as instructors telling them what to do. In other words, the children may have even believed that they might be scolded or punished if they didn't follow the model's lead. Last, Bandura (1965) found that showing the model being punished for attacking the bobo doll decreased modeled behaviors in child participants. Yet the punishments themselves appeared to involve considerable aggressive behavior. As described in the original text (Bandura, 1965, p. 591):

> For children in the model-punished condition, the reinforc-
> ing agent appeared on the scene [this occurs after the chil-
> dren watched the model hit the bobo doll] shaking his finger

menacingly and commenting reprovingly, "Hey there you big bully. You quit picking on that clown. I won't tolerate it." As the model drew back he tripped and fell, and the other adult sat on the model and spanked him with a rolled up magazine while reminding him of his aggressive behavior. As the model ran off, cowering, the agent forewarned him, "If I catch you doing that again, you big bully, I'll give you a hard spanking. You quit acting that way."

From this description it is reasonable to wonder what we can conclude when it appears that children are willing to imitate aggression against an object, but viewing violence against an actual person inhibits their aggression. However one interprets the meaningfulness of the bobo doll studies, there is little doubt that they had considerable impact on the media effects debate.

The Telecommunications Act of 1996 mandated a new technology, the V-chip, into televisions. The intent of the V-chip was, in the words of President Bill Clinton, who signed the act into law, "handing the TV remote control back to America's parents so that they can pass on their values and protect their children" (CNN, 1996). Television producers were also required to develop a code for objectionable content that would warn parents about the shows on television. They could then use the V-chip to block shows with content they considered objectionable. The V-chip became something of a flop, however, and is used by only a minority of parents (15% according to the Kaiser Family Foundation, 2004). It's unclear why the V-chip, trumpeted as empowering parents, has been met with such apathy. Many have complained that the ratings for content used for television are difficult to decipher, and, although televisions come with instructions on using the V-chip, many consumers may fail to read them. Other parents may simply feel they don't need a chip to help them regulate their children's television viewing. A follow-up Kaiser Family Foundation (2007) study found that the majority of parents felt competent in monitoring their children's viewing habits, whether or not they used the V-chip. Perhaps not surprisingly, the television ratings have been condemned by the conservative activist group Parents Television Council (2007) for being too lenient regarding violent and sexual content.

The Filthy Fifteen

Roughly during this same time, music came under scrutiny. For at least a decade, with the counter-culture movement of the 1960s and the advent of heavy metal music in the early 1970s, music lyrics began to involve more sexually explicit language, violence, and profanity. By the 1980s, some politicians felt that things had gotten too extreme.

The result was the founding of the Parents Music Resource Center (PMRC) by several women connected to Washington politicians. The movement was particularly associated with Tipper Gore, wife of future Vice President (and then Senator) Al Gore. The PMRC was successful in pressing for congressional hearings on music lyrics in the mid 1980s, claiming such lyrics were damaging to youth. The PMRC also released a "Filthy Fifteen" list of bands and songs they felt were particularly egregious. On the list were acts ranging from Prince to Madonna to Judas Priest to Twisted Sister to Cyndi Lauper. For instance, Lauper's song "She Bop" was included on the list, because the "bopping" in question referred to masturbation. Apparently the PMRC was concerned Lauper would get teens running around masturbating like crazy, as if they needed Lauper's help for that. Most of these rock acts are, 30 years later, considered "classic" or tame.

Using the same threat of censorship waged against the movie, comic book, and television industries, the PMRC pressured the recording industry to provide a Parental Advisory sticker on albums or songs with explicit lyrics. Whether the advent of this sticker was a success is debatable. Certainly it provided content labels for parents, but arguably it also provided a "forbidden fruit" incentive for youth to be attracted to controversial media. This may, if anything, have accelerated the profanity in music as controversy is profitable and there's little evidence to suggest youth today hear fewer explicit lyrics than in the past.

17

The Age of Video Games

Video games as a new medium entered the fray in the late 1970s with the popularity of arcade games and the release of the Atari 2600 home console in 1977. Most early games were quite primitive and highly pixilated, although person-on-person violence did begin to emerge fairly quickly. In arcades, the game *Death Race* (1976), which involved driving a car over humanoid "gremlins," had earlier raised considerable controversy. On personal computers and game consoles, games such as *Swashbuckler* (1982), *Chiller* (1986), *Castle Wolfenstein* (1981), and *Spy vs. Spy* (1984) began introducing person-on-person violence, some rather surprisingly graphic. Controversy emerged pretty quickly with the surgeon general claiming in the early 1980s that video games were a leading cause of family violence (Cooper & Mackie, 1986).

Video games weren't the only interactive media to come under scrutiny at this time. The paper-and-pencil, role-playing game *Dungeons and Dragons* (see Cardwell, 1994), which involved playing as knights or wizards, led some to speculate that the game was so immersive it might lead to aggression, suicide, or psychosis. Little research actually examined the potential impact of *Dungeons and Dragons,* although there appears to be little evidence that the emergence of the game touched off a youth violence wave. Very likely the game took so long to play (hours for any given session) that experimental studies of the game were simply not feasible.

The late 1980s and early 1990s saw a new class of video games with better graphics and increased person-on-person violence. These included *Street Fighter* (1987), *Mortal Kombat* (1992), *Wolfenstein 3D* (1992) and, finally, *Doom* (1993). Games such as these included new levels of graphic, person-on-person violence that were not possible in the earlier pixilated games.

Fears about such games promoting real-life violence appeared realized following the Columbine High School massacre of 1999. Two adolescents, Eric Harris and Dylan Klebold, killed 12 students and a teacher before committing suicide. It was widely reported in the news media that Harris and Klebold had been fans of the violent shooter game *Doom*.

By this time, Congress had already held hearings on video game violence. Consistent with previous hearings on other media, these hearings prodded the video game industry to form the Entertainment Software Ratings Board (ESRB) to rate all video games for violent and other potentially offensive content. The ESRB content labels appear on all commercially available games. The ESRB ratings system has actually been rated as one of the best media ratings systems by the Federal Trade Commission (FTC; 2007). Not all have been happy with the ESRB ratings system, however. At about the same time the FTC praised the ESRB system, the antimedia advocacy group National Institute of Media and the Family (NIMF) claimed that the ESRB standards were not strict enough (2007). The ESRB shot back that it was the NIMF report that was flawed and inconsistent with the FTC's generally supportive appraisal of the ESRB (Gamepolitics.com, 2007). The NIMF has since ceased to operate.

As one issue for debates on video game and other violent media, the crime waves of the 1970s and 1980s began to dissipate in the early 1990s (Federal Bureau of Investigation, 1951–2012), including among youth (Childstats.gov, 2015). School shootings, despite receiving increased attention, were also on the decline (see also Bureau of Justice Statistics, 2008, for university crime data), although mass shootings remain at a steady rare level (Fox & DeLateur, 2014). It has been observed that, by the 1990s, almost all young males play violent games (Griffiths & Hunt, 1995), questioning the meaningfulness of reported "links" between violent video games and some school shooters. Also, regarding school shootings, in a report by the United States Secret Service and United States Department of Education (2002), school shooters appeared to have fairly average to low-average interest in violent media, and that an interest in violent media was not a good predictor of school shootings.

Nonetheless, horrifying mass shootings continue to fuel debates about violent video games. The 2012 shooting at Sandy

Hook Elementary School, wherein the shooter, Adam Lanza, was rumored to be a heavy player of violent video games, reawakened public debates regarding such games. However, the final investigation report by the state of Connecticut revealed that he was more interested in nonviolent video games such as *Dance, Dance Revolution* (State's Attorney for the Judicial District of Danbury, 2013).

As the new millennium unfolds, media of all sorts remain controversial. We are probably seeing an increased liberalization of sexuality, violence, profanity, and just about everything else, while technological innovations continue at a rapid pace. New media, such as social media, have begun to create new concerns. With such a heavy rate of technological progress, it is unlikely that debates over media effects will diminish in the short term. In the following chapters we look at some of those media and the debates that focus on them.

REFERENCES

Augustine. (397). *Confessions.* Retrieved October 1, 2008, from http://www.ccel.org/ccel/augustine/confessions.toc.html

Bandura, A. (1965). Influence of models' reinforcement contingencies on the acquisition of imitative response. *Journal of Personality and Social Psychology, 1,* 589–595.

Blummer, H. (1933). *Movies and conduct.* New York, NY: Macmillan.

Bureau of Justice Statistics. (2008). *Campus law enforcement, 2004-2005.* Retrieved April 2, 2008, from http://www.ojp.usdoj.gov/bjs/abstract/cle0405.htm

Bushman, B., & Anderson, C. (2001). Media violence and the American public. *American Psychologist, 56,* 477–489.

Cardwell, J. (1994). The attacks on role-playing games. *Skeptical Inquirer, 18,* 157–165.

Centerwall, B. (1989). Exposure to television as a risk factor for violence. *American Journal of Epidemiology, 129,* 643–652.

Charlton, T., Gunter, B., & Coles, D. (1998). Broadcast television as a cause of aggression? Recent findings from a naturalistic study. *Emotional and Behavioral Difficulties: A Peer-Reviewed Journal, 3,* 5–13.

Childstats.gov. (2015). *America's children: Key national indicators of well-being, 2015.* Retrieved July 26, 2015, from http://www.childstats .gov/

CNN. (1996). *Clinton praises TV execs' pledge.* Retrieved from http://cgi .cnn.com/ALLPOLITICS/1996/news/9602/29/clinton.tv/

Cohen, L., & Felson, M. (1980). Social change and crime rate trends: A routine activity approach. *American Sociological Review, 44,* 588–608.

Coleman, K. (1990). Fatal charades: Roman executions staged as mythical enactments. *Journal of Roman Studies, 80,* 44–73.

Cooper, J., & Mackie, D. (1986). Video games and aggression in children. *Journal of Applied Social Psychology, 16,* 726–744.

Cumberbach, G. (2007). Media effects: Continuing controversies. In D. Albertazzi & P. Cobley (Eds.), *The media.* London, UK: Pearson Education.

Daniell, D. (2004). *Oxford dictionary of national biography.* Oxford, UK: Oxford University Press.

Division 46. (2014). *Society for media psychology and technology.* Retrieved from http://www.apa.org/divisions/div46

Federal Bureau of Investigation. (1951–2012). *Uniform crime reports.* Washington, DC: U.S. Government Printing Office.

Federal Trade Commission. (2007). *Marketing violent entertainment to children.* Retrieved April 2, 2008, from http://www.ftc.gov/ reports/violence/070412MarketingViolentEChildren.pdf

Fox, J., & DeLateur, M. (2014). Mass shootings in America: Moving beyond Newtown. *Homicide Studies, 18*(1), 125–145. doi:10.1177/ 1088767913510297

Gamepolitics.com. (2007). *ESRB: Video game report card flawed, contradicts government findings.* Retrieved April 2, 2008, from http://gamepolitics.com/2007/12/04/esrb-video-game-report-card-flawed-contradicts-govt-findings

Gauntlett, D. (2005). *Moving experiences: Understanding television's influences and effects.* Luton, UK: John Libbey.

Griffiths, M., & Hunt, N. (1995). Computer game playing in adolescence: Prevalence and demographic indicators. *Journal of Community and Applied Social Psychology, 5,* 189–193.

Griswold, C. (2003). Plato on rhetoric and poetry. *The Stanford Encyclopedia of Philosophy.* Retrieved March 25, 2008, from http://plato .stanford.edu/archives/spr2004/entries/plato-rhetoric/

21

Grossman, D. (1995). *On killing: The psychological cost of learning to kill in society.* New York, NY: Little, Brown.

Hallo, W., & Simpson, W. (1971). *The ancient Near East: A history.* San Diego, CA: Harcourt Brace.

Kaiser Family Foundation. (2004). *Parents, media and public policy.* Retrieved April 2, 2008, from http://www.kff.org/entmedia/7156.cfm

Kaiser Family Foundation. (2007). *Parents, children, and media: A Kaiser Family Foundation survey.* Retrieved from http://kff.org/other/poll-finding/parents-children-media-a-kaiser-family-foundation/

Kirschenbaum, M. (2007). How reading is being reimagined. *Chronicle of Higher Education, 54*(15), B20.

Kottler, J. A. (2011). *The lust for blood: Why we are fascinated by death, murder, horror, and violence.* Amherst, NY: Prometheus Books.

Lowery, S., & DeFleur, M. (1995). *Milestones in mass communication research: Media effects* (3rd ed.). New York, NY: Longman.

Luskin, B. (2013). The media psychology effect. *Psychology Today.* Retrieved from http://www.apa.org/divisions/div46/Luskin,%20B.,%20Defining%20Media%20Psychology,%20Psychology%20Today,%202012.pdf

McCall, G., & Shields, N. (2008). Examining the evidence from small-scale societies and early prehistory and implications for modern theories of aggression and violence. *Aggression and Violent Behavior, 13*, 1–9.

McLuhan, M., & Fiore, Q. (1967). *The medium is in the message.* Corte Madera, CA: Gingko Press.

National Institute of Media and the Family. (2007). *12th annual Media-wise video game report card.* Retrieved April 2, 2008, from http://www.mediafamily.org/research/report_vgrc_2007.shtml

National Jousting Association. (2008). *The medieval tourney.* Retrieved October 1, 2008, from http://www.nationaljousting.com/history/medieval.htm

Parents Television Council. (2007). *The ratings sham II.* Retrieved from http://www.parentstv.org/PTC/publications/reports/ratingsstudy/exsummary.asp

Pearson, G. (1983). *Hooligan: A history of respectable fears,* London, UK: Macmillan.

Pike, A., Hoffmann, D., Garcia-Diez, M., Pettitt, P., Alcolea, J., De Balbin, R., . . . Zilhao, J. (2012). U-series dating of paleolithic art in 11 caves in Spain. *Science, 336*, 1409–1413.

Pinker, S. (2011). *The better angels of our nature: Why violence has declined*. New York, NY: Viking.

Prest, T. (1847). *Varney the Vampire*. Retrieved March 28, 2008, from http://etext.lib.virginia.edu/toc/modeng/public/PreVarn.html

Rutledge, P. (2010). *What is media psychology? And why you should care*. Retrieved from http://www.apa.org/divisions/div46/Rutledge_ What-is-Media-Psychology.pdf

Savage, J. (2008). The role of exposure to media violence in the etiology of violent behavior: A criminologist weighs in. *American Behavioral Scientist, 51,* 1123–1136.

Seneca. (64). *Epistulae morales ad Lucilium*. Retrieved October 1, 2008, from http://www.martinfrost.ws/htmlfiles/moral_epistles.html

Sherkat, D., & Ellison, C. (1997). The cognitive structure of a moral crusade: Conservative Protestantism and the opposition to pornography. *Social Forces, 75,* 957–980.

State's Attorney for the Judicial District of Danbury. (2013). *Report of the State's Attorney for the Judicial District of Danbury on the shootings at Sandy Hook Elementary School and 36 Yogananda Street, Newtown, Connecticut on December 14, 2012*. Danbury, CT: Office of the State's Attorney Judicial District of Danbury.

Tertullian. (200). *De spectaculis*. Retrieved October 1, 2008, from http://www.tertullian.org/lfc/LFC10-13_de_spectaculis.htm

Tilley, C. (2012). Seducing the innocent: Fredric Wertham and the falsifications that helped condemn comics. *Information & Culture, 47*(4), 383–413. doi:10.1353/lac.2012.0024

Trend, D. (2007). *The myth of media violence: A critical introduction*. Malden, MA: Blackwell.

United States Secret Service and United States Department of Education. (2002). *The final report and findings of the Safe School Initiative: Implications for the prevention of school attacks in the United States*. Retrieved November 12, 2007, from http://www.secretservice .gov/ntac/ssi_final_report.pdf

Wells, C. (1995). *The Roman Empire*. Cambridge, MA: Harvard University Press.

Wertham, F. (1996). *Seduction of the innocent*. Mattituck, NY: Amereon. (Original work published 1954)

Woolley, J., & Van Reet, J. (2006). Effects of context on judgments concerning the reality status of novel entities. *Child Development, 77,* 1778–1793.

Theories and Methods of Media Effects

Theories in science are used to organize existing data and provide hypotheses or routes for new data collection. Imagine, for instance, you had three pieces of scientific data. First, people who eat more vegetables than candy bars live longer. Second, people who eat more candy bars than vegetables gain much more weight. Third, candy bars have more fats and sugars than do vegetables. You might come up with the theory that fats and sugars are unhealthy for you, leading to weight gain, which puts potential fatal strain on the body. You could test the theory further by examining other classes of food, meats high in fat, for instance, or by doing experiments with animals such as mice. This is a relatively simplistic example, of course, but it's what theories basically do: organizing existing data and presenting testable hypotheses that could be used to further test the theory.

Theories in science are not used the same way we use the term in everyday life, that is, to imply a semieducated guess. Theories are not guesses but are (one hopes) based on data. That is why we have a "Theory of Evolution" that, of course, is based on a century and a half of data. Calling it a "theory" does not mean it's a shaky guess. In science there are very few "facts," and the only "laws" are in the physical/chemical sciences. Certainly, nothing in the social sciences approaches that level.

Theories are not "true"; indeed, they can never really be proven true, only proven false. A strong theory is simply one that hasn't *yet* been proven to be false. Some theories do overstay their usefulness, however. This happens because it's not always clear how much disconfirmatory evidence is required for a theory to be considered *falsified* or untrue. Scholars who have invested years in promoting a particular theory, or whose reputations have become identified with that theory, can become quite defensive about it, even as data begins to suggest it may have been wrong. This can lead to the development of what I call *undead theories* or theories that continue to be popular despite considerable evidence suggesting they are wrong (Ferguson & Heene, 2012). Periods in which a field switches from one theoretical model to another can be quite tumultuous and acrimonious, periods that are called *paradigm change* (Kuhn, 1970).

Over the years, a number of theories have been proposed for how media and consumers may interact. Much of the theoretical struggle has been between what is sometimes called the limited-effects theory (e.g., Katz & Lazarsfeld, 1955) of media effects and the hypodermic needle model (Berger, 1995). The hypodermic needle model essentially indicated that media had direct, predictable causal effects on consumers who were passive "sitting ducks." By contrast, the limited-effects model suggested that media effects were more subtle and often idiosyncratic, with consumers interpreting media very differently from one another. There are also some theories, such as Moral Panic Theory (Gauntlett, 2005), which do not necessarily fit well into this basic dichotomy. In this chapter we study some of these basic theoretical approaches as well as the methodologies used in media research to examine them.

HYPODERMIC NEEDLE MODELS

The hypodermic needle model or models (as in recent decades several similar models on different media topics arguably fall under the umbrella) posit general, direct relationships between media consumption and consumer behavior. Sometimes also referred to as "magic bullet" theories of media effects, such theories posit media messages as something directly "injected" into consumers who are passive recipients without conscious control of the resultant behaviors. Essentially, this is the "monkey see, monkey do" approach to media effects. This approach became particularly popular in the 1930s, corresponding with both the Payne Fund studies of movie violence and the behaviorist movement in psychological science. The early 20th-century behaviorists believed, putting it a bit simply, that human behavior was mechanistic, responding unconsciously to external influences in ways beyond the individual's control.

However, the core beliefs of the hypodermic needle approach were probably nothing new. We've already seen that the essential element of media having a corruptive influence on audiences has been with us, in some form, since at least the time of the ancient Greeks. The theorists of the early 20th century merely put these ideas into the more formal structure of scientific theory.

Probably few events typified the beliefs of the hypodermic needle approach of the early 20th century more than the famous Orson Welles radio broadcast of *War of the Worlds* in 1938. Using the format of a news radio show, Welles acted out a fictional invasion of Earth by Martians. As has been reported in many social psychology and communication textbooks, this radio broadcast terrified millions, many of whom ran off into the woods to save

27

themselves or were saved from committing suicide by more rational colleagues. The Orson Welles broadcast of *War of the Worlds* had one of the most dramatic audience impacts in history.

Only it never happened. Well, the radio show did. Only, according to new investigation, it was neither terribly popular the night it was broadcast nor did it touch off even a temporary nationwide panic (Pooley & Socolow, 2013). No verified cases of people running into the woods or attempting suicide are known. The show may have "terrified" some people in the sense that modern horror movies do today, but little evidence of a credulous audience believing in a Martian invasion wholesale has emerged. As happens with many urban legends, the notoriety of *War of the Worlds* grew as the actual event receded in memory, replaced by more elaborate and interesting but ultimately unverifiable memories. But, like another urban legend, the murder of Kitty Genovese, which was inaccurately reported to have been witnessed by many do-nothing bystanders (see Manning, Levine, & Collins, 2007), it has become a parable, useful for illustrating a scientific theory, so long as one doesn't allow pesky things like historical accuracy to get in the way.

The hypodermic needle approach is arguably popular for two reasons. First, it is fairly simple and straightforward and feels like "common sense," at least to some people ("common sense," of course, has little scientific value and is known to be inaccurate; see Lilienfeld, Lynn, Ruscio, & Beyerstein, 2009. Part of this is because people tend to view their own opinions as "common sense" whatever they may be, and contrary opinions as "nonsense.") Second, the hypodermic needle model tends to fit well with culture-war issues over what media is acceptable or not. Since such culture wars often focus on the potential for morally objectionable media to "harm" children or other groups, the hypodermic needle model fits in well. This observation doesn't make the theory either right or wrong; it just helps to explain its enduring popularity.

Within academic circles, the hypodermic needle approach ebbed a bit during the mid-20th century (despite the 1950s fervor over comic books) but was revived by the bobo doll experiments of Bandura, which purported to show children mimicking aggressive behaviors witnessed in videos. Whether the bobo doll experiments really generalize to any kind of influence of media on real-life aggressive motivations is unclear (the kids, after all, may have mimicked what they saw because they believed the videos were instructions, not because the kids actually felt aggressive), but, with Bandura paradigms, social science tended to focus now on social learning.

In fairness, Bandura's approach to social modeling isn't exactly a hypodermic needle approach. Indeed, Bandura argued that individuals, the social world, and an individual's biology all influenced one another in a complex pattern, something he called *triadic reciprocal determination* (Bandura, 1986). Bandura has also demonstrated an interest in human agency (Bandura, 2006), in which humans control their own behavior in conjunction with the social system in which they live. I'm certainly no biographer of Bandura, but it seems that his perspective on human behavior was quite complex, and reducing it to the simplicity of the hypodermic needle approach would be unfair.

Nonetheless, the development of the social cognitive approach that came out of Bandura's theories postulated the development of cognitive "scripts" as an intermediate link between environmental stimuli and behavior. The basic way of thinking of such scripts is in terms of cognitive shortcuts our brains use to respond to social situations in an automatic fashion. For instance, when someone you don't know well asks, "Hey how's it going?" Most of us respond with something like "Good, thanks," whether we're really having a good day or not. We are, in essence, following a script. According to this theoretical approach, we can learn such scripts from multiple sources: family, friends, and, potentially, the media. Few scholars would argue that these scripts don't develop at all. But there is debate about what circumstances are sufficient to form them, how automatic or consciously controlled they are, and whether they transfer easily from one situation to another. Does the child who learns to mimic light-saber battles from the *Star Wars* films in his or her play also use scripts learned from *Star Wars* in situations that less resemble the movie than do imaginative play?

The hypodermic needle approaches, revived since the time of the bobo doll studies, have branched out a bit into specific theories for individual topic areas. Several of the main areas follow.

Media Violence

Hypodermic needle theories of media violence on aggression tend to fall within a broad range of social cognitive theories of aggression. A number of related theories, involving the development and activation of aggressive scripts, affective arousal, and desensitization have been developed over the past few decades, although these seem to have congealed into something called the General Aggression Model (GAM; DeWall, Anderson, & Bushman, 2011). The GAM (or previously the General Affective Aggression Model) represents an attempt to integrate and build upon the numerous previous social cognitive models of aggression, incorporating both affective and cognitive components of previous models. Gradually (although unofficially), the affective side of the model has been deemphasized in more recent discussions (indeed, affective was dropped from the name), and some authors have argued that the influence of violent media on affect has been difficult to demonstrate (Ballard, Visser, & Jocoy, 2012; Ramos, Ferguson, & Frailing, in press).

The GAM thus particularly emphasizes the development of cognitive scripts. Watching media violence results in the development of scripts involving aggressive responses to ambiguous stimuli. The more media violence exposure, the more deeply rooted and easily activated are these aggressive scripts. Therefore, over time, people exposed to media violence will be more likely to respond to minor provocations with aggressive behavior and also to become less empathic and more desensitized to the suffering of others.

Within the field of media violence, the GAM almost certainly continues to enjoy dominance as of this writing, although it is seldom used in other areas such as criminology. However, the GAM (and other social cognitive models of aggression) have been controversial because of several issues and built-in assumptions.

First, the GAM does make a nod to the possibility that biological or personality factors may contribute to aggression. However, the GAM does little to explain these variables. Nor does the GAM appear to allow for such variables to have much impact on the links between media violence and behavioral aggression. Although advocates of the GAM allow that some individuals may be more influenced by media violence than others, they are also quite explicit in saying that no one is "immune" to the predictable effects of media violence (e.g., Anderson, Bushman, Donnerstein, Hummer, & Warburton, 2014). That is to say, the GAM is explicit in predicting general, universal effects.

Second, the GAM has relied on the assumption that the human brain treats fictional violence in the same manner as it does real-world violence. Some advocates of the GAM have been quite explicit in stating that media violence should have the same impact as exposure to violence in real life or in the home (Bushman & Huesmann, 2014). Other scholars have suggested that such a primitive reaction of the human brain making no distinction is unlikely and unsupported by evidence (Elson & Ferguson, 2014; Gauntlett, 2005).

There are other issues with the GAM's assumptions (see Ferguson & Dyck, 2012), including the assumption that aggression is primarily cognitive in nature, the assumption that aggression is primarily learned (and that our default response to behavior would be nonaggressive if not otherwise learned), and the failure of the GAM to provide clear, falsifiable predictions about real-world behavior. For instance, consider an experiment when the brains of teenagers are scanned while they play a violent video game. If the brains of the teens become more active over time, it would be possible to argue that they are

31

becoming agitated and thus prone to greater aggression. If their brains become less active, it would be possible to argue they are becoming desensitized and thus prone to greater aggression. In other words, any outcome could, with creativity, fit within the GAM model.

Despite these concerns, the GAM certainly remains the most-often used theory of aggression within media psychology itself. Proponents argue that the data on the GAM is solid and the theory is, essentially, beyond repute. Putting any theory under scrutiny is a normal part of the scientific process. Whether the GAM survives that scrutiny will be told over time.

Body Dissatisfaction

Related to body dissatisfaction, Social Comparison Theory (SCT; Festinger, 1954), at its most basic level, suggests simply that we form opinions about ourselves by evaluating how we compare to those around us. For instance, a child may form opinions about how smart he or she is by comparing his or her grades to those of other students in a class. As it has been applied to media and body dissatisfaction, SCT suggests that we form opinions about our own attractiveness by comparing ourselves to others, including media figures. Thus, for women seeing a bevy of thin, beautiful actresses on TV or in magazines, those women may feel less beautiful by comparison and become increasingly dissatisfied with their bodies.

As with the social cognitive theories of media violence, SCT enjoys considerable dominance within the field of media and body dissatisfaction. Once again, it fits very well with the "concern" view of media effects. It is not uncommon to hear scholars claim that the evidence for SCT, as it applies to media, is definitive. However, meta-analyses generally suggest that media effects on body dissatisfaction are fairly small (Grabe, Ward, & Hyde, 2008; Groesz, Levine, & Murnen, 2002; Holmstrom, 2004), and effects may be limited to women with preexisting body dissatisfaction (Ferguson, 2013; Roberts & Good, 2010).

Cultivation Theory

The third hypodermic needle approach to receive considerable attention is the cultivation theory or hypothesis. Particularly associated with communication researcher George Gerbner (1998), this theory focuses less on behaviors and more on ideas. In essence, cultivation theory focuses on the degree to which our ideas about the world are developed through exposure to events in the media. As a very basic idea, if you watch local news channels and, night after night, the news focuses on violent crimes occurring in your local city, you might begin to develop the belief that violent crime is rising, despite evidence that violent crime has been declining for decades (Federal Bureau of Investigation, 1951–2012).

Cultivation from media tends to work best in the absence of conflicting information from the real world. For instance, having just been informed about actual crime statistics, one hopes you now will become rather resistant to misleading information from news media or other sources. Like most hypodermic needle approaches, cultivation has endured its share of controversy and debate (e.g., Newcomb, 1978), although other researchers continue to express that it is doing rather well as a theory (e.g., Morgan & Shanahan, 2010). We talk about cultivation a bit more when we get into news media, but my own perception is that cultivation theory, particularly when applied to news media, actually remains one of the strongest of the hypodermic needle approaches. It is probably most accurate to state that some, but not all, media promote cultivation for some, but not all, viewers (Cohen & Weimann, 2000).

Perhaps one of the greatest obstacles for the hypodermic needle models is not so much the unreasonableness of their propositions but rather the highly ideological way in which they have often been presented by their supporters (Ferguson, 2013; Gill, 2012; Grimes, Anderson, & Bergen, 2008; Steinberg & Monahan, 2011). That is to say, supporters of hypodermic needle models often state that evidence is conclusive for their theories, neglecting to inform readers of research results contrary to their reviews. This "citation bias" is considered a questionable researcher practice (Babor & McGovern, 2008) and is likely a consequence of the degree to which hypodermic needle models often coincide with well-meaning advocacy goals devoted to protecting media consumers. Nonetheless, a certain dishonesty often creeps into such claims and, when these claims are ultimately challenged, can do harm to the credibility of media psychology science (Hall, Day, & Hall, 2011; Steinberg & Monahan, 2011).

LIMITED-EFFECTS THEORIES

As opposed to hypodermic needle approaches, which assume that media consumers are passive and essentially helpless recipients of media messages, limited-effects theories posit the consumers as active shapers of their own media experience. That is to say, media users are active in both selecting the media that they consume and, perhaps more importantly, interpreting its meaning. These theories don't rule out the possibility for media to influence us. However, media consumers are much more active in the process, seeking out media in order to get a particular effect from it rather than simply being unwittingly manipulated by media. Further, according to such theories, media can have very different influences from one person to the next. Lastly, according to limited-effects theories, the influence of media is much less dramatic than assumed under hypodermic needle approaches. For instance, hypodermic needle models often take seriously the potential for thin-image media to contribute to clinical eating disorders, or even shooter games to contribute to mass shootings. Limited-effects theories would consider such dramatic impacts unlikely.

Limited-effects theories, like hypodermic needle models, tend to be very similar as a group on some of those core assumptions. They differ a bit mainly in how they are applied to real-life issues and whether they come from psychological or communication science traditions.

Uses and Gratifications Theory

Uses and Gratifications Theory, a theory that comes out of the communications tradition (Sherry, Lucas, Greenberg, & Lachlan, 2006), posits that media users play a crucial role in the media experience. As a critical element of UGT, media users aren't accidently or randomly exposed to different types of media but are attracted to them in advance, often because of particular emotional responses or outcomes we already associate with such media. Consider scary movies, for instance. The hypodermic needle approach would assume that such movies would provoke fear and aggression in us. Being scared and angry is not typically our notion of fun; however, why would we ever watch such films in the first place? Undoubtedly, many people *don't* watch scary movies because they don't enjoy being frightened. But other people get a very different response from such movies; for example, the adrenaline rush that comes with momentary fear is fun, particularly when it's a social event (Kottler, 2011). That adrenaline rush is followed by relief, laughter, and reflection. In other words, it's simplistic to say that we merely mimic what we see in the media; rather, we reflect on it and approach it or avoid it given our individual proclivities.

From this approach, even discussing topics such as "media violence" may be rather simplistic. For instance, consider literature. Stephen King novels, Shakespearean tragedies, the Bible, and the sadistic writings of the Marquis de Sade are all "violent media," but we would hardly consider these works to seriously all occupy a single conceptual space. Nonetheless, we often treat debates on media from such simplistic approaches.

Research has increasingly made clear that exposure to media is not accidental. Rather, we seek out particular forms of media depending on what we think they will do for us. Scholars have known for some time that personality determines media choices (e.g., Rentfrow, Goldberg, & Zilca, 2011) as well as do moral proclivities (Tamborini et al., 2013). Thus different people are drawn to different media and may respond to such media very differently. The Bible is an excellent example of this. Technically, the Bible is violent media, even God-sanctioned violence. But clearly, most people don't go to the Bible for aggression. Many people go to it to learn how to love others better or to be a better person or to find comfort during difficult times. However, some people may use the Bible or other religious texts as rationale for their hatred of others who are different from them. Some murderers have even claimed the Bible inspired them. Of course, various unhinged individuals have claimed that a whole variety of media from *Catcher in the Rye* (Mark Chapman) to Jodie Foster in *Taxi Driver* (John Hinckley, Jr.) to the Beatles's *Helter Skelter* (Charles Manson) inspired them, so people can sometimes be rather creative in finding messages that suit their proclivities.

Other research has indicated that our moods matter. Typically referred to as *mood management*, such approaches indicate that we seek out media that we believe will change our moods to whatever we would like them to be (Bowman & Tamborini, 2013). For instance, in one study, we found that people who played a lot of violent games actually were better at handling stress than those who did not (Ferguson & Rueda, 2010). This fits rather well with studies of youth who commonly indicate that they use games to reduce stress (Olson, Kutner, & Warner, 2008). We may be particularly prone to selecting media that are likely to move us to a more positive mood from a negative one (Dillman-Carpentier et al., 2008). Of course what works for one person may be very different from what works for another. Things are rather complicated under limited-effects theories!

Self-Determination Theory

A related theory, which comes from the psychological tradition, is Self-Determination Theory (SDT; Przybylski, Rigby, & Ryan, 2010). While UGT focuses on the degree to which individuals select media then interpret it according to their own personalities and desires, SDT focuses on motivations. Specifically, SDT suggests that we seek out media in order to meet certain needs that are not met well in everyday life. In particular, we seek out media to meet social, autonomy, and competence needs.

The gist of SDT is that, to put it bluntly, ordinary life sometimes is very difficult. Working a day job, shuffling papers from one side of the desk to another, the average person doesn't necessarily get much opportunity to really feel part of something important or like he or she has had the opportunity to make a difference. By getting a lot accomplished in a media universe, the individual can meet those needs vicariously—or perhaps by using video games, even act out scenarios that involve autonomy, influence, and competence, perhaps in a social environment. These motivations appear to be a big driver of video game experience in particular (Przybylski, Weinstein, Murayama, Lynch, & Ryan, 2012). It's also not surprising that video gaming is often a very social activity (Lenhart et al., 2008). Far from being the domain of loners, gaming appears to be an excellent space for the meeting of social needs, although that may be particularly true for individuals who have difficulty meeting social needs in real life (Durkin, 2010).

Studies with youth support the SDT approach to video game use (Colwell, 2007; Ferguson & Olson, 2013). Some studies have likewise indicated that motivational issues such as frustration (Przybylski, Deci, Rigby, & Ryan, 2014) and competitiveness (Adachi & Willoughby, 2011) are better predictors of aggressive behavior following game play than is violent content.

Like UGT, SDT suggests that we need to look deeper than mere content to understand how media and consumers interact. Media psychology is complex, subtle, and idiosyncratic, and very much dependent upon a user shaping the experience rather than direct impact of certain types of content.

The Catalyst Model

I include the Catalyst Model (Ferguson et al., 2008) here because it focuses on the degree to which media inform criminal acts, although it is more a theory of violence than media effects. The Catalyst Model is a diathesis/stress model of violence; that is to say, the theory suggests that genetics and early childhood environment interact to cause more aggressive personalities. Those aggressive personalities are more prone to violence throughout life, particularly under times of stress. Nothing terribly controversial there.

The Catalyst Model, unlike the hypodermic needle approaches, makes a clear difference between the impact of real-life exposure to violence and exposure to media violence. In particular, the Catalyst Model specifically suggests that humans distinguish between real and fictional violence, and that fictional violence is too distal or weak to have much developmental effect. Fictional violence just doesn't have enough direct impact on us to cause us to change our behavior. Real-life violence, by contrast, can have a very dramatic impact and thus is more likely to shape behavior. Therefore, the Catalyst Model is quite different from hypodermic needle approaches, which tend to hold fictional and real-life violence as being similar (Bushman & Huesmann, 2014).

A variation of the Catalyst Model (Ferguson, Winegard, & Winegard, 2011) has also been proposed for female body dissatisfaction, although, overall, the Catalyst Model is most used toward violent behavior issues. The Catalyst Model suggests that, while media has little to no impact on the motivation to commit crimes, media may provide *stylistic catalysts* wherein once an individual has decided to commit a crime, he or she may adopt specific elements from media. For instance, a criminal may try to hide evidence in a way learned from a crime drama. Consider, too, James Holmes, who dressed up in Joker-like garb and went on a shooting spree at a Colorado theater showing a "Batman" movie. If we could wave a magic wand and remove all media violence from the world, would Holmes have still committed the shooting? According to the Catalyst Model, yes, he just wouldn't have dressed up as the Joker, since removing the media only accomplishes removing the stylistic catalyst.

In fairness, the Catalyst Model is a newer model in media studies and doesn't see nearly as much use as the hypodermic needle models or even other limited-effects models. However, independent research with actual criminal inmates suggests that the Catalyst Model is superior to the hypodermic needle approach in understanding how media interacts with criminal behavior (Surette, 2014).

MORAL PANIC THEORY

The last theoretical perspective we'll discuss is Moral Panic Theory. Moral Panic Theory is not so much concerned with how the media does or does not influence us but more with how society reacts to media, particularly new media. Put simply, Moral Panic Theory suggests that society often overreacts to new media, proclaiming significant but often nonexistent public health crises. More crucially, these social narratives, at least initially, provide incentives for scholars, politicians, and journalists to promote the moral panic, often by misinforming the general public about the research data on the new media.

Moral Panic Theory was initially proposed by Cohen (1972), who suggested that society responds to perceived crises by constructing "folk devils" who can be blamed for the panic. Such moral panics often focus on crime-related issues, as well as youth. Thus we often see politicians or journalists claim that youth are doing naughty things "younger and younger" all the time. I've been hearing them my entire lifetime and, if they were true, babies ought to be coming out of the womb with a pistol in one hand and a joint in the other.

Historically, new media have often been the target of moral panics, with the presumption that certain "at risk" groups might be "harmed" by them. Youth are particularly thought of as needing "protection," although women and immigrant groups have also sometimes been thought of as unable to distinguish fact from fiction (Kirschenbaum, 2007). Everything from dime novels to Greek plays, to the waltz, to jazz music, to comic books, to rock and roll, to *Dungeons and Dragons*, to movies, television, video games, and the Internet have been subject to moral panics.

Moral Panic Theory suggests that this isn't just an accident. Rather, society forms an impression about a new form of media, then incentivizes journalists, politicians, and scholars, at least in the short term. Recent examples of moral panics over video games are an excellent example. Particularly after mass shootings such as the 2012 Sandy Hook Elementary School massacre, it is not uncommon to see a bevy of politicians, journalists, and scholars wringing their hands about the dangers of violent video games. Politicians call for "studies" (usually making clear what they want the conclusion of those "studies" to be) or propose legislation regulating or taxing video games. This allows politicians to look like they are doing something while targeting the low-hanging fruit of a media form most older adults don't understand well (Przybylski, 2014). By hyping sensationalist headlines, journalists get more "page clicks" or new subscribers. Scholars also benefit by getting their names in the news, political prestige and influence, professional prestige by taking on the naughty media industry, or grant funding (it's harder, after all, to get a grant arguing that something *isn't* a pressing social problem). In some cases, this can potentially lead to questionable researcher practices (QRPs) on the part of scholars. For instance, Frederic Wertham, who criticized comic books in the 1950s, has recently been called out for manipulating and fabricating data (Tilley, 2012).

This cyclical pattern of journalists, scholars, and politicians feeding a moral panic was described by Gauntlett (2005) in the Moral Panic Wheel presented in Figure 2.1. According to Gauntlett, once society has made up its mind about a new media, it cherry-picks sources of data to support that preexisting belief and ignores sources of data that don't conform. Again, with mass shooters we can readily see that pattern. Many mass shootings are perpetrated by older, even elderly men such as 59-year-old John Houser who shot up a theater in Louisiana on July 23, 2015, yet the issue of video game violence is simply ignored in such cases. When a shooter is a young male, society leaps to the assumption that video games were a factor. When it turns out that even some

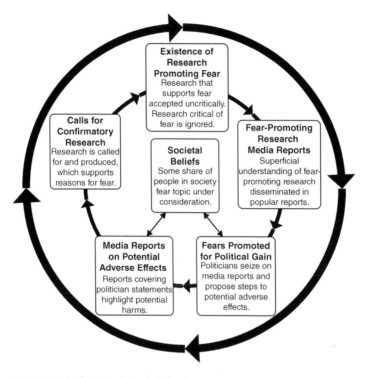

FIGURE 2.1 The Moral Panic Wheel.
Note: Based on Gauntlett (2005). Design by Andrew Przybylski.

young males, such as the Virginia Tech shooter or the Sandy Hook shooter, don't fit that assumed profile, society grudgingly moves on, often with little comment. In fact, the idea that video game violence contributes to mass shootings has been called a "myth" by criminologists (Fox & DeLateur, 2014). Nonetheless, the belief is resistant and may not change until, in effect, gamers age into the power structure of society. By then, the new generation will simply begin to pick on new media favored by the next younger generation. This is something I call the "Goldilocks Effect": the belief every generation has that the generation of elders before them were too conservative and the generation of youth after them too out of control. Every generation thinks it got media "just right."

41

The impact of scholars following along with a moral panic is long term. As indicated earlier, eventually the younger generation ages into the power structure and is much less likely to take seriously claims that the media it grew up with are harmful. Few people think comic books cause harm to juveniles anymore, or that Cyndi Lauper was a source of sexual immorality due to her "She Bop" song, or that Ozzy Osbourne caused teens to commit suicide. When the course shifts, scholars who staked their reputations on the "harm" view, such as Frederic Wertham, switch from being darlings of society to examples of overzealous moral advocacy masquerading as science. This can damage the reputation of media psychology science in the long term.

CONCLUSIONS

At present, no single paradigm defines media psychology. Some scholars continue to approach media psychology from a hypodermic needle perspective, others from a limited-effects perspective. These struggles between paradigms are often the source of intense debates. As Moral Panic Theory suggests, struggles between paradigms may be made more acute due to societal moral concerns over media, which may provide incentives for scholars to adopt more antimedia paradigms. At present, theoretically, media psychology remains a bit muddled!

REFERENCES

Adachi, P. C., & Willoughby, T. (2011). The effect of video game competition and violence on aggressive behavior: Which characteristic has the greatest influence? *Psychology of Violence, 1*(4), 259–274. doi:10.1037/a0024908

Anderson, C., Bushman, B., Donnerstein, E., Hummer, T., & Warburton, W. (2014). *SPSSI research summary on media violence.* Retrieved from http://www.spssi.org/index.cfm?fuseaction=page .viewPage&pageID=1899&nodeID=1

Babor, T. F., & McGovern, T. (2008). Dante's *Inferno*: Seven deadly sins in scientific publishing and how to avoid them. In T. F. Babor, K. Stenius, S. Savva, & J. O'Reilly (Eds.), *Publishing addiction science: A guide for the perplexed* (2nd ed., pp. 153–171). Essex, UK: Multi-Science Publishing Company.

Ballard, M., Visser, K., & Jocoy, K. (2012). Social context and video game play: Impact on cardiovascular and affective responses. *Mass Communication and Society, 15*(6), 875–898.

Bandura, A. (1986). *Social foundations of thought and action: A social cognitive theory.* Englewood Cliffs, NJ: Prentice-Hall.

Bandura, A. (2006). Toward a psychology of human agency. *Perspectives on Psychological Science, 1*(2), 164–180. doi:10.1111/j.1745-6916.2006.00011.x

Berger, A. A. (1995). *Essentials of mass communication theory.* London, UK: Sage.

Bowman, N., & Tamborini, R. (2013). "In the Mood to Game": Selective exposure and mood management processes in computer game play. *New Media and Society, 17*(3), 375–393.

Bushman, B. J., & Huesmann, L. (2014). Twenty-five years of research on violence in digital games and aggression revisited: A reply to Elson and Ferguson (2013). *European Psychologist, 19*(1), 47–55. doi:10.1027/1016-9040/a000164

Cohen, J., & Weimann, G. (2000). Cultivation revisited: Some genres have some effects on some viewers. *Communication Reports, 13*(2), 99–114.

Cohen, S. (1972). *Folk devils and moral panics.* London, UK: MacGibbon and Kee.

Colwell, J. (2007). Needs met through computer game play among adolescents. *Personality and Individual Differences, 43*(8), 2072–2082. doi:10.1016/j.paid.2007.06.021

DeWall, C., Anderson, C. A., & Bushman, B. J. (2011). The general aggression model: Theoretical extensions to violence. *Psychology of Violence, 1*(3), 245–258. doi:10.1037/a0023842

Dillman-Carpentier, F., Brown, J., Bertocci, M., Silk, J., Forbes, E., & Dahl, R. (2008). Sad kids, sad media? Applying mood management theory to depressed adolescents' use of media. *Media Psychology,* *11,* 143–166.

Durkin, K. (2010). Videogames and young people with developmental disorders. *Review of General Psychology, 14*(2), 122–140. doi:10.1037/a0019438

Elson, M., & Ferguson, C. J. (2014). Does doing media violence research make one aggressive? The ideological rigidity of social cognitive theories of media violence and response to Bushman and Huesmann (2013), Krahé (2013), and Warburton (2013). *European Psychologist, 19*(1), 68–75.

Federal Bureau of Investigation. (1951–2012). *Uniform crime reports.* Washington, DC: U.S. Government Printing Office.

Ferguson, C. J. (2013). In the eye of the beholder: Thin-ideal media affects some but not most viewers in a meta-analytic review of body dissatisfaction in women and men. *Psychology of Popular Media Culture, 2*(1), 20–37.

Ferguson, C. J., & Dyck, D. (2012). Paradigm change in aggression research: The time has come to retire the General Aggression Model. *Aggression and Violent Behavior, 17*(3), 220–228. doi:10.1016/j.avb.2012.02.007

Ferguson, C. J., & Heene, M. (2012). A vast graveyard of undead theories: Publication bias and psychological science's aversion to the null. *Perspectives on Psychological Science, 7*(6), 550–556.

Ferguson, C. J., & Olson, C. K. (2013). Friends, fun, frustration and fantasy: Child motivations for video game play. *Motivation and Emotion, 37*(1), 154–164. doi:10.1007/s11031-012-9284-7

Ferguson, C. J., & Rueda, S. M. (2010). The Hitman study: Violent video game exposure effects on aggressive behavior, hostile feelings and depression. *European Psychologist, 15*(2), 99–108.

Ferguson, C. J., Rueda, S. M., Cruz, A. M., Ferguson, D. E., Fritz, S., & Smith, S. M. (2008). Violent video games and aggression: Causal relationship or byproduct of family violence and intrinsic violence motivation? *Criminal Justice and Behavior, 35,* 311–332.

Ferguson, C. J., Winegard, B., & Winegard, B. M. (2011). Who is the fairest one of all? How evolution guides peer and media influences on female body dissatisfaction. *Review of General Psychology, 15*(1), 11–28.

Festinger, L. (1954). A theory of social comparison processes. *Human Relations, 7*(2), 117–140.

Fox, J., & DeLateur, M. (2014). Mass shootings in America: Moving beyond Newtown. *Homicide Studies, 18*(1), 125–145. doi:10.1177/1088767913510297

Gauntlett, D. (2005). *Moving experiences: Understanding television's influences and effects.* Luton, UK: John Libbey.

Gerbner, G. (1998). Cultivation analysis: An overview. *Mass Communication and Society, 3,* 175–194.

Gill, R. (2012). Media, empowerment and the "sexualization of culture" debates. *Sex Roles, 66,* 736–745.

Grabe, S., Ward, L., & Hyde, J. (2008). The role of the media in body image concerns among women: A meta-analysis of experimental and correlational studies. *Psychological Bulletin, 134*(3), 460–476.

Grimes, T., Anderson, J., & Bergen, L. (2008). *Media violence and aggression: Science and ideology.* Thousand Oaks, CA: Sage.

Groesz, L. M., Levine, M. P., & Murnen, S. K. (2002). The effect of experimental presentation of thin media images on body satisfaction: A meta-analytic review. *International Journal of Eating Disorders, 31,* 1–16.

Hall, R., Day, T., & Hall, R. (2011). A plea for caution: Violent video games, the Supreme Court, and the role of science. *Mayo Clinic Proceedings, 86*(4), 315–321.

Holmstrom, A. (2004). The effects of media on body image: A meta-analysis. *Journal of Broadcasting and Electronic Media, 48,* 186–217.

Katz, E., & Lazarsfeld, P. F. (1955). *Personal influence: The part played by people in the flow of mass communications.* New York, NY: Free Press.

Kirschenbaum, M. (2007). How reading is being reimagined. *Chronicle of Higher Education, 54*(15), B20.

Kottler, J. A. (2011). *The lust for blood: Why we are fascinated by death, murder, horror, and violence.* Amherst, NY: Prometheus Books.

Kuhn, T. (1970). *The structure of scientific revolutions.* Chicago, IL: University of Chicago Press.

Lenhart, A., Kahne, J., Middaugh, E., MacGill, A., Evans, C., & Vitak, J. (2008). *Teens, video games and civics.* Retrieved July 26, 2015, from http://www.pewinternet.org/2008/09/16/teens-video-games-and-civics/

Lilienfeld, S., Lynn, S., Ruscio, J., & Beyerstein, B. (2009). Mythbusting in introductory psychology courses: The whys and the hows. In S. A. Meyers & J. R. Stowell (Eds.), *Essays from E-xcellence in teaching* (Vol. 9). Retrieved February 6, 2012, from http://teachpsych.org/ebooks/eit2009/index.php

Manning, R., Levine, M., & Collins, A. (2007). The Kitty Genovese murder and the social psychology of helping: The parable of the 38 witnesses. *American Psychologist, 62*(6), 555–562. doi:10.1037/0003-066X.62.6.555

Morgan, M., & Shanahan, J. (2010). The state of cultivation. *Journal of Broadcasting & Electronic Media, 54*(2), 337–355. doi:10.1080/08838151003735018

Newcomb, H. (1978). Assessing the violence profile studies of Gerbner and Gross: A humanistic critique and suggestion. *Communication Research, 5*(3), 264–282. doi:10.1177/009365027800500303

Olson, C. K., Kutner, L. A., & Warner, D. E. (2008). The role of violent video game content in adolescent development: Boys' perspectives. *Journal of Adolescent Research, 23*(1), 55–75. doi:10.1177/0743558407310713

Pooley, J., & Socolow, M. (2013). The myth of the *War of the Worlds* panic. *Slate.* Retrieved from http://www.slate.com/articles/arts/history/2013/10/orson_welles_war_of_the_worlds_panic_myth_the_infamous_radio_broadcast_did.html

Przybylski, A. K. (2014). Who believes electronic games cause real world aggression? *Cyberpsychology, Behavior, and Social Networking, 17*(4), 228–234. doi:10.1089/cyber.2013.0245

Przybylski, A. K., Deci, E., Rigby, C. S., & Ryan, R. M. (2014). Competence-impeding electronic games and players' aggressive feelings, thoughts, and behaviors. *Journal of Personality and Social Psychology, 106*(3), 441–457.

Przybylski, A. K., Rigby, C. S., & Ryan, R. M. (2010). A motivational model of video game engagement. *Review of General Psychology, 14*(2), 154–166.

Przybylski, A. K., Weinstein, N., Murayama, K., Lynch, M. F., & Ryan, R. M. (2012). The ideal self at play: The appeal of video games that let you be all you can be. *Psychological Science, 23*(1), 69–76. doi:10.1177/0956797611418676

Ramos, R., Ferguson, C. J., & Frailing, K. (in press). Violent entertainment and cooperative behavior: Examining media violence effects on cooperation in a primarily Hispanic sample. *Psychology of Popular Media Culture.*

Rentfrow, P. J., Goldberg, L. R., & Zilca, R. (2011). Listening, watching, and reading: The structure and correlates of entertainment preferences. *Journal of Personality, 79*(2), 223–258. doi:10.1111/j.1467-6494.2010.00662.x

Roberts, A., & Good, E. (2010). Media images and female body dissatisfaction: The moderating effects of the Five-Factor traits. *Eating Behaviors, 11*(4), 211–216. doi:10.1016/j.eatbeh.2010.04.002

Sherry, J. L., Lucas, K., Greenberg, B. S., & Lachlan, K. A. (2006). Video game uses and gratifications as predictors of use and game preference. In *Playing video games. Motives, responses, and consequences* (pp. 213–224). Mahwah, NJ: Lawrence Erlbaum Associates.

Steinberg, L., & Monahan, K. C. (2011). Adolescents' exposure to sexy media does not hasten the initiation of sexual intercourse. *Developmental Psychology, 47*(2), 562–576. doi:10.1037/a0020613

Surette, R. (2014). Cause or catalyst: The interaction of real world and media crime models. *American Journal of Criminal Justice.* doi:10.1007/s12103-012-9177-z

Tamborini, R., Eden, A., Bowman, N. D., Grizzard, M., Weber, R., & Lewis, R. J. (2013). Predicting media appeal from instinctive moral values. *Mass Communication & Society, 16*(3), 325–346. doi:10.1080/15205436.2012.703285

Tilley, C. (2012). Seducing the innocent: Fredric Wertham and the falsifications that helped condemn comics. *Information and Culture, 47*, 383–413.

Advertising Effects

dvertisements are rather like the mosquitoes of the media universe: annoying and pesky and sometimes carrying disease but, on some level, a critical part of the ecosystem. Advertisements do sometimes work to make themselves amusing, but they occupy a different niche from fictional media. Advertisements differ from fictional media in that they are purposely intended to change behavior. Fictional media may sometimes seek to inspire or give thought, and some producers of fictional media may hope they encourage behavior change in others, but as a whole, fictional media doesn't have that specific purpose. By contrast, advertisements almost universally intend some level of behavior change, although most such behaviors are quite minor. And advertisements provide an economic backbone for much of the media we consume. Broadcast television is "free" because of the presence of advertisements and even pay-for-consumption media costs are kept lower by the presence of advertisements. Put simply, without lucrative advertisements we'd pay more for our media.

But even the best produced advertisements are repetitive, and we tend to get bored quickly watching the same thing over and over. Thus, advertisements are not looked upon with favor. Further, the behavior change that advertisements often encourage is not always the best for us. From advertisements for cigarettes to alcohol, to sugary foods and drinks, we are bombarded with enticements to do things that are not in our best interest. In this chapter we consider several related issues:

1. How influential are advertisements on our behavior?
2. What "tricks" do advertisers use to influence behavior?
3. How do the influences of advertisements compare to fictional media?

WHAT IS ADVERTISING?

First, it is important to understand what it is we're discussing. Advertising is a subset of marketing. The American Marketing Association (AMA) defines marketing as: "Marketing is the activity, set of institutions, and processes for creating, communicating, delivering, and exchanging offerings that have value for customers, clients, partners, and society at large" (American Marketing Association, 2007). Advertising is a direct communication that falls under the umbrella of marketing in which a product and its benefits (or alleged benefits) are proclaimed through various forms of media. Although we tend to think of television commercials primarily when we think of advertisements, advertisements can take many forms, from print or radio ads, to banners on the sides of trucks or on billboards, to more subtle forms such as product placement in movies, television, or video games. Advertisements are designed to make the public aware of a product, as well as to provide a pitch for why that particular product is superior to its competitors.

Although we think of advertisements as selling products such as food, soda, cars, and so forth, that's not always the case.

Some advertisements sell not products but ideas. Political ads are an excellent example of these in which politicians running for office or advocating for a particular cause try to convince voters to vote their way (and not for that other candidate who clearly is an incompetent liar). Other ads are purely ideological, trying to convince the consumer of a particular life course. Examples may be ads that try to convince you to stop smoking, wear your seatbelt, donate to charity, or convert to their religion. Such ads are often well intentioned (after all, who would argue people should smoke more and wear their seatbelts less), but clearly intended to nudge the consumer's behavior onto a particular life path.

Advertisements are controversial on multiple levels. Part of this is aesthetic. After all, advertisements can be intrusive, unattractive, and repetitive. Although there are certainly examples of advertisements with great artistic merit, for the most part they do not seem to add to the beauty of the world. But advertisements are also controversial for the degree to which they may mislead consumers by overemphasizing benefits and de-emphasizing potential problems with their products, or by contributing to problems, such as the obesity epidemic, in modern society. Many of the debates that focus around advertisements come as a tug-of-war between the need to protect the public from faulty or misleading messages and free speech.

Far from being a modern invention, advertising has a long historical past. There are records going back to the ancient Egyptians (Presbrey, 2000) using papyrus for hand flyers and poster-type advertisements. The Romans advertised for political campaigns. They also used visual advertisements, such as symbols of pubic hair to lead travelers to prostitutes along pathways marked with footprints. Through most of history, advertisements had to be either visual or auditory (e.g., town criers) since the majority of the populace were illiterate.

Advertising really began to increase in the 19th century with the advent of the industrial age. Populations increased, and more and more products came on the market. Some producers were skeptical of the worth of advertising, but competition was fierce, and the impact of advertisement in product branding soon proved its worth (Cadbury, 2011). Of course, some advertisers realized they needn't always tell the whole truth in their advertisements. False advertisements tried to entice consumers with lofty but untrue claims of benefits and to hide weaknesses or financial liabilities with their products. So-called *snake oil* was an example of this. Snake oils are a term for a variety of 19th-century medical treatments that were often advertised as if they cured a long host of ailments when, in fact, they did nothing or even were harmful in some cases. These snake oils and other forms of false advertisements highlighted the need to balance free speech with consumer protection.

By the 20th century, advertisements began to change into the modern form we see today. Early 20th-century advertisements tended to be dense, wordy affairs. Soon, things changed with advertising increasingly drawing upon the theories of classical conditioning, pioneered by J. B. Watson. In his Little Albert experiment, Watson, an academic psychologist, demonstrated that a toddler could be conditioned to fear a white rat by pairing exposure to the rat with loud noises (Watson & Rayner, 1920). After an adulterous affair forced him to leave academia, Watson joined the advertising industry, bringing his conditioning theories to bear (Burnham, 1994). The long, wordy, informative advertisements of the past became part of history, now pairing a product with something else we already like, such as attractive people, excitement, humor, and so on. With modern advertisements we might even be left wondering, "That was a great ad, but what does the product do?"

FALSE ADVERTISEMENTS

False advertising is defined here as advertisements that include information known or suspected by the advertiser to be false, or the omission of information that the advertiser would have reason to suspect would change consumers' decisions in order to manipulate consumer choices (Olson & Dover, 1978). That's a fancy way of saying that advertisers purposely say things they know aren't true or leave out crucial information in order to make it more likely you'll buy their product. Although many of us tend to think of all advertisements as potentially misinformative, research suggests that a fair percentage of people accept information in advertisements uncritically, particularly if the advertisements put them in a good mood (LaTour & LaTour, 2009). Of course, even run-of-the-mill advertisements are trying to manipulate mood and use noninformative tricks such as *testimonials* in which some random person (often an actor) gushes about how the product essentially changed his or her life. Testimonials are very persuasive but actually are utterly meaningless from an empirical point of view. Even if the testimonial is *not* an actor, a single individual or even group of selected individuals attributing their life happiness to a product could be misattributed.

False advertising takes many forms, but I'll list out a few here and see if you've ever come across any of these:

1. **False claims of benefits.** This is the most obvious example, such as the snake oil claims mentioned earlier. A product advertises itself or suggests it will give you a particular benefit despite little empirical evidence for such benefits. The flip-side is a product that evidence suggests is harmful, but the advertiser fails to disclose that potential harm. Even in an age of greater regulation, this practice remains common, with many advertisers trying to skirt the line of implying certain benefits, often by using vague terms without making direct claims. An herbal remedy that claims to "restore the energy balance in your body" might be such an example. One might assume from such a claim that the remedy would make you feel better or have more energy, even though the product never directly claimed that, and there is little empirical evidence for such claims.

2. **Hidden fees.** "Get our new cell-phone plan for only $10 a month, and make unlimited calls and texts!" Great deal,

right? Who could believe it? Well, don't. You'll never really get that $10/month plan. Want to make long-distance calls? Well that's an extra $30/month. Oh, don't forget roaming charges. Oh, and we forgot to mention the taxes, installment fees, monthly maintenance fees, and so forth. Always read the fine print! Airlines have actually been rather famous for this with low advertised fares that neglect to mention taxes and other fees, for say, an actual reserved seat or checked baggage.

3. **Manipulation of terms such as "organic," "light," "natural," and so on.** The classic example in this case was the use of terms like "mild" or "filtered" to describe cigarettes that killed you just fine regardless of being "mild." The use of such terms is now prohibited by the Food and Drug Administration (2013). However, many such terms that are ill defined are used to convey a naturalness of food items that may not survive careful scrutiny. This may allow food producers to charge a premium for high-demand, unadulterated food without needing to bother with more expensive production costs. Use of the term "organic" has since been regulated by U.S. law, but many other terms may be ill defined and misleading. One example of this was Kashi All-Natural Cereal, which was found to be loaded with synthetic products (Weinmann & Bhasin, 2011).

4. **Misleading illustrations.** Have you ever purchased a frozen dinner featuring a luxurious-looking, mouthwatering meal only to open it and find a few pale, tasteless patties? This approach is, again, fairly common with food items that are shown as larger or fresher than the actual product you get.

5. **Bait-and-switch.** Bait-and-switch occurs when advertisers advertise a particular, low-cost product that, in fact, doesn't exist. Phrases such as "for as low as . . . " should be a warning, as they're not promising the low cost, just saying that the range of costs could be as low as 'X.' Typically, once people have bothered to go to a store, they are easier to persuade to purchase a higher price item than they initially intended.

These are just a few examples of false advertisement techniques. False advertisement is risky, potentially subjecting a company to fines and ridicule. However, advertisers often try to guess how far they can push the envelope. As the saying goes, if it sounds too good to be true, it probably is!

SUBLIMINAL ADVERTISING AND BACKMASKING

Another issue people sometimes worry about is subliminal advertising. Subliminal advertising refers to advertisers putting some form of stimuli into an advertisement that is too subtle or brief to be consciously detected. For instance, a television advertisement might include a single frame of a naked adult in the middle of a cereal commercial. The typical frames-per-second rate for television is at least 24, so one frame passes too quickly to be noticed by human perception. But the idea is that, even if not noticed consciously, the image is recorded somewhere in the brain. Thus, the alluring image of the naked adult may unconsciously make you want the cereal more. There have been some examples of this actually happening with advertisements, particularly with furtive bits of subtle sexuality thrown into advertisements that are hard to notice without either slowing down frame rates or being extremely observant in print ads.

The idea of advertisers subliminally manipulating us is, of course, alarming. The good news is that the idea behind subliminal advertising is largely hooey. Studies indicate that subliminal advertisement simply doesn't work (Broyles, 2006; Trappey, 1996). So, we may be influenced by advertisers, but not through any secretly planted mind tricks.

A similar idea that was popular, particularly during the 1970s and 1980s, was *backmasking*. The idea of backmasking was that certain bands (ranging from Queen, to Styx, to Led Zeppelin, to Judas Priest) incorporated backward lyrics into their music, often involving satanic lyrics or enticements to immoral or even suicidal behavior. Such claims typically turned out to be false, with the backward lyrics more in the mind of the perceiver than in reality (Vokey & Read, 1985). Several states nonetheless passed legislation attempting to regulate backmasking. Of course, some bands *have* employed backmasking of lyrics, a phenomenon that probably increased because of the controversy rather than decreased. Most such efforts appear to be in jest, in effect, poking fun at the controversy. The evidence that such backmasking of lyrics causes people to join satanic cults, commit suicide, or otherwise do anything at all, is effectively zero.

PRODUCT PLACEMENT AND VIRAL ADVERTISEMENT

One form of advertising that has been controversial is product placement. In traditional advertisement, you know that you're seeing an advertisement whether it's a TV commercial or print ad. With product placement, you aren't necessarily aware you've been pitched to unless you're alert for it. Product placement is the positioning of branded products in fictional media such as television or movies. Probably the most famous example is the extra terrestrial's fascination with Reese's Pieces in the *ET* movie. In fact, placement is common and a big business.

With product placement, brands pay media producers to put their products into fictional media. Sometimes this is subtle, such as simply having a character drink a particular brand of soda or use a particular brand of computer (Apple shows up a lot, its logo easily recognized). Product placements can also be rather blatant. Perhaps you've watched a television show in which the characters suddenly launch into a discussion of the merits of the car they're driving, even though this conversation has nothing to do with the plot of a show. How effective product placements are seems to depend on our state of mind, with subtle product placements more effective when we're "ego depleted" or essentially tired after a long day (Gillespie, Joireman, & Muehling, 2012). However, product placement can be a risky strategy and can decrease brand loyalty if it comes across in a negative way (Gibson, Redker & Zimmerman, 2014). Basically, people don't like to think they're being tricked, which is one of the bigger controversies about product placement. Product placement likely works like most advertising, by increasing brand loyalty through familiarity and positive associations. But it often feels more insidious since we're not aware we're being advertised to.

Viral advertisement is advertising that relies less on traditional outlets such as television or radio and instead seeks to become edgy enough to be passed along via word-of-mouth from one consumer to another. Viral advertisements may use social platforms such as YouTube where they can avoid the limitations of typical television. If an advertisement is cool or funny enough, people will pass it along for its entertainment value, thus doing the advertiser's work for them at a fraction of the cost of marketing on television or in print. For instance, viral ads with high-intensity comedic violence tend to be particularly successful (Brown, Bhadury, & Pope, 2010), probably because they push the envelope on what can be seen on TV. With viral advertising, the quality of the ad itself is often more important than the brand, but the brand benefits from the exposure (Huang, Su, Zhou, & Liu, 2013). Viral advertising is also a much more interactive and social process, giving the ad the benefit of positive associations with these phenomena. The risk for viral advertisements is simply that they will never catch on and end up being ignored.

ADVERTISING TO CHILDREN

One other area that is controversial is advertisement directed at children. If you've ever watched children's programming, you'll see kids are bombarded with a variety of flashing, colorful ads marketing all manner of toys and sugary foods. Many people consider this to be unfair, given that children don't always understand the purposes of advertisements and are less likely to critically evaluate them. Of course, young children aren't going to hail a cab and set off with a twenty in their pocket to buy a box of Chocolate Coated Sugar Bombs. Marketing to children, particularly young children, tends to work through *pester power* in which parents give in to children who nag them for a particular product.

Children are thought of as being particularly vulnerable given that they are less adept than adults at reality testing. However, children's reality testing is complex and not exactly as awful as many people assume. Although the ability to distinguish reality from fantasy is a skill that children develop over time, evidence suggests that that one of the basic functions, namely, the ability to use context, begins to develop fairly early (Boerger, Tullos, & Woolley, 2009; Corriveau, Kim, Schwalen, & Harris, 2009; Woolley & Van Reet, 2006), and that such skills are generally well developed prior to the teen years (Tullos & Woolley, 2009). The effectiveness of childhood reality testing can perhaps be best demonstrated by the ability of middle elementary–aged children in the United States to reliably reject the plausibility of Santa Claus despite being misinformed on the issue by the entirety of society, their own parents, and the presence of Santa "in real life" at malls and parties. By the time a child is in middle school, they are probably about as effective as an adult at distinguishing reality from fiction, an important point we return to later in the book. But for the moment, we might expect that the impact of advertising might be particularly potent on very young children.

This is, in fact, exactly what we see. In one study of advertisement effects on eating choices, some students and I brought children of varying ages from 3 to 12 into our research laboratory and had them watch cartoons. Between the cartoons were three commercials. Two commercials were for unrelated things, but the middle commercial was for a McDonald's food item. Some kids saw an advertisement for unhealthy French fries, others for healthier Apple Dippers. Following this, children were given the opportunity to select a coupon for either Apple Dippers or French fries. Children were also randomized to have their parents read a script in which they either encouraged the child to select either the healthy option or whichever option they wanted more. We wanted to see what the impact of a brief commercial was on eating choices, and whether the effect of the commercial was mitigated by parental influences. We found that young children (3–5) tended to be most influenced by the advertisements middle-grade children (6–8) tended to accept their parents' suggestions and older children (9–12) could care less what either the advertisement or their parents suggested and did their own thing! Thus, in this study, we were able to chart the developmental course of advertising and parental influences on healthy eating choices. Advertisements are most influential on the very young, which we might have expected from the work on reality testing (Ferguson, Contreras, & Kilburn, 2014).

So we see that children appear to develop a "fiction detector" rather early in life. But advertisements generally try to work around those fiction detectors by claiming to be true. Advertisers are known to deliberately employ strategies to get around children's fiction detecting (Bezbaruah & Brunt, 2012) which, again, makes such advertising controversial. Given the obesity problems in many industrialized nations, marketing of unhealthy food products to children has been particularly controversial, although advertising strategies are just one facet of a broader and more complex problem (Buijzen, Schuurman, & Bomhof, 2008). This obesity problem has been particularly influential in leading to calls for the regulation of advertisements directed at children, although the effectiveness of potential regulation in tackling obesity is debated (Dhar & Baylis, 2011; Kent, Dubois, & Wanless, 2011).

REGULATION OF ADVERTISING

The issue of advertisements directed toward children coupled with the obesity epidemic in Western nations raises the question of when advertisements could be regulated. Direct advertising of unhealthy food to children is only part of the obesity crisis, and probably a small part, but if limiting advertisements directed at children could help in even a small way, would it be worth it? What about the free-speech rights of the advertisers themselves? At what point do we want government to limit what we, whether individuals or businesses, can say even if it is ostensibly for our own good? Although you might agree with the issue of advertisements toward children and obesity, I think we could see that it would be easy to draw up a long list of "naughty" advertisements we might be better without. What about direct advertisements of medications to consumers, encouraging patients to pressure their doctors into prescribing medications they might not need? Or advertisements for things like alcohol or, for that matter, sunny vacations at the beach, when both alcohol and sun consumption are both associated with disease? If it were true, as some claim (although we see later such claims are debated), that even PG-13 rated movies are associated with societal violence, should we prohibit advertisements for many movies "for our own good"? The province of Quebec in Canada at one time proposed banning advertisements for cars and snowmobiles that featured fast driving (Thenewspaper.com, 2007). Although it's often possible to provide a rational argument for why one product's advertisements should be regulated, it's not clear where that slippery slope might end, and who gets to decide when it's "for our own good" that we don't receive certain advertisements.

Within the United States, the Federal Trade Commission is responsible for most advertisement regulation. Much of their efforts focus on issues related to deceptive advertising. Related to industry-specific regulation, the industry most regulated is, by far, the cigarette industry.

In the early days of television, cigarette ads were common. Many of these can still be viewed online on channels such as YouTube. Classic examples include jaunty cigarettes dancing, healthy, happy young people enjoying adventurous activities while smoking, and, of course, the Marlboro Man, whose image equated smoking with rugged masculinity.

Regulation of tobacco advertisements began in the 1960s as the public health consequences of smoking became clear. Initially, the Federal Communications Commission required television and radio stations that ran tobacco ads to also run, at no cost, public service announcements regarding the health risks of smoking (Wagner, 1971). By 1970, Congress passed the Public Health Cigarette Smoking Act, which required warning labels on cigarette packages and also banned cigarette ads from television and radio. Initially, these efforts seemed to have little impact. The FTC reported to Congress in 1981 that warning labels had little impact on consumers, resulting in more rigorous standards for warning labels (Centers for Disease Control and Prevention, 2000). Tobacco producers shifted to marketing to children, introducing child-friendly cartoon characters such as Joe Camel (Fischer, Schwartz, Richards, Goldstein, & Rojas, 1991). The 2009 Family Smoking Prevention and Control Act further prohibited tobacco advertising at cultural events such as sports and concerts. The Federal Drug Administration sought to use the act to force cigarette makers to include graphic images of diseased individuals along with warning labels on packages. Such efforts have been found to be unconstitutional by U.S. courts, although they are permitted in other nations. Through litigation settlements, tobacco advertisement on public transportation and billboards is prohibited in most (but not all) states, and tobacco is not advertised in magazines likely to be used by minors for research purposes (e.g., news magazines such as *Time* or *Newsweek*). Other countries are even more stringent, such as the United Kingdom where almost all tobacco advertising is banned.

Like tobacco, alcohol advertising is regulated in many nations, typically focused on banning advertisements directed at minors or promising health or behavioral benefits of alcohol.

In the United States, alcohol has avoided much regulation because of the tight control of advertising standards by the alcohol industry itself. The industry is careful not to market to minors (Federal Trade Commission, 2003), thus avoiding much of the condemnation that fell upon the cigarette industry.

COMPARING ADVERTISEMENTS TO FICTIONAL MEDIA

One last cautionary note before we move further. In public debates on other forms of media, particularly fictional media, fictional media are often compared to advertisements. A slightly exaggerated version of this might go like, "If advertisers spend billions of dollars each year to change our behavior, why can't video games make us mass murderers, or sexy media cause teens to get pregnant?" This type of argument, which has some initial appeal, is based on a logical fallacy, or error of logical argument, called *false equivalence.* In other words, the argument rests on the assumption that advertising and fictional media influences are similar, or that the behavioral outcomes are similar.

In fact, there are many reasons to reject such a line of argument. First, related to behavioral outcomes, for advertisements to be successful and profitable, they need result in only relatively minor forms of behavioral change. For instance, a successful ad need not even get you to switch from drinking water to soda. A successful ad need only convince people who are *already* soda drinkers to switch to or remain loyal to the ad's brand. This is far different from the kinds of profound behavioral changes, such as violence, the development of clinical eating disorders, or rampant immorality, worried over for fictional media.

Second, the two forms of media are far different in composition and intent. Advertisements are *designed* to influence behavior (Figure 3.1), and advertising companies invest considerable resources in researching how to be effective at behavioral change.

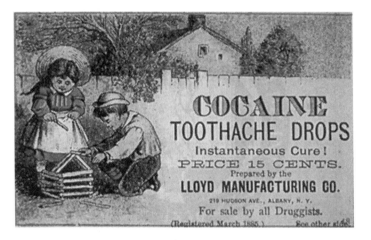

FIGURE 3.1 Cocaine advertisement from the 19th century.

Fictional media, by contrast, is typically less concerned with behavioral change. True, some fiction may seek to get consumers to consider an issue or even persuade, but their efforts are typically subtler and less specifically designed. And fictional media typically makes little effort to convince consumers it is *true*, whereas advertisements tend to project a kind of *truthiness*. We may know that advertisements can be deceptive, but they at least try to convince us they're telling the unvarnished truth. There are good reasons to think that our brains will process messages from fictional media and advertising differently. Thus, although the effects of both advertising and fictional media are important to consider and research, we can't begin a scientific investigation with such a clumsy assumption of false equivalence. Each purported media effect needs to be studied independently, and if the data support one effect but not the other, such is life.

CONCLUSIONS

Just like mosquitoes, advertisements aren't going away anytime soon. Overall, research indicating that advertisements have at least some impact on some people's behavior for some things is quite strong. Indeed, the research on advertisement impact is probably the strongest of the topics we cover in the book. Henceforth, however, we move into fiction and news media, where greater controversy often lies.

REFERENCES

American Marketing Association. (2007). *Definition of marketing.* Retrieved November 23, 2008, from http://www.marketingpower .com/AboutAMA/Pages/DefinitionofMarketing.aspx

Bezbaruah, N., & Brunt, A. (2012). The influence of cartoon character advertising on fruit and vegetable preferences of 9- to 11-year-old children. *Journal of Nutrition Education and Behavior, 44*(5), 438–441. doi:10.1016/j.jneb.2011.03.139

Boerger, E., Tullos, A., & Woolley, J. (2009). Return of the Candy Witch: Individual differences in acceptance and stability of belief in a novel fantastical being. *British Journal of Developmental Psychology, 27,* 953–970.

Brown, M. R., Bhadury, R. K., & Pope, N. I. (2010). The impact of comedic violence on viral advertising effectiveness. *Journal of Advertising, 39*(1), 49–65. doi:10.2753/JOA0091-3367390104

Broyles, S. J. (2006). Misplaced paranoia over subliminal advertising: What's the big uproar this time? *Journal of Consumer Marketing, 23*(6), 312–313. doi:10.1108/ 07363760610701841

Buijzen, M., Schuurman, J., & Bomhof, E. (2008). Associations between children's television advertising exposure and their food consumption patterns: A household diary-survey study. *Appetite, 50*(2–3), 231–239. doi:10.1016/j.appet.2007.07.006

Burnham, J. C. (1994). John B. Watson: Interviewee, professional figure, symbol. In J. Todd & E. Morris (Eds.), *Modern perspectives on John B. Watson and classical behaviorism* (pp. 65–73). Santa Barbara, CA: Greenwood Press.

Cadbury, D. (2011). *The chocolate wars: The 150-year rivalry between the world's greatest chocolate makers.* New York, NY: Public Affairs.

Centers for Disease Control and Prevention. (2000). *2000 Surgeon General's Report—Reducing tobacco use.* Retrieved from http://web.archive.org/web/20070427165525/http://www.cdc.gov/tobacco/data_statistics/sgr/sgr_2000/highlights/highlight_labels.htm

Corriveau, K., Kim, A., Schwalen, C., & Harris, P. (2009). Abraham Lincoln and Harry Potter: Children's differentiation between historical and fantasy characters. *Cognition, 113,* 213–225.

Dhar, T., & Baylis, K. (2011). Fast food consumption and the ban on advertising targeting children: The Quebec experience. *Journal of Marketing Research, 48*(5), 799–813. doi:10.1509/jmkr.48.5.799

Federal Trade Commission. (2003). *Alcohol marketing and advertising.* Retrieved from http://www.ftc.gov/sites/default/files/documents/reports/alcohol-marketing-and-advertising-federal-trade-commission-report-congress-september-2003%2falcohol08report.pdf

Ferguson, C. J., Contreras, S., & Kilburn, M. (2014). Advertising and fictional media effects on healthy eating choices in early and later childhood. *Psychology of Popular Media Culture, 3*(3), 164–173. doi:10.1037/ppm0000016

Fischer, P., Schwartz, M. P., Richards, J. W., Goldstein, A. O., & Rojas, T. H. (1991). Brand logo recognition by children aged 3 to 6 years. Mickey Mouse and Old Joe the Camel. *Journal of the American Medical Association, 266*(22), 3145–3148.

Food and Drug Administration. (2013). *Light, low, mild or similar descriptors.* Retrieved from http://www.fda.gov/TobaccoProducts/Labeling/Labeling/MisleadingDescriptors/default.htm

Gibson, B., Redker, C., & Zimmerman, I. (2014). Conscious and non-conscious effects of product placement: Brand recall and active persuasion knowledge affect brand attitudes and brand self-identification differently. *Psychology of Popular Media Culture, 3,* 19–37.

Gillespie, B., Joireman, J., & Muehling, D. D. (2012). The moderating effect of ego depletion on viewer brand recognition and brand attitudes following exposure to subtle versus blatant product placements in television programs. *Journal of Advertising, 41*(2), 55–65. doi:10.2753/JOA0091-3367410204

Huang, J., Su, S., Zhou, L., & Liu, X. (2013). Attitude toward the viral ad: Expanding traditional advertising models to interactive advertising. *Journal of Interactive Marketing, 27*(1), 36–46. doi:10 .1016/j.intmar.2012.06.001

Kent, M., Dubois, L., & Wanless, A. (2011). Food marketing on children's television in two different policy environments. *International Journal of Pediatric Obesity, 6*(2-2), e433–e441. doi:10.3109/ 17477166.2010.526222

LaTour, K. A., & LaTour, M. S. (2009). Positive mood and susceptibility to false advertising. *Journal of Advertising, 38*(3), 127–142. doi:10.2753/JOA0091-3367380309

Olson, J., & Dover, P. (1978). Cognitive effects of deceptive advertising. *Journal of Marketing Research, 15,* 29–38.

Presbrey, F. (2000). The history and development of advertising. *Advertising and Society Review, 1*(1). Retrieved from http://muse .jhu.edu/login?auth=0&type=summary&url=/journals/asr/ v001/1.1presbrey.html

Thenewspaper.com. (2007). *Canada: Quebec may ban fast car ads.* Retrieved from http://www.thenewspaper.com/news/21/2129.asp

Trappey, C. (1996). A meta-analysis of consumer choice and subliminal advertising. *Psychology & Marketing, 13*(5), 517–530. doi:10.1002/ (SICI)1520-6793(199608)13:5<517::AID-MAR5>3.0.CO;2-C

Tullos, A., & Woolley, J. (2009). The development of children's ability to use evidence to infer reality status. *Child Development, 80,* 101–114.

Vokey, J. R., & Read, J. (1985). Subliminal messages: Between the devil and the media. *American Psychologist, 40*(11), 1231–1239. doi:10.1037/0003-066X.40.11.1231

Wagner, S. (1971). *Cigarette country.* New York, NY: Praeger Publishers.

Watson, J. B., & Rayner, R. (1920). Conditioned emotional reactions. *Journal of Experimental Psychology, 3,* 1–14.

Weinmann, K., & Bhasin, K. (2011). 14 False advertising scandals that cost brands millions. *Business Insider.* Retrieved from http:// www.businessinsider.com/false-advertising-scandals-2011-9 ?op=1#ixzz34XCp8adi

Woolley, J., & Van Reet, J. (2006). Effects of context on judgments concerning the reality status of novel entities. *Child Development, 77,* 1778–1793.

The Boob Tube:
Media and Academic
Achievement

For decades, televisions have been referred to as "boob tubes." This slang term arose from the common belief that time spent in front of a television made one stupid, as if the television set magically drained intelligence out of viewers. The "tube" side of the slang term referred to the huge (by today's standards) cathode-ray tubes that powered the viewing screen in the Stone Age of television. This basic belief persists, that time spent on entertainment media, particularly visual media (books are somewhat immune, although perhaps not comic books or trashy romances), is associated with reduced intelligence or academic performance. On the other hand, some investigators are examining whether newer forms of media can be used to promote learning. This idea is the basis for shows such as *Sesame Street*. In this chapter we examine these concerns and beliefs and elucidate to what degree consuming entertainment media actually influences our academic achievement.

THE SCOPE OF THE ISSUE

If people, children or adults, were in the habit of consuming moderate amounts of media, the issue might largely be moot. However, evidence is pretty clear that the average person in an industrialized nation consumes copious amounts of media, particularly visual media. The consumption of media is typically referred to as *screen time*. Screen time is any time spent in front of various visual media, whether televisions, computers, video game consoles, or smartphones. The notion of screen time initially referred to entertainment media, although screens have become increasingly integrated into our lives, and we interact with screens continuously at work, at school, and as part of our social lives. Thus, when we consider how much time we spend in front of screens, we must remember that these figures no longer refer exclusively to screens for entertainment but the complete integration of screens as essential parts of our lives. We can see this with the smartphone, a device that can be used for communication, for work, for education, and for entertainment, perhaps simultaneously! How do we figure such a device properly when calculating screen time?

Much of the attention focuses on television and, by any estimate, we watch a lot of television. According to the Bureau of Labor Statistics (2013), the typical child watches about 24 to 25 hours of television each week and, in a typical year, spends more time watching television than in school (although the long summer break factors into this presumably). The average person, over the course of his or her life, will have spent 9 "blissful" years watching television. According to a 2010 report by the Kaiser Family Foundation, teens spend about 7.5 hours a day on "screen time," much of which is driven by mobile devices. This number must be qualified by observing, once again, that devices such as smartphones are more integrated into our social and even educational lives, and so a direct comparison with passive TV viewing of two generations ago may be risky, but nonetheless we can see that screens are an important part of our lives and the lives of youth today. What's more, the Kaiser report suggests that heavy users have more academic problems than light users of screens.

WHAT'S THE EVIDENCE?

The Kaiser report accurately notes that correlation does not mean causation however, so let's look a bit closer at the evidence regarding screen time and academic performance. Given that correlations are observed between screen time and reduced academic performance (although more on this later), it's not unreasonable to wonder about causal influences. However, it's also quite possible that there may be a selection effect in play. Perhaps more disadvantaged families engage in more screen time. Lower-income families, where parents may need to spend more time working, may have both difficulty providing the same level of educational opportunities for their children and may also use screens more as babysitters, given their need to work or from exhaustion following long hours at work. Or both could be true, with certain families selecting more television, which, in turn, makes academic achievement worse!

Let's look at the correlational evidence first. Given the hype regarding screen time and academic performance, data on the relationship suggests that such effects, even correlational, are fairly modest. In one characteristics example, Sharif, Wills, and Sargent (2010) followed a large sample of middle school youth for 2 years. They found that screen time did correlate with academic problems. However, controlling for other variables, such as parental practices and the child's self-control, reduced these correlations such that screen time had no direct relationship with school performance. The authors did find several indirect relationships, wherein screen time did correlate with school performance through moderator variables such as substance abuse or behavior problems, but these indirect relationships were very small, ranging from $r = .05$ to .12 (or, roughly speaking, suggesting that overlapping variance between screen time and intermediate outcomes ranged from about a quarter of a percentage point to just over 1%). Not very much at all. Although the authors were able to predict almost 48% of the variance in school problems, most of this seems to have come from demographic variables such as gender and socioeconomic status. This same general pattern is replicated throughout the literature. Television viewing is associated with small correlations predicting reduced academic achievement (Hancox, Milne, & Poulton, 2005), whereas in other studies (Schmidt, Rich, Rifas-Shiman, Oken, & Taveras, 2009) these small correlations disappeared once other variables, particularly involving family circumstances, were controlled. Similar results are found for videogames, where pathological gaming (a tendency to overdo gaming at the expense of other activities, which we talk about in the next chapter) is associated with academic problems, but nonpathological gaming, no matter how many hours played, is not (Skoric, Teo, & Neo, 2009). Some research has, in fact, indicated a curvilinear relationship for video game exposure (Przybylski, 2014), with the best outcomes seen for moderate gamers as compared to either heavy gamers or children who don't play video games at all.

Thus, to summarize the research, it appears that small correlations between screen time and reduced academic performance do exist. However, it's less clear whether this link is causal or an artifact that is due to other factors. The correlational evidence seems to lean toward the latter explanation, that it's less the media damaging academic achievement and more that heavy media viewing is symptomatic of other structural problems.

Experimental studies of media's influence on academics are few, which is not surprising. Ethically, we can't cause kids to fail school in the name of science. So what experimental studies that do exist are somewhat difficult to generalize to real life. However, a few have tackled the issue of media's impact on academics. In one example of a study trying to address this issue, Lillard and Peterson (2011) randomized children to watch either a fast-paced cartoon (*SpongeBob SquarePants*) and/or an educational show, or to perform a controlled drawing task. The authors assessed the children's executive functioning immediately after. Children who had recently watched *SpongeBob SquarePants* had reduced executive functioning (the ability to plan) compared to the other two groups. The authors interpret this as a possible sign that exposure to fast-paced television cartoons may make it difficult for children to remain focused on the comparatively slower paced and boring instructions of their school teachers. However, the authors didn't provide evidence for any long-term impact. It's not unreasonable to think kids might be in a different frame of mind following various types of tasks. Whether this has a long-term ramification remains unclear. Other experimental studies have generally indicated null effects for television exposure, suggesting that exposure to television, including educational videos for infants, neither helped much nor hindered early language or academic development (Richert, Robb, Fender, & Wartella, 2010; Robb, Richert, & Wartella, 2009).

THE *BABY EINSTEIN* DEBACLE

Perhaps one of the most fascinating cases of push-and-pull between the claims of media industries and media scholars is the case of *Baby Einstein*. The *Baby Einstein* videos are a series of videos designed for infants that combine images, puppets, and pleasant music in a way that is intended to be intellectually stimulating for young, developing minds. Even the use of the Einstein

71

name (for which royalties are paid) implies that watching the videos would improve a child's intelligence.

The degree to which watching media with educational content can boost intelligence has always been controversial. For instance, in one famous experiment, listening to classical music was demonstrated to cause temporary increases in spatial intelligence, something subsequently referred to as the "Mozart Effect" (Rauscher, Shaw, & Ky, 1993). However, the Mozart Effect proved difficult to replicate and is now generally considered to be erroneous despite having become something of a cultural meme (Chabris, 1999).

So too were the implicit claims of *Baby Einstein* videos controversial, particularly in light of long-standing recommendations by the American Academy of Pediatrics (see Council on Communications and Media, 2011, but more on this later) for babies to avoid media altogether until age 2. By 2007 several pediatricians (Zimmerman, Christakis, Meltzoff, 2007) published a correlational article that purported to show that watching baby videos was associated with language delays for young infants (under 18 months) although not for older infants. This article raised a hue and cry over the purported "harm" of such videos. Disney, current owner of the Baby Einstein Company, denied that the product was harmful but offered refunds to any purchasers unhappy with it. The University of Washington (2007) issued a press release accompanying this study and quoted one of the authors, Dr. Christakis, as claiming that baby videos "may in fact be harmful."

So, do we have here a case of the media industry foisting a faulty product on us with exaggerated claims, and academic pediatricians riding to our rescue? Not so fast. What then ensued was a maelstrom that backfired on the pediatricians. The findings of Zimmerman et al. (2007) were not well replicated in other studies. One review on this topic (Courage & Setliff, 2009) concluded "it is premature either to condemn television and video material as a source of harm to the developing infant brain or to promote it as a viable source of early learning" (p. 76).

In 2010 William Clark, one of the cofounders of the *Baby Einstein* product line, sued the University of Washington to gain access to the data for the 2007 Zimmerman et al. paper, as well as an earlier 2004 paper (Christakis, Zimmerman, DiGiuseppe, & McCarty) by the same two lead authors (Lewin, 2010). Despite the fact that the 2007 study was federally funded, there are concerns about how strongly the University of Washington supported transparency in scientific research. The 2004 dataset is said to be lost, and the university reportedly refused to release the 2007 dataset until compelled by court order. The information turned over to William Clark and his wife Julia reportedly included emails documenting disagreements between the researchers regarding the null effects for the older children. The Clarks have also alleged methodological discrepancies in the different databases they received.

So the University of Washington and the authors of the Zimmerman et al. study *went to court* to try to prevent their data from becoming public. And lost. This is a rather remarkable example of nontransparency for a federally funded research project. With the dataset now publically available, however, because of court order, I became interested in the matter. With coauthor Brent Donnellan, I filed a Public Information Act request and obtained a copy of the Zimmerman et al. (2007) dataset. In our reanalysis (Ferguson & Donnellan, 2014), we concluded that the original authors had handled their data sloppily, that, depending upon how the data were analyzed, it was possible to show that baby videos helped, harmed, or had no impact on language development, and that the worst outcomes for language development, ironically, were for infants who watched no television at all (in compliance with the American Academy of Pediatrics' [AAP] recommendations). We stated that we found the Zimmerman et al. (2007) and University of Washington (2007) claims of "harm" due to baby videos to be unwarranted.

Thus, we see that media producers sometimes make exaggerated claims about their product's usefulness. However, the academic community too often turns around and mimics that behavior, only in the opposite direction by making exaggerated claims of harm. Although concerns expressed by scholars are often in good faith, it may also often be the case that scholars experience *warning bias* in that their reputations are enhanced (along with grant funding) by drawing attention to pressing societal ills that they will, of course, fix. The lesson is, buyer beware, whether you're buying media products or academic claims about those media products.

THE AMERICAN ACADEMY OF PEDIATRICS POLICY STATEMENT

Despite the inconsistent nature of some of the research, the American Academy of Pediatrics (AAP) has a long-standing policy suggesting the infants under age 2 should not watch any television or screens at all (Council on Communications and Media, 2011). This policy statement presents the research in this area as more solid and consistent than it actually is. How did this come to be? Policy statements by professional advocacy organizations are presented as factual truths but, in fact, often reflect politics and the internal ideology of the group in question. That is to say, policy statements often reflect what is good for the group issuing them, rather than a factual truth. Further, among the council members who drafted the statement was Dimitri Christakis, coauthor on some of the articles critical of media including the *Baby Einstein* research noted earlier. Too often, professional advocacy groups like the AAP allow authors heavily invested in a particular theoretical position to, in essence, review their own work and declare it beyond further debate. That must be nice, but it shouldn't be mistaken for a credible, objective review by disinterested scholars.

As we see in later chapters, the AAP has released a host of policy statements on media issues, almost all of questionable quality. These have ranged from media violence to "Facebook Depression" (the belief that time spent on social media causes depression). All have been criticized for excessive alarmism, misrepresenting the science, failing to cite articles that disconfirm the AAP's policy, and allowing authors with ideological or sometimes financial conflicts of interest to write the AAP's policy statements.

As noted earlier, reanalyzing the evidence from Zimmerman et al. (2007), which the AAP cites in support of its policy, suggests that total media abstinence is associated with declines, not advances, in language learning in toddlers. The policy has also been criticized as simply being unrealistic (Poniewozik, 2011). Such critics argue that the AAP's policy puts unrealistic demands on parents to constantly enrich their babies through face-to-face contact, which succeeds mainly in making parents feel guilty when they are unable to achieve such a high standard. In this sense the AAP is likely experiencing something I call *sanctimony bias*, which occurs when academics (or other society elites) propose a behavior that few people can live up to as an ideal. Such a proposition may make the proposers feel good (through sanctimoniousness), but serves little other real purpose.

Naturally, everything is good in moderation. Babies certainly should be enriched through face-to-face time, and television or other screens at any age should be used in moderation in combination with adequate socialization time, exercise, and brain-enriching activities. But the AAP's zero-screen-time recommendation appears to rest both on shaky science and unrealistic expectations of most parents. There is little to suggest that ignoring it should be high on a parent's list of main worries.

EDUCATIONAL MEDIA?

It stands to reason that if vacuous entertainment media is a potential source for reduced academic readiness, designing educational content for television or other media can reverse this trend. This is the concept behind a wealth of educational television shows ranging from *Sesame Street* to the UK's *Horrible Histories*, and entire networks have been constructed around educational ideas (although some have slipped increasingly into reality television). Similarly, many books or even video games (*Math Blaster, Oregon Trail*) have been constructed with the hope of fostering education.

Concerns about quality educational television for minors resulted in the Children's Television Act of 1990, which required that U.S. broadcast channels (those that use government-owned airwaves such as NBC, Fox, CBS, and ABC, but not cable stations) broadcast a minimum of 3 hours of educational programming each day. A 1999 analysis of the Children's Television Act (Woodard, 1999) suggested that the impact of the Act had been modest, overall.

Is educational television actually helpful? Again, it depends on whom you ask and what your standards of evidence are. The AAP would prefer that children watch no television at all, including educational programming, particularly before age 2 (although, again, whether this recommendation itself is sound is debatable). In one of the most compelling long-term studies that argue for the value of educational programming, Anderson, Huston, Schmitt, Linebarger, and Wright (2001) found that watching educational television was associated with better academic performance and higher creativity, as well as with lower aggression, particularly for boys. Curiously, and jumping ahead to a later discussion, watching violent television had no impact on aggression, although it was associated with slightly lower grades. Here, once again, effect sizes were fairly small, however, suggesting that the impact of educational television isn't necessarily dramatic. Researcher Deborah Linebarger (Linebarger, Kosanic, Greenwood, & Doku, 2004; Linebarger & Wainwright, 2007) has noted that well-designed educational programs can foster learning in young children, but not all educational shows are created the same, and the best are designed to match the learning styles of children.

The advent of video games, not surprisingly, has led to the development of "serious games," which might foster academic achievement with compelling game play (e.g., Annetta, 2010).

However, a curious thing happened with video games. Some evidence began to suggest that violent action games might actually promote some kinds of cognitive development! A fairly wide body of evidence (e.g., McDermott, Bavelier, & Green, 2014; Spence & Feng, 2010) has suggested that playing shooter games improves a variety of cognitive tasks known collectively as visuospatial cognition. Such tasks are probably more colloquially known as "hand-eye coordination," although they actually include a wider range of skills, such as attention, processing, and conceptualization of visual material. Such skills would be valuable in a spectrum of careers from engineering to surgery, and there is even some evidence to suggest that playing violent action games makes for better surgeons (Rosser, Lynch, Haskamp, Gentile, & Yalif, 2007)!

This research on video games and visuospatial cognition has also been controversial, however. Boot, Blakely, and Simons (2011) contend that the potential for spurious effects in this realm has been high, with inadequate control groups, demand characteristics (hypothesis guessing), and other methodological issues common in experimental studies. We see that such issues are common to many studies of video game violence, whether on positive or negative outcomes, so it is best, perhaps, to avoid getting too excited about such games, one way or another.

One other issue bears mentioning. Few doubt that encouraging children to read can boost their academic skills. But in one of my recent studies (Ferguson, 2014), *why* children read may be surprisingly important. In this study, which had to do with reading "banned books" (books that have been controversial for one reason or another), I found that children's reading for pleasure, but *not* assigned school readings, correlated with better academic performance. So, when encouraging children to read, it may be more productive to allow them to follow their fancy and develop a love for reading . . . anything . . . rather than foisting *Moby Dick* or *The Grapes of Wrath* on them.

CONCLUSIONS

The degree to which time spent on screens contributes to academic problems in youth has been an ongoing controversy. In general, it appears that time spent watching television or playing video games has a small correlation with lower academic achievement, but that this correlation largely disappears once other factors are controlled. That is to say, it's difficult to definitively claim that screen time *causes* reductions in academic functioning. Other evidence has suggested that the relationship between screen time and academic achievement is curvilinear, with worst outcomes both for overusers and those who don't use screens at all, even at young ages. So the old maxim of "everything in moderation" appears to hold. More to the point, efforts to eliminate screen time altogether from children's lives may not only be unrealistic but actually counterproductive.

As such, trying to tie screen time directly to academic difficulties may not be very helpful. However, some children and adults do demonstrate patterns of media use that are obsessive and pathological. Sometimes called media addictions, these patterns of use can indeed impair academic performance. It is to this issue that this book now turns.

REFERENCES

Anderson, D. R., Huston, A. C., Schmitt, K. L., Linebarger, D. L., & Wright, J. C. (2001). Early childhood television viewing and adolescent behavior: The recontact study. *Monographs of the Society for Research in Child Development, 66*(1), vii–147. doi:10.1111/1540-5834.00120

Annetta, L. A. (2010). The "I's" have it: A framework for serious educational game design. *Review of General Psychology, 14*(2), 105–112. doi:10.1037/a0018985

Boot, W. R., Blakely, D. P., & Simons, D. J. (2011). Do action video games improve perception and cognition? *Frontiers in Psychology, 2,* 226. doi:10.3389/fpsyg.2011.00226

Bureau of Labor Statistics. (2013). *Television watching statistics.* Retrieved from http://statisticbrain.com/television-watching-statistics

Chabris, C. (1999). Prelude or requiem for the "Mozart effect"? *Nature, 400,* 826–827. doi:10.1038/23608

Christakis, D., Zimmerman, F., DiGiuseppe, D., & McCarty, C. (2004). Early television exposure and subsequent attentional problems in children. *Pediatrics, 113*(4), 708–713.

Council on Communications and Media. (2011). Media use by children younger than 2 years. *Pediatrics, 128*(5), 1040–1045.

Courage, M., & Setliff, A. (2009). Debating the impact of television and video material on very young children: Attention, learning, and the developing brain. *Child Development Perspectives, 3*(1), 72–78.

Ferguson, C. J. (2014). Is reading "banned" books associated with behavior problems in young readers? The influence of controversial young adult books on the psychological well-being of adolescents. *Psychology of Aesthetics, Creativity, and the Arts, 8*(3), 354–362. doi:10.1037/a0035601

Ferguson, C. J., & Donnellan, M. B. (2014). Is the association between children's baby video viewing and poor language development robust? A reanalysis of Zimmerman, Christakis, and Meltzoff (2007). *Developmental Psychology, 50*(1), 129–137.

Hancox, R., Milne, B., & Poulton, R. (2005). Association of television viewing during childhood with poor educational achievement. *JAMA Pediatrics, 159,* 614–618.

Kaiser Family Foundation. (2010). *Daily media use among children and teens up dramatically from five years ago.* Retrieved from http://kff.org/disparities-policy/press-release/daily-media-use-among-children-and-teens-up-dramatically-from-five-years-ago/

Lewin, T. (2010). "Baby Einstein" founder goes to court. *The New York Times.* Retrieved December 22, 2011, from http://www.nytimes.com/2010/01/13/education/13einstein.html

Lillard, A., & Peterson, J. (2011). The immediate impact of different types of television on young children's executive functioning. *Pediatrics, 128,* e1–e6.

Linebarger, D. L., Kosanic, A. Z., Greenwood, C. R., & Doku, N. (2004). Effects of viewing the television program *Between the Lions* on the emergent literacy skills of young children. *Journal of Educational Psychology, 96*(2), 297–308. doi:10.1037/0022-0663.96.2.297

Linebarger, D. L., & Wainwright, D. K. (2007). Learning while viewing: Urban myth or dream come true? In S. R. Mazzarella (Ed.), *20 questions about youth and the media* (pp. 179–196). New York, NY: Peter Lang.

McDermott, A. F., Bavelier, D., & Green, C. (2014). Memory abilities in action video game players. *Computers in Human Behavior, 34*, 69–78. doi:10.1016/j.chb.2014.01.018

Poniewozik, J. (2011). I let my babies watch TV. And I regret nothing! *Time.* Retrieved from http://entertainment.time.com/2011/10/19/i-let-my-babies-watch-tv-and-i-regret-nothing

Przybylski, A. (2014). Electronic gaming and psychosocial adjustment. *Pediatrics, 134*, e716–e722. doi:10.1542/peds.2013-4021d

Rauscher, F., Shaw, G., & Ky, C. (1993). Music and spatial task performance. *Nature, 365*, 611. doi:10.1038/365611a0

Richert, R. A., Robb, M. B., Fender, J. G., & Wartella, E. (2010). Word learning from baby videos. *Archives of Pediatrics & Adolescent Medicine, 5*, 432–437. doi:10.1001/archpediatrics.2010.24

Robb, M. B., Richert, R. A., & Wartella, E. A. (2009). Just a talking book? Word learning from watching baby videos. *British Journal of Developmental Psychology, 27*, 27–45. doi:10.1348/026151008X320156

Rosser, J. C., Lynch, P. J., Haskamp, L., Gentile, D. A., & Yalif, A. (2007). The impact of video games in surgical training. *Archives of Surgery, 142*, 181–186.

Schmidt, M., Rich, M., Rifas-Shiman, S., Oken, E., & Taveras, E. (2009). Television viewing in infancy and child cognition at 3 years of age in a US cohort. *Pediatrics, 123*(3), e370–e375.

Sharif, I., Wills, T. A., & Sargent, J. D. (2010). Effect of visual media use on school performance: A prospective study. *Journal of Adolescent Health, 46*(1), 52–61. doi:10.1016/j.jadohealth.2009.05.012

Skoric, M. M., Teo, L., & Neo, R. (2009). Children and video games: Addiction, engagement, and scholastic achievement. *Cyberpsychology & Behavior, 12*(5), 567–572. doi:10.1089/cpb.2009.0079

Spence, I., & Feng, J. (2010). Video games and spatial cognition. *Review of General Psychology, 14*(2), 92–104. doi:10.1037/a0019491

University of Washington. (2007). *Baby DVDs, videos, may hinder, not help, infants' language development.* Retrieved December 22, 2011, from http://www.washington.edu/alumni/uwnewslinks/200709/videos.html

Woodard, E. (1999). *The 1999 state of children's television report.* Annenberg School of Public Policy. Retrieved from http://www.annen bergpublicpolicycenter.org/Downloads/Media_and_Developing_ Child/Childrens_Programming/19990628_State_of_Children/ childrensTVreport1999.pdf

Zimmerman, F. J., Christakis, D. A., & Meltzoff, A. N. (2007). Associations between media viewing and language development in children under age two years. *Journal of Pediatrics, 151*(4), 364–368.

Media Addiction

As a general rule, if it's fun, someone is going to overdo it. We hear lots of talk about people becoming addicted to a wide range of pleasurable activities, whether sex, food, gambling, or even exercise. Probably there are some people who are even "addicted" to activities society encourages, such as attending religious services, but "addictions" tend to have a moral component to them, so "religion addiction" doesn't get much attention. In fact, at present, the *Diagnostic and Statistical Manual of Mental Disorders* (*DSM-5*; American Psychiatric Association, 2013) recognizes only one *behavioral* addiction (in addition to the addictions to various substances ranging from caffeine to heroin), namely gambling addiction. However, one condition, "Internet Gaming Disorder," has been proposed as a possible category for future study. This chapter concerns itself with the concept of media addiction, how prevalent it is, and the controversies surrounding it.

MEDIA ADDICTION: BASIC ISSUES

That some people watch too much television or play too many video games is probably not news to anyone. On a basic level, overindulging in too much screen time can be negative to the extent that it takes us away from other activities or contributes to a sedentary lifestyle. But what do we mean that someone is "addicted" to media? How does such an addiction relate (or not) to addictions to substances such as tobacco or heroin?

On a very basic level, a lot remains unknown about media addictions. Primarily that's because there remains considerable disagreement about actually how to define it. Should we assume that media addictions function similarly to substance addictions or, for that matter, gambling addiction? Or do some symptoms of those disorders not translate very well to media addictions? For instance, thinking about substance use or gambling often when not engaged in those activities is typically considered symptomatic of addiction. But would thinking about playing your favorite video game during the day be particularly unusual or symptomatic of an addiction? Don't people often think about their hobbies while they're not engaged in them?

So let's try to define what an addiction is. According to the American Society of Addiction Medicine (2011),

> Addiction is a primary, chronic disease of brain reward, motivation, memory and related circuitry. Dysfunction in these circuits leads to characteristic biological, psychological, social and spiritual manifestations. This is reflected in an individual pathologically pursuing reward and/or relief by substance use and other behaviors. Addiction is characterized by inability to consistently abstain, impairment in behavioral control, craving, diminished recognition of significant problems with one's behaviors and interpersonal relationships, and a dysfunctional emotional response. Like other chronic diseases, addiction often involves cycles of relapse and remission. Without treatment or engagement in recovery activities, addiction is progressive and can result in disability or premature death.

A bit of a long definition, but it essentially says that people with addictions lack the capacity to moderate their use of some substance or engage in some behavior and continue in that pattern of behavior to a degree that it causes notable impairment. Relating this to media use, we would thus say that someone has a media addiction if they continue using media and are unable to moderate their use of it to the point that it impairs their functioning in other realms. So, if you are addicted to telenovelas, you might watch them continuously even when you know you should stop, to the point that you fail to do your homework, go to school or to work, and you fail your classes and lose your job.

Impairment of functioning in other realms thus is key to addiction along with dysfunction in behavioral regulation. Someone is not addicted to video games merely because they spend a lot of time playing video games. So long as they are getting to their classes and/or job and are reasonably happy, it's not an addiction, no matter how long they play. Indeed, time spent on media, by itself, is generally not a good indicator of whether someone is addicted or not (Ferguson, Coulson, & Barnett, 2011).

The first difficulty of defining media addiction has come with properly delineating the symptoms of media addiction. One tactic a lot of folks have used is to migrate symptoms of gambling addiction to media use (McCormack, Shorter, & Griffiths, 2013). Thus, in addition to symptoms related to impairment of functioning, we see symptoms such as getting into arguments with family over the behavior or thinking about the behavior while engaged in other activities. However, this has set up some controversy about whether assuming equivalence between gambling addiction and media addiction works or may result in spuriously high prevalence estimates. For instance, arguing with your spouse about having lost thousands of dollars is clearly a problem, whereas arguing with your parents about when to turn off the television may be rather developmentally normal for children. And, as noted earlier, thinking about gambling when not gambling may be a sign of a problem, but thinking about your favorite television show or video game throughout the day may, again, be relatively normal. If you begin to identify relatively normal behaviors as "symptoms" of some problem, prevalence rates can get spuriously high.

PREVALENCE

Prevalence refers to the proportion of individuals who experience a particular problem condition, either during a specific time period or over a lifetime. This is contrasted with a different word you'll sometimes hear called *incidence*, which is the number of *new* cases only over a period of time. In this discussion we talk about the prevalence of media addiction.

Regarding television, relatively little attention has been paid to the concept of television addiction despite (or perhaps because of) the heavy viewing habits of the average individual (Kubey, 2009). As Kubey notes, throughout the industrialized world, the average person spends approximately 2 to 3 hours *a day* watching television. If that's the norm, delineating "addiction" may be difficult! As early as the 1950s, some clinicians did report cases of television addiction (Meerloo, 1954). The relaxing nature of television was thought to potentially foster dependence in some individuals, particularly with preexisting susceptibility to addiction (McIlwraith, Jacobvitz, Kubey, & Alexander, 1991). Scholars continue to speculate about television addiction (e.g., Sussman & Moran, 2013). But the reality is that, despite considerable consternation over violence on television (covered in a subsequent chapter), research on television addiction, as compared to more recent concerns about Internet and video game addiction, has always been thin.

Why this may be is an interesting question, and we can only speculate. One possibility is that heavy use of television actually became rather normative quite quickly. Further, unlike video game use, television use was quickly adopted by older generations. As we see, many fears of media are promoted by older generations who don't use new media and think its use is a waste of time. However, if older generations are using a particular form of media, they may see it as worthwhile and be less inclined to endorse its problematic nature. Or put simply, people may not have worried too much about television addiction because older people were just as inclined to indulge in television as the young.

This can be contrasted with video games and the Internet, where a clear, generational divide exists (Przybylski, 2014). Older generations were not as quick to embrace these technologies, particularly video games, and so it's common to see a lot of cross-generational suspiciousness, much of which is bread by unfamiliarity. When younger generations embrace new technology in broad swaths, it makes it seem to older generations as if an epidemic of addiction has occurred, even if most use is particularly healthy. As compared to television addiction (or the nonexistent research on things like "book addiction"), there is considerable research on video game and Internet addiction.

As mentioned, scholars don't agree on the criteria and symptoms of video game or Internet addiction. Therefore, there are a number of different survey instruments available for measuring these constructs, few of which have been properly validated. Because these different measurement instruments have different assumptions about what constitutes "addiction," this makes getting reliable prevalence estimates rather difficult. Indeed, across a fair number of studies, you find prevalence estimates ranging from near zero through to nearly 20%!

Most scholars agree that *some* users of new technology experience something like an addiction, but that it's probably rather rare. For video game addiction, across studies, that number appears to be somewhere between 1% to 4% of gamers (Desai, Krishnan-Sarin, Cavallo, & Potenza, 2010; Ferguson et al., 2011; Haagsma, Pieterse, & Peters, 2012). Similar prevalence figures have been found for Internet addiction (Kuss, Griffiths, & Binder, 2013; Kuss, van Rooij, Shorter, Griffiths, & van de Mheen, 2013). So these conditions do seem to occur although not in the vast majority of users.

So, in the absence of clearly delineated clinical symptoms of media addiction, what should people look for in themselves or parents in their children? The most basic answer to this is simply interference. Is the media activity interfering with other life responsibilities, and is the individual having difficulty moderating media use despite the obvious negative repercussions? Simply using media a lot, even hours and hours a day, is not an addiction if the person is otherwise able to meet his or her other responsibilities. Indeed, time spent on media is usually not a good indicator of problems (Skoric, Teo, & Neo, 2009). Scholars also acknowledge a difference between *engaged* users of media who may consume copious amounts of media without showing problem behavior and *problem* users for whom media use interferes with other life responsibilities (Charlton & Danforth, 2007).

Therefore, if someone continues using media despite obvious negative consequences (e.g., missing work, not doing homework, eliminating other social activities they used to enjoy, etc.), this could be indicative of a potential problem. In many cases the problem may be fairly minor. Indeed even in the prevalence figures noted earlier, scholars are usually cautious to say that these 1% to 3% of media users are not radically out-of-control people engaged in prostitution or crime to support their media habits (as sometimes happens with substance addictions), but people for whom their media use has resulted in suboptimal performance in other areas. Looking at sensationalized television, extreme cases of people whose lives are completely shattered, or even parents who allowed their babies to starve because they couldn't tear themselves away from media, are sometimes highlighted. But these cases are extremely rare, and it's safe to say there were likely other things going wrong for those individuals prior to media entering the picture. However, this brings us to the next question: Is media addiction something specific to media, or indicative of other, underlying mental health problems?

THE CHICKEN OR THE EGG: ADDICTION OR UNDERLYING MENTAL HEALTH ISSUE?

One reasonable question is whether media addiction is something unique or merely symptomatic of underlying preexisting problems. Or, put another way, does media take individuals who are reasonably healthy and convert them to addicts, or does media addiction merely signal underlying problems that had nothing to do with media? It's a difficult question, of course. Even with substance abuse, individuals may experience differing degrees of susceptibility, but most scholars agree that substances ranging from tobacco to heroin have inherent physiologically addicting qualities. Is media similar to this?

Well, obviously media doesn't have the potential to directly change our biochemistry in the way that ingested or injected substances can. But media can have inherent reward structures that may influence our brains' pleasure centers (more on this later). Of course that can be said for just about anything "fun." Many scholars feel that the reward structure for gambling, particularly it's intermittent reinforcement schedule (in which you win small amounts unpredictably every now and again, so it always feels like the next pull or hand may be the lucky one) makes gambling particularly addictive for a behavior at least (Parke & Griffiths, 2004), which probably also helps to explain the inclusion of gambling addiction as the only behavioral addiction in the *DSM-5*.

Do media have the right kind of reinforcement schedules to make them as addictive as gambling? This is an issue that is debated among scholars, and you certainly find commentary suggesting that, particularly for video games, they are designed to be addictive (e.g., Trenholm, 2013). Certainly, makers of all media try to find ways to make their products more compelling. As a fiction author, I was taught to end chapters halfway through a critical scene to keep readers reading on to the next chapter, for instance. So media producers, of course, don't want to make boring products that don't engage consumers. Scholars or activists who call for producers to make less engaging products will seem hopelessly out of touch. But my perception is that most forms of media work more on a continuous, not intermittent, reinforcement schedule, which is not as addictive as what you'd see in gambling. Granted, media may have high points (cliffhangers, big boss fights, etc.), but overall the experience is continuously positive. So, I find the evidence for direct comparisons with gambling addiction and certainly substance addictions to be unwarranted.

Similarly, evidence seems to be mounting that media addictions (probably similar to sex addictions, food addictions, exercise addictions, etc.) result from a preexisting dysfunction in behavioral moderation (e.g., Desai et al., 2010; Ferguson & Ceranoglu, 2014). For instance, in one recent longitudinal study I conducted of youth with psychiatrist Attila Ceranoglu, we found that video game addiction tended to arise from preexisting attention- and impulse-control problems, but not the inverse. In other words, the mental health symptoms came first, then the media addiction. Evidence here remains preliminary, however, and much debate remains. Of course, exposure to certain types of media or the Internet may make preexisting symptoms even worse (Kuss et al., 2013), but more data on this issue is necessary. At present, it is probably reasonable to assert, however, that media addiction arises mainly in individuals with preexisting problems or personality structures that make them susceptible to behavior-modulation problems for pleasurable behaviors.

THIS IS YOUR BRAIN ON THE INTERNET (OR *CANDY CRUSH*, OR *WORLD OF WARCRAFT*, ETC.)!

One question people seem to be fascinated with is the degree to which media addictions can be compared to addictions to illicit substances such as cocaine or heroin. For instance, we occasionally see news articles quoting various experts saying that video games are as addictive as things like heroin, are linked to suicides, and are "the scourge of our generation" (Rundle, 2014). Such stories usually point out that video games influence dopamine-producing areas of the brain that handle pleasure and rewards, similar areas as are stimulated by illicit drugs. Sometimes such stories will rely on brain scans, such as through fMRI studies (the fMRI is a scanning machine that can measure brain activity). So, are media addictions similar to addictions to cocaine and heroin?

The answer is a little bit of *yes* and a whole lot of *no*. Addictions can all have some similarities on basic behavioral and neurochemical levels. However, there is a difference of degree. Simply put, a greater proportion of people exposed to cocaine or heroin (or nicotine) develop addictions than do people exposed to media like video games or television, and the drug addictions tend to be much deeper and more impactful. Comparisons with heroin and cocaine are simply sensationalistic and have been used not with just media but with everything from Oreo cookies and tanning booths to being in a position of power over others (Koebler, 2013). Such sensationalistic claims take a certain kernel of truth and blow it out of proportion.

As mentioned earlier, anything that is pleasurable, be it eating those Oreo cookies, playing video games or using the Internet, exercising, or using narcotics, activates certain areas of the brain associated with pleasure. People with preexisting issues in behavior modulation can experience difficulties limiting any of these activities, that much is true. However, making direct comparisons assumes that all potential addictions are equal merely because they involve the same areas of the brain. For instance, the National Institute on Drug Abuse (2008) notes that "natural" rewards like food or sex (and presumably media) increase dopamine levels from about 150% to 200% of normal levels. Drugs vary in their effects on dopamine. Nicotine brings on a jolt that's only about 225% of normal, not much more than sex, but cocaine can raise dopamine to roughly 350% of normal levels, and amphetamines can bring dopamine levels up near 1000% of normal! So making direct comparisons between media and illicit drugs is more than a little misleading. There's an element of truth there, but sensationalistic claims paper over some important differences.

It should also be noted that the use of fMRI imagines can be sensationalistic as well. Presenting pictures of two different groups of people with different areas of their brains lit up can be rather dramatic. However, fMRI research has often been controversial, and some scholars have claimed that the statistics behind such images remain questionable (e.g., Vul, Harris, Winkielman, & Pashler, 2009). One researcher demonstrated it was possible to get positive brain-scan images from a dead trout put through an fMRI machine (Bennett, Baird, Miller, & Wolford, 2009). Of course, statistics and research tools of all sorts can be abused in promoting bogus beliefs, and fMRI is not unique in this respect. But it is a reminder that even impressive-looking pictures may not be the clear-cut answer to a question they are presented to be.

CONCLUSIONS

Media addictions appear to be real issues that can have an important impact on the functioning of some individuals. Fortunately, they appear to be rare, and evidence of an "epidemic" of such cases has not emerged. Nor are such behavioral addictions comparable to addictions to substances but probably are simply a part of a spectrum of behavioral addictions that can latch onto any activity that individuals find pleasurable. Further, it appears likely that such behavioral addictions arise mainly in individuals with preexisting mental health issues and may be more symptomatic of deeper problems than being a unique syndrome of their own.

REFERENCES

American Psychiatric Association. (2013). *Diagnostic and statistical manual of mental disorders* (5th ed.). Arlington, VA: American Psychiatric Press.

American Society of Addiction Medicine. (2011). *Definition of addiction.* Retrieved from http://www.asam.org/for-the-public/definition-of-addiction

Bennett, C., Baird, A., Miller, M., & Wolford, G. (2009). *Neural correlates of interspecies perspective taking in the post-mortem Atlantic salmon: An argument for multiple comparisons correction.* Retrieved from http://prefrontal.org/blog/2009/06/human-brain-mapping-2009-presentations

Charlton, J. P., & Danforth, I. D. W. (2007). Distinguishing addiction and high engagement in the context of online game playing. *Computers in Human Behavior, 23*(3), 1531–1548. doi: 10.1016/j.chb.2005.07.002

Desai, R. A., Krishnan-Sarin, S., Cavallo, D., & Potenza, M. N. (2010). Video-gaming among high school students: Health correlates, gender differences, and problematic gaming. *Pediatrics, 126*(6), e1414–e1424. doi:10.1542/peds.2009-2706

Ferguson, C. J., & Ceranoglu, T. A. (2014). Attention problems and pathological gaming: Resolving the "chicken and egg" in a prospective analysis. *Psychiatric Quarterly, 85*(1), 103–110. doi:10.1007/s11126-013-9276-0

Ferguson, C. J., Coulson, M., & Barnett, J. (2011). A meta-analysis of pathological gaming prevalence and comorbidity with mental health, academic and social problems. *Journal of Psychiatric Research, 45*(12), 1573–1578.

Haagsma, M. C., Pieterse, M. E., & Peters, O. (2012). The prevalence of problematic video gamers in The Netherlands. *Cyberpsychology, Behavior, and Social Networking, 15*(3), 162–168. doi:10.1089/cyber.2011.0248

Koebler, J. (2013). No, Oreos aren't as addictive as cocaine. *Motherboard.* Retrieved from http://motherboard.vice.com/blog/no-oreos-arent-as-addictive-as-cocaine

Kubey, R. W. (2009). Addiction to television: With commentary on dependence on video games and the Internet. In A. Browne-Miller

(Ed.), *The Praeger international collection on addictions, Vol. 4: Behavioral addictions from concept to compulsion* (pp. 27–51). Santa Barbara, CA: Praeger/ABC-CLIO.

Kuss, D. J., Griffiths, M. D., & Binder, J. F. (2013). Internet addiction in students: Prevalence and risk factors. *Computers in Human Behavior, 29*(3), 959–966. doi:10.1016/j.chb.2012.12.024

Kuss, D. J., van Rooij, A. J., Shorter, G. W., Griffiths, M. D., & van de Mheen, D. D. (2013). Internet addiction in adolescents: Prevalence and risk factors. *Computers in Human Behavior, 29*(5), 1987–1996. doi:10.1016/j.chb.2013.04.002

McCormack, A., Shorter, G. W., & Griffiths, M. D. (2013). Characteristics and predictors of problem gambling on the internet. *International Journal of Mental Health and Addiction, 11*(6), 634–657. doi:10.1007/s11469-013-9439-0

McIlwraith, R., Jacobvitz, R. S., Kubey, R., & Alexander, A. (1991). Television addiction: Theories and data behind the ubiquitous metaphor. *American Behavioral Scientist, 35*(2), 104–121. doi:10.1177/0002764291035002003

Meerloo, J. M. (1954). Television addiction and reactive apathy. *Journal of Nervous and Mental Disease, 120,* 290–291. doi:10.1097/00005053-195412030-00018

National Institute on Drug Abuse. (2008). *Addiction science: From molecules to managed care.* Retrieved from http://www.drugabuse.gov/publications/addiction-science/why-do-people-abuse-drugs/natural-rewards-stimulate-dopamine-neurotransmission

Parke, J., & Griffiths, M. (2004). Gambling addiction and the evolution of the "near miss." *Addiction Research & Theory, 12*(5), 407–411. doi:10.1080/16066350410001728118

Przybylski, A. K. (2014). Who believes electronic games cause real-world aggression? *Cyberpsychology, Behavior and Social Networking, 17*(4), 228–234. doi:10.1089/cyber.2013.0245

Rundle, M. (2014). Video games "as addictive as heroin" claims *The Sun.* Do you agree? *Huffington Post.* Retrieved from http://www.huffingtonpost.co.uk/2014/07/08/video-games-addictive-heroin_n_5567147.html

Skoric, M. M., Teo, L., & Neo, R. (2009). Children and video games: Addiction, engagement, and scholastic achievement. *Cyberpsychology & Behavior, 12*(5), 567–572. doi:10.1089/cpb.2009.0079

Sussman, S., & Moran, M. B. (2013). Hidden addiction: Television. *Journal of Behavioral Addictions*, 2(3), 125–132. doi:10.1556/JBA .2.2013.008

Trenholm, R. (2013). *Video games should be made less addictive, say experts*. Retrieved from http://www.cnet.com/news/video-games-should-be-made-less-addictive-say-experts

Vul, E., Harris, C., Winkielman, P., & Pashler, H. (2009). Puzzlingly high correlations in fMRI studies of emotion, personality, and social cognition. *Perspectives on Psychological Science*, 4(3), 274–290. doi:10.1111/j.1745-6924.2009.01125.x

Banned Books

n 2013, a concerned parent asked the Toronto Public Library to remove a book from its shelves. The book, marketed toward young children, contained considerable violence, the complaining patron said. What's more, the book appeared to advocate that children engage in violence specifically toward their parents. The library, apparently insensitive to the plague of child-on-parent violence, declined to remove the book. Thus it remains, an instigation to child-perpetrated cruelty, available to even the youngest of children. The book? The 1963 classic *Hop on Pop* by Dr. Seuss (Stampler, 2014).

Coverage of the attempt to ban Dr. Seuss was, not surprisingly, met largely with ridicule, but it reflects a continual trend: efforts to ban a wide variety of books, including many marketed to children and youth, from school or public libraries because of their perceived objectionable content. Such content may involve anything from sex (including merely positive portrayals of homosexuality) and violence to drug use, to occult references, to disrespect toward authority. Many popular books, from *The Adventures of Huckleberry*

Finn through the *Harry Potter* series, have been targets of these attempted bannings. In modern times, in the United States, most such attempts fail, and it is probably more accurate to say that these books have been *challenged*, although the American Library Association (ALA) still uses the term "banning," and I'll continue with that tradition here (American Library Association, 2013).

Nonetheless, outright banning of books has occurred throughout U.S. history and still occurs across much of the rest of the world, including in some other industrialized democracies. Books contain ideas, and some individuals are threatened by those ideas. Typically, people fear that exposure to the ideas in books will cause some people (particularly youth, women, minorities, and the lower classes) to become more rebellious, licentious, or aggressive. In honor of this phenomenon of book banning, the ALA holds a "Banned Book Week" with observations in many public libraries each year, usually in late September/early October.

A BRIEF HISTORY OF BANNED BOOKS

Since the creation of the Gutenberg printing press in the mid-15th century, there has been tension between the spread of ideas through books and the need to control information. It would be a mistake to imply that censorship originated with the mass production of books through the printing press. Censorship and the strict control of ideas has been common to authoritarian (and even many democratic) regimes throughout history. But the sudden increase in the availability of books gave the issue new urgency. The slow rise of literacy in the 15th century, combined with mass book production, challenged the religious and political elites and their control of ideas.

Perhaps not surprising, much early censorship in the West was pushed by the Roman Catholic Church (as well as Protestant equivalents). In the mid-16th century, the Roman Catholic

Church published (and maintained until 1966) the *Index Librorum Prohibitorum* (ILP, or list of banned books), which constituted a list of books considered heretical, erroneous, or immoral. The ILP included many scientific works that were considered erroneous because they appeared to conflict with the teachings of the church on issues such as the geocentric (versus heliocentric) solar system. Many intellectuals, from Copernicus to Galileo to Kant to Descartes, found their works on the list. The ILP was only spottily enforced as individual nations typically set up their own lists of prohibited works and censorship regimes. Nonetheless, the ILP was only officially discontinued in 1966.

The experience of William Tyndale is perhaps illustrative of the seriousness to which censorship was taken during the Reformation. In the early 1500s, Tyndale translated the Bible into English, a crime punishable by death at the time. The Catholic Church was concerned that unofficial translations would contain "errors" that would portray the Church in a negative light. Tyndale was arrested in 1535 and executed for his translations.

Book bannings and burnings have long been part of authoritarian regimes, whether aristocratic, fascist, or communist. Notable incidents include the "Bonfire of the Vanities" in Renaissance Florence, burnings by fascist regimes in 20th-century Germany, Spain, and Greece, as well as by communist regimes in Russia, China, and other parts of Asia. Salman Rushdie's *The Satanic Verses* were burned by Islamist regimes and groups worldwide, and the author was condemned to death by the regime in Iran (Rushdie went into hiding in England for many years). However, book burnings have also occurred in democratic nations, often at the instigation of popular movements rather than governments. Perhaps most notably, the *Harry Potter* series has been subject to several burnings by religious groups and, in 2010, the Dove World Outreach Center, a conservative Christian organization in Florida, burned a copy of the Qur'an despite worldwide condemnation.

Even the U.S. government has been involved in book burnings and bannings. During the 20th century many books, such as *Tropic of Cancer*, were banned in the United States because of their perceived "obscene" sexual material. In the 1964 decision *Grove Press, Inc. v. Gerstein*, the U.S. Supreme Court greatly restricted the government's ability to ban books for their content.

The object of such bannings should be plain. Supporting book banning is not necessary to prevent oneself from reading a book. One need only not buy it. Book bannings are intended to prevent *others* from reading a book. That is to say, book bannings are motivated by fear of the material contained within the book. They are often couched in the language of protection, namely, that certain vulnerable groups, whether youth, women, minorities, or the lower classes, need to be "protected" from the influence of such books. Ironically, even in the area of media research, some scholars have appeared to advocate censorship, maintaining that journalists should not speak to others whose views differ from their own (e.g., Prot & Gentile, 2014). I would humbly submit that endorsement of censorship would seem to indicate lack of faith in one's own beliefs, that they might so easily be challenged by the written word.

HARRY POTTER: HARMLESS FICTION OR INVITATION TO DEVIL WORSHIP?

In recent memory, probably few books have come to epitomize the debates on banned books more than the *Harry Potter* series, written by J. K. Rowling. The series, aimed at youth but also popular with adults, follows the adventures of a young orphan boy as he grows up being educated in the ways of wizardry at Hogwarts Academy while fighting the minions of his evil nemesis, Voldemort. I won't get into the specifics of the series, however, the key element of controversy is the fact that a young boy is learning to be a wizard.

These occult themes, if they can be called that, have led to multiple calls for the books to be banned from schools and public libraries in the United States, mainly by conservative groups, as well as various Christian denominations in Europe and by some Muslim countries in the Middle East. The argument raised in such objections is that the *Harry Potter* books provide a model by which youth may be led into practicing pagan religions based on witch-craft such as Wicca (an organized religion based loosely on European pagan beliefs). The books themselves don't mention Wicca and present magic use as an innate ability to be trained, with no actual religious context. Nonetheless, the books haven't always sat well with conservative religious elements. In the United States, efforts to ban the books have been largely unsuccessful, although the series was banned from schools in some Middle Eastern countries (e.g., BBC, 2002). Coverage of the topic from the *700 Club* (2008) is probably fair in understanding concerns from Christian conservatives about the books. The arguments advanced by the *700 Club* and others are, effectively, similar to arguments raised by psychologists that kids will mimic violence or sex seen on television or read in books. The main difference is that the *700 Club*'s moral agenda isn't hidden as "science."

Of course, moral opponents of the *Harry Potter* series certainly took the series rather seriously and at face value. It's unclear why children, who can begin to distinguish reality from fiction at a young age (e.g., Boerger, Tullos, & Woolley, 2009), would seek to "learn" wizarding behaviors that are actually presented as largely innate in the book series. Nor is it clear why they would do so in the context of a religion such as Wicca, which is never mentioned in the books. But, alas, moral panics are inevitably founded upon belief in the extraordinary power of media to induce blind mimicry in the huddled masses.

EDGY YOUNG-ADULT FICTION

Books that are challenged are very often books that are targeted toward youth, yet still contain edgy content such as sexuality (as in *The Absolutely True Diary of a Part-Time Indian*), violence (as the child-on-child violence of *The Hunger Games*), occult themes (as in *Harry Potter*), profanity (including use of racial slurs in *The Adventures of Huckleberry Finn*), and drug references (as in *Thirteen Reasons Why*). Books that highlight homosexual relationships, such as *And Tango Makes Three*, a children's book about a same-sex pairing of two male penguins who raise a chick together, are also commonly challenged.

Concerns that books marketed toward youth were including too much edgy or salacious content were voiced in one 2011 *Wall Street Journal* book review (Gurdon, 2011). This review, which reiterated concerns that youth might mimic what they read, set off considerable debate by strongly criticizing the dark content of many young-adult books. In writing about the controversies over that dark content, Alexie (2011) also notes, however, that this may often be counterproductive. Children lose the opportunity to discuss, with adults, issues and material they will inevitably encounter or have already encountered in their real lives. And books may provide an opportunity for children to explore their own conflicts with relatable characters.

To be sure, some evidence does suggest that books targeted toward youth are becoming edgier, including more profanity, for instance (Coyne, Callister, Stockdale, Nelson, & Wells, 2012). And books are often raised as a contrast to newer media, such as video games, with the implication that newer, interactive media may have more harmful effects than books (an argument that has been repeatedly rejected by the U.S. courts). Curious, however, relatively little research has actually been done on the impact of banned books on adolescent well-being.

DO BANNED BOOKS HARM MINORS?

The relative dearth of research on books is probably the result of several factors. First, for the moment, newer media such as video games, social media, and old standbys such as movies and television, tend to get most of the focus. And people may be particularly reluctant to talk about anything that sounds like censorship of books, as compared to other media. Further, whereas a laboratory study can show someone a television show or have them play a video game for a relatively short period of time, asking research participants to read entire books is time prohibitive. Thus, helpful research studies are few.

In one study on books, Coyne, Ridge, Stevens, Callister, and Stockdale (2012) examined the influence of reading book passages on physical and relational aggression in two laboratory experiments. Results indicated that participants tended to model what they had read. This study represents an important and well-done first step in this field. However, its ability to answer questions about the influence of books on youth is limited in several ways. Most notably, this study was conducted with college students, who may have been well aware of media effects theories, in a laboratory environment that may have been subject to demand characteristics. Further, laboratory aggression measures often have difficulty answering questions about real-life aggression, given the limitations of these measures (Elson, Mohseni, Breuer, Scharkow, & Quandt, 2014). Last, the experiments considered passages from books taken out of context rather than the actual experience of reading a complete literary work for pleasure. The intent is not to be unduly critical of an important and illuminating study, far from it. Rather, the intent is acknowledged that there is certainly room for more research examining the potential influence of content in books in other ways.

One correlational study of youth by the same research team (Stockdale, Coyne, Nelson, & Padilla-Walker, 2013) suggested that reading books about aggressive behavior is associated with physical and relational aggression among middle school students. However, this study had numerous serious issues with it. First, the authors engaged in "citation bias," that is, the tendency to cite only articles that support the author's personal views and ignore articles which do not thus presenting a distorted and dishonest view of the research field. They did this by presenting the research on media violence as being more consistent than it actually is. As noted earlier, this behavior is considered bad science (Babor & McGovern, 2008) and can generally serve as a red flag that the authors have something of an axe to grind, which can prejudice their research findings. Further, respondents were asked to rate both their own aggression and the amount of aggression in the books. This method is problematic for two reasons; first, because such ratings are subjective, and second, by pairing the predictor and outcome measures in such a fashion, the authors prime their participants about their hypotheses, setting up "demand characteristics" that can cause spurious correlations. Last, relying on responses only from one respondent type, in this case youth, sets up "single-responder bias" in which respondents can guess hypotheses and respond accordingly, creating spurious correlations (Baumrind, Larzelere, & Cowan, 2002). Put simply, the small correlations found in this study are probably best explained by methodological weaknesses of the study itself.

This study hasn't replicated well either. In a more recent study (Ferguson, 2014), I examined kids' exposure to various "banned" books, and the association of such exposure with aggression, prosocial behavior, and mental health problems in teens. Unlike the Stockdale et al. (2013) study, I did not ask teens to rate the amount of aggression in the books. Further, I obtained data on mental health issues from primary caregivers, helping to avoid the single-responder bias. In this case, reading banned books was associated with more prosocial behavior among teens and not problems with violent or nonviolent crime commission. However, reading such books was associated with mental health symptoms, as rated by the primary caregivers, but this relationship was not linear. The correlation was driven not by the entire sample but by a small cluster of mainly girls who voraciously consumed banned books and who also tended to have higher levels of mental health symptoms. In other words, reading banned books was not associated with any problems for the vast majority of readers. Whether the books caused the mental health symptoms, or whether the girls used books cathartically, is unclear from correlational data.

This study had one further interesting outcome. Namely, reading for pleasure but not assigned readings from school was associated with higher grade point averages (GPAs). So, although the data is correlational, it may be that encouraging reading anything that is fun may be more valuable for kids than is assigning "classics" for children (ages 12–18) to read.

CONCLUSIONS

At present, there is little good data to suggest that reading books, even those with edgy content, is particularly harmful to minors. Further, the benefits of reading anything may be enough that discouraging reading even of edgy books may do more harm than good. This is unlikely to stop further protests, attempted bannings, and the occasional academic tongue-clucking about books, however. As with all media, authors, even authors marketing toward youth, may feel tempted to push the envelope on what can be written.

At the same time, book bannings invariably look bad to history and outsiders once the emotion that drives them has passed. Most people in Western countries are opposed to censorship, particularly of books, and book burnings have typically become so associated with authoritarian regimes that people are particularly sensitive about this topic. This doesn't mean that some attempts to ban certain books won't continue. Books are ultimately ideas and ideas are power, and there will always be those motivated to control the flow of power in words. It is for this reason that the American Library Association holds a Banned Book Week each year, typically in late September or early October. Those interested in learning more are encouraged to attend one of these events at your local library and support free-speech rights for everyone.

REFERENCES

Alexie, S. (2011). Why the best kids books are written in blood. *The Wall Street Journal.* Retrieved from http://blogs.wsj.com/speakeasy/2011/06/09/why-the-best-kids-books-are-written-in-blood

American Library Association. (2013). *Frequently challenged books of the 21st century.* Retrieved from http://www.ala.org/bbooks/frequentlychallengedbooks/top10

Babor, T. F., & McGovern, T. (2008). Dante's *Inferno:* Seven deadly sins in scientific publishing and how to avoid them. In T. F. Babor, K. Stenius, S. Savva, & J. O'Reilly (Eds.), *Publishing addiction science: A guide for the perplexed* (2nd ed., pp. 153–171). Essex, UK: Multi-Science Publishing Company.

Baumrind, D., Larzelere, R., & Cowan, P. (2002). Ordinary physical punishment: Is it harmful? Comment on Gershoff (2002). *Psychological Bulletin, 128*(4), 580–589. doi:10.1037/0033-2909.128.4.580

BBC. (2002). *Emirates ban Potter book.* Retrieved from http://news.bbc.co.uk/2/hi/entertainment/1816012.stm

Boerger, E., Tullos, A., & Woolley, J. (2009). Return of the Candy Witch: Individual differences in acceptance and stability of belief in a novel fantastical being. *British Journal of Developmental Psychology, 27,* 953–970.

Coyne, S. M., Callister, M., Stockdale, L. A., Nelson, D. A., & Wells, B. M. (2012). "A helluva read": Profanity in adolescent literature. *Mass Communication & Society, 15*(3), 360–383. doi:10.1080/15205436.2011.638431

Coyne, S. M., Ridge, R., Stevens, M., Callister, M., & Stockdale, L. (2012). Backbiting and bloodshed in books: Short-term effects of reading physical and relational aggression in literature. *British Journal of Social Psychology, 51,* 188–196. doi:10.1111/j.2044-8309.2011.02053.x

Elson, M., Mohseni, M., Breuer, J., Scharkow, M., & Quandt, T. (2014). Press CRTT to measure aggressive behavior: The unstandardized use of the competitive reaction time task in aggression research. *Psychological Assessment.* doi:10.1037/a0035569

Ferguson, C. J. (2014). Is reading "banned" books associated with behavior problems in young readers? The influence of controversial young adult books on the psychological well-being of adolescents. *Psychology of Aesthetics, Creativity, and the Arts, 8*(3), 354–362. doi:10.1037/a0035601

Gurdon, M. (2011, June). Darkness too visible. *Wall Street Journal.* Retrieved from http://online.wsj.com/article/SB10001424052702 303657404576357622592697038.html

Prot, S., & Gentile, D. (2014). Applying risk and resilience models to predicting the effects of media violence on development. In J. Benson (Ed.), *Advances in child development and behavior* (Vol. 46, pp. 215–244). Waltham, MA: Elsevier.

700 Club. (2008). Harry Potter witchcraft repackaged interview. Retrieved from http://www.youtube.com/watch?v=GUlNjr9NXrA

Stampler, L. (2014). Grinch wants Dr. Seuss' *Hop on Pop* banned. Retrieved from http://time.com/#81560/dr-seuss-hop-on-pop-ban-toronto

Stockdale, L. A., Coyne, S. M., Nelson, D. A., & Padilla-Walker, L. M. (2013). Read anything mean lately? Associations between reading aggression in books and aggressive behavior in adolescents. *Aggressive Behavior, 39*(6), 493–502.

Media and Body Dissatisfaction

edia has to sell, and in order to sell it has to be appealing. This basic tenet is true for fictional media, news media, advertising media, and online media. If people don't watch it, read it, or listen to it, the media in question is unsuccessful and won't survive. As a result, media producers attempt to ascertain what media will sell best and pander to the interests of the public. Safe bets are better than new risks, which is why movie and video game sequels seem so appealing, and truly new ideas often seem so rare.

Visual media, such as movies, television, magazines, and video games, appeal to numerous human interests, including drama, violence, love, and inspiration. Visual media commonly also tap into our basic interest in viewing beautiful people as one method to attract viewership. This can be observed in police drama shows such as the *CSI* or *Criminal Minds* series. These shows depict gorgeous (male and female) police officers often chasing equally attractive criminals. As someone who has worked with law enforcement personnel and provided mental health services in a jail, I can assure readers that they would be disappointed by the gulf between the attractiveness of people in television crime dramas and their real-life counterparts! In fairness, one could probably say the same about college professors in the movies and in real life.

Our societal fascination with beauty drives much of media strategy. The result is that viewers are exposed to a constant stream of higher-than-average attractive people unmatched by real life and, for many viewers, unmatched by their own appearance. What impact does this have on viewers, if any? It's not very difficult to find anecdotes in our personal lives of people who become irritated by unrealistically pretty people on television or in magazines, or who say that seeing such images may, at least in the moment, make them feel bad about their own appearance. But to what degree do unrealistically attractive people contribute to *body dissatisfaction* (the technical term for being unhappy with one's own appearance to one degree or another)? Are there certain features, such as unrealistic thinness (or the *thin ideal*), that most contribute to body dissatisfaction, or is attractiveness in general the issue? And to what extent does any link between media and body dissatisfaction contribute to more serious clinically diagnosed eating disorders?

Even as I ask these questions, I suspect many readers would have strong opinions on these questions. However, the data isn't always clear, and the answers are nuanced. As with many areas of media psychology, there are gulfs between the data and the pronouncements of advocates and some scholars. But neither is media entirely off the hook. My own perception is that the impact of media on body image and body dissatisfaction is probably the second-most controversial area in media psychology (nothing remotely comes close to the acrimony seen in the field of media violence!), but I will provide an overview of this field, warts and all.

BODY DISSATISFACTION AND EATING DISORDERS: WHAT THEY ARE AND HOW THEY DIFFER

Before we discuss what media effects may exist, we have to first understand what it is that people think media may have an effect on. Two related, but separate, issues are discussed as potentially being influenced by attractive images in media (*thin-ideal* media in particular): *body dissatisfaction* and *eating disorders*, particularly anorexia nervosa (AN) and bulimia nervosa (BN), both of which are conceptualized as arising from body dissatisfaction (the main difference being AN involves a significant and unhealthy reduction in weight, whereas BN involves a binge/purge pattern that does not necessarily entail weight loss). Although the etiology of eating disorders is complex, body dissatisfaction is generally conceptualized as an originating issue for many if not most (some people may develop AN for ascetic reasons) cases of eating disorders (Fallon, Harris, & Johnson, 2014; Lindner, Tantleff-Dunn, & Jentsch, 2012). Nonetheless, body dissatisfaction and eating disorders remain distinct clinical constructs.

This can be observed simply in the prevalence of the two conditions. Most data suggest that body dissatisfaction is relatively common. For instance, a recent survey (Fallon et al., 2014) found that body dissatisfaction was reported by between 13% and 34% of women and between 9% and 28% of men. These numbers actually represent a decline in reported prevalence rates, which had reached levels of approximately 50% for women by the 1990s (Cash & Henry, 1995). By contrast, prevalence data for eating disorders make it clear that they are quite rare—a review of the literature by Hoek and van Hoeken (2003) estimates that the prevalence of anorexia among young females is roughly .3% and that the rate of bulimia is about 1%. Thus, we must be careful not to make direct inferences equating body dissatisfaction with AN or BN. In most of this chapter, I refer to body dissatisfaction, because that is where most of the evidence

111

regarding potential media effects is. Since eating disorders are relatively rare, they are trickier to study. There are some studies examining eating disorder symptoms in nonclinical populations, but there are, in fact, no studies at all directly examining the impact of media on clinically diagnosed eating disorders (Ferguson, 2013).

WHY WOULD MEDIA INFLUENCE BODY DISSATISFACTION?

The notion that media could have some kind of impact on body dissatisfaction is probably fairly intuitive for many readers. However, it's worth examining how this may happen. Like many media-effects approaches, arguments for media effects on body dissatisfaction are still often presented as hypodermic-needle approaches, albeit with some nuances. Many scholars view media effects in this realm through the lens of *social comparison theory*, in which we have a tendency to compare our own worth to that of others (Myers, Ridolfi, Crowther, & Ciesla, 2012). Originally proposed in 1954 by Festinger, social comparison theory suggests that our self-evaluation is relative to our evaluation of others. We can probably see this easily in our own lives, as we ask ourselves if we are as attractive, as talented, or as intelligent as those around us. When we are around others who seem, perhaps, a little inferior to ourselves, that makes us feel good. When we are around others who appear to be "better" than us on some level, that can make us feel bad. Sometimes college students experience this—many college students are among the brightest in their high schools, but once they are around a bunch of other smart college students, they begin to doubt their own abilities.

So social comparison theory isn't limited just to attractiveness or to media. And it's fairly "common sense" to believe (not that common sense always turns out to be "true"; see Lilienfeld,

Lynn, Ruscio, & Beyerstein, 2009), and difficult to argue against, that we engage in some level of social comparison regularly. Further, social comparison is even consistent with evolutionary psychology to the extent that there may be practical ramifications in how we compare to others regarding our relative "mate value," or how attractive we are to potential mates (Ferguson, Winegard, & Winegard, 2011). But to what extent do we use the media for social comparison? We probably don't worry much whether we're smarter than characters on television or in books. But is beauty different?

A further theoretical issue is what is sometimes called the *internalization of thin ideals* (Vartanian & Dey, 2013). Thin-ideal internalization focuses more narrowly than does social comparison theory on the thinness of models on television and in magazines. The argument is that seeing such unrealistic thinness represented over and over can create body dissatisfaction (and it doesn't help when magazines further Photoshop even those actresses and models!). Thin-ideal internalization suggests that the issue is not simply that we compare ourselves to attractive people on television or in magazines, but that a cultural obsession specifically with thinness is driving body dissatisfaction and, by extension, the unhealthy eating seen in restrictive eating disorders. Some analyses (e.g., Owen & Laurel-Seller, 2000) suggest that models' figures decreased in size over the 20th century, becoming increasingly and unrealistically thin. Thus, is thinness the critical variable we should be focused on when considering media effects?

As mentioned, the issue has probably attracted even more attention due to some high-profile Photoshopping scandals in which already-attractive actresses were digitally altered to be even thinner than they are. For instance, a 2009 cover shot of Demi Moore on *W* magazine was altered poorly so as to make it look as if she were missing a chunk of her left thigh. A 2010 cover of *Ralph Lauren* altered an already-thin model to look like little more than a scarecrow. Actresses and singers from Tina Fey (2011 *InStyle*) to Katy Perry (2010 *Rolling Stone*) have been subjected to similar silly airbrushing. If such naturally beautiful women can't make it untouched to the covers of magazines, how does anyone else stand a chance to meet these crazy beauty standards?

WHAT IMPACT DOES MEDIA ACTUALLY HAVE?

There's pretty good evidence that mass media, particularly U.S. media, is fairly obsessed with beauty. Granted, the media is likely pandering to what people want to see (although it's curious to see British television, where more average-looking actors and actresses seem more common in a cross-cultural comparison). But does that merely reflect culture's obsession with beauty, or is there some causal impact there? Deciding that a particular attribute should be "beautiful" probably wasn't simply arbitrary on the part of media producers; after all, what advantage is there for media companies in picking extraordinary thinness as "beautiful" at the expense of women's health? And there is good evidence that standards of beauty tend to shift in response to internal social changes within a society (Ferguson, Winegard, & Winegard, 2013), related to every-thing from food availability to freedom to choose marriage part-ners to average nuptial age. Finding beauty in larger figures, for instance, tends to be more common in societies with less food availability—some degree of corpulence is thus seen as an indica-tor of health, whereas the inverse is true in food-rich societies.

It is certainly not uncommon to hear scholars claim that clear and convincing evidence exists to link thin-ideal media to body dissatisfaction (e.g., Tiggemann, 2014), and this notion was repeated (if a bit clumsily) by the American Psychological Asso-ciation (2007) in their policy statement on the sexualization of girls. Here, though, we see how advocacy-driven sound bites are not always the most accurate representations of the actual data.

Part of the problem is that much of the data contains seri-ous flaws that mainly benefit the hypothesis that effects exist

114

(Ferguson, 2013). For example, most studies pair the indepen-dent variables (e.g., measures of media consumption) very closely with dependent measures (e.g., body dissatisfaction inventories) so that it's easy for respondents to guess the hypoth-esis of the study. Imagine if you were asked several questions about whether the shows you watch or magazines you read tend to have lots of pictures of thin models, and immediately were asked how you felt about your own body. This type of methodol-ogy introduces what are called *demand characteristics*, in which respondents may (consciously or unconsciously) respond how they think they should rather than in accordance with how they actually feel. In another common issue, many media studies compare reactions toward images of thin models with reactions toward images of nonhuman objects such as household goods. Naturally, we don't compare ourselves to lamps or mops, so this type of manipulation is rather "cheating." It would be more valu-able to compare reactions to thin models, first to reactions to attractive but average-sized women, then to reactions to women who are of average appearance altogether. Without doing so, we haven't really isolated the variables of interest (thinness, attrac-tiveness). Yet, surprisingly few studies employ such methods, and those that do seem least likely to find evidence for effects (e.g., Ferguson, Munoz, Contreras, & Velasquez, 2011; Hayes & Tantleff-Dunn, 2010; Veldhuis, Konijn, & Seidell, 2014).

Further, data from existing studies appears to be much less consistent than is often advertised (including in the APA's policy statement). Across meta-analytic reviews, the effects for media on body dissatisfaction, even without controlling for other variables, is typically very small, with effect sizes ranging from approximately $r = .08$ through .19 (Ferguson, 2013; Grabe, Ward, & Hyde, 2008; Holmstrom, 2004; Want, 2009). That's saying that thin-ideal media exposure is able to predict from roughly 0.64% to 3.6%, without controlling for other possible variables that might explain those relationships. That's not much. And the results from individual studies are inconsistent, although some studies with inconsistent results have a tendency to market themselves as more supportive of their hypotheses than they actually are (Ferguson, 2013).

Part of the issue may have simply been focusing too much on general effects on all women or girls. Also, the subjects in many studies are solely college students, who arguably are not always the best samples to work with, particularly when they may have been exposed already to a lot of talk about media effects. A more promising line of inquiry may be in examining whether women and girls with preexisting, high levels of body dissatisfaction may be influenced by thin-ideal media, whereas other women are not. In my 2013 meta-analysis, this appeared to be the case. Most women, in fact, are not "harmed" by thin-ideal media, although a minority of women with preexisting body dissatisfaction may be. Other studies have found that women with certain neurotic personality profiles may be influenced by media, whereas most other women are not (Roberts & Good, 2010).

Nonetheless, I haven't always been able to replicate this effect either. In one recent longitudinal study of teen girls, I wasn't able to find any evidence that watching thin actresses in television shows had an influence on body dissatisfaction, even in girls with preexisting issues (Ferguson, Munoz, Garza, & Galindo, 2014). Media had no effect at all . . . on anyone. The only exception was that involvement with social media tended to increase girls' sense of being in competition with other girls, which in turn led to more body dissatisfaction. But interactions on social media are arguably far different from viewing traditional media like television.

This leads us to evidence that suggests that the social comparison we see through peer comparisons are more powerful than media effects. Observing that we compare ourselves with peers is neither surprising nor necessarily mutually exclusive with media effects (Shroff & Thompson, 2006). Yet the effects for peers are clearly more dramatic than for media. For instance, in an important study (Clark & Tiggerman, 2008), media exposure to thin models was found to have little direct influence on body dissatisfaction in preadolescent girls (bivariate r between media exposure and body esteem was only $-.08$ for magazines and $-.09$ for television). By comparison, the influence of peers on body dissatisfaction was significant (bivariate $r = -.20$). A subsequent path analysis suggested that media messages may be transmitted through peers rather than from media directly, although moderator/mediator effects can often be spuriously used to try to "rescue" effects that were not found directly. Other studies have also found active peer effects to be among the strongest influences on body dissatisfaction in young girls (Dohnt & Tiggemann, 2005; Taylor et al., 1998).

Research with adolescents similarly suggests that active peer influences are among the strongest influences on body dissatisfaction (Jones, Vigfusdottir, & Lee, 2004; Paxton, Schutz, Wertheim, & Muir, 1999; Shroff & Thompson, 2006). For instance, in the path analysis conducted by Jones et al. (2004), media influences had no direct relationship with body dissatisfaction and only a weak, indirect relationship through internalization of thin ideals ($\beta = .13$). By contrast, direct effects for peer criticism ($\beta = .31$) and indirect effects for appearance conversations (conversations about looks among peers) through internalization of thin ideals were far stronger ($\beta = .44$). Similarly, McCabe and Ricciardelli (2005) found that girls' body dissatisfaction was influenced by their mothers and female friends but not by media. A recent meta-analysis of appearance-related teasing, body dissatisfaction, and disordered eating found an overall effect size of $r = .37$ between weight-related teasing and body dissatisfaction in females and an effect size of $r = .33$ between appearance-related teasing and body dissatisfaction (Menzel et al., 2010). These effects are small to moderate but are considerably larger (about three to five times larger in regard to explained variance) than media effects using the highest ($r = .19$) meta-analytic estimate.

Why peer influences would have more influence than media influences is explained by evolutionary psychology. Theories of body dissatisfaction that take an evolutionary approach consider body dissatisfaction to be a rational reaction to actual mate competition (Abed, 1998; Ferguson, Winegard, & Winegard, 2011). That is to say, we worry about our appearance because we would like to attract mates, and if we are less desirable than our peers, potential mates may select them instead of us! Worrying about this state of affairs, at least to some extent, may be rather normal. Further, since we are competing with those around us, not with people on television or in magazines, our peers are more likely to make us worry than are the people in the media. This does not mean that media has no influence at all, just that we would expect it to be much smaller than for peer influences, and this is precisely what we see in research.

WHAT ABOUT FOR MEN?

Most of the research on body dissatisfaction has focused on women, probably because eating disorders tend to be far more prevalent in women (American Psychiatric Association, 2013). Women, arguably, are also judged on appearance to a greater degree than men. Indeed, evolutionary psychologists have even framed this in terms of a mating exchange wherein, effectively, women exchange appearance for men's worldly goods or resources (Buss, 1989). So, for men, it's better to be rich than good looking (I sometimes call this the Donald Trump phenomenon).

But it's absurd to suggest that women don't care at all about men's appearances. Indeed, women's preference in mates may depend on whether they are currently seeking short-term or long-term partners (Gangestad, Garver-Apgar, Simpson, & Cousins, 2007). Thus, men are not immune to appearance issues of body dissatisfaction.

Nonetheless, studies of body dissatisfaction in males are far less frequent than for females. Much of the focus for males has been on what's been called the *muscularity ideal*, or the perception that males should have strapping, muscular physiques. Consider the way men are drawn in comic books, as an extreme example, almost inhuman in the degree of muscularity of their physiques. Some studies have found evidence for the muscularity ideal (e.g.,

Agliata & Tantleff-Dunn, 2004), although overall evidence is weaker than for media effects on women (Ferguson, 2013). This may be because body dissatisfaction issues for men may be diffuse, less likely to focus on a single issue such as muscularity. For instance, speaking as a height-challenged fellow myself, being short may be an issue related to body dissatisfaction in men (particularly given the perception many women prefer tall men). What is interesting about that is that, unlike thinness, for which dieting holds some hope (although admittedly futile for many), there's nothing at all to be done about adult height. Nonetheless, research looking at other issues, such as height as a source of body dissatisfaction in men, is minimal.

CONCLUSIONS

The issue of media effects on body dissatisfaction is a complex one. Unfortunately, too often, hyperbole about media effects in this realm has often outpaced the actual data. Over 200 studies have examined media effects on body dissatisfaction. However, the quality of many of these studies is low. Further, evidence for any impact on clinically diagnosed eating disorders is absent, in part because of the difficulty in locating samples of individuals with such rare clinical disorders.

So the answer to the question of whether media impacts body dissatisfaction is "it depends." Media representations of attractive others probably remind at least some people to worry about their bodies, particularly people who have already been worrying about their bodies. But evidence that media is a root cause of body dissatisfaction in our society is comparatively lacking. Most people, women or men, don't seem to experience profound effects due to exposure to attractive others in media, and body dissatisfaction appears to be gradually declining in society rather than increasing in recent years. Peers, rather than media, appear to have a more important influence on our body dissatisfaction.

So perhaps it is most accurate to say that media representations of attractive others may have small, temporary effects on some people who are already predisposed to worry over their bodies. But it is unlikely that this worry originated from the media or that most of us are being influenced in a profound way. Nonetheless, much research still needs to be done, particularly whether thinness (or muscularity for men) truly is the critical component for media effects, or whether we simply tend to compare ourselves to attractive others in general. Given, however, that media audiences tend to enjoy watching attractive actors and actresses, we are unlikely to see much change in the media, at least in the short term.

REFERENCES

Abed, T. R. (1998). The sexual competition hypothesis for eating disorders. *British Journal of Medical Psychology, 71*, 525–547.

Agliata, D., & Tantleff-Dunn, S. (2004). The impact of media exposure on males' body image. *Journal of Social and Clinical Psychology, 23*(1), 7–22. doi:10.1521/jscp.23.1.7.26988

American Psychiatric Association. (2013). *Diagnostic and statistical manual of mental disorders* (5th ed.). Arlington, VA: American Psychiatric Press.

American Psychological Association. (2007). *Report of the APA task force on the sexualization of girls.* Retrieved November 10, 2009, from http://www.apa.org/pi/wpo/sexualization_report_summary.pdf

Buss, D. M. (1989). Sex differences in human mate preferences: Evolutionary hypotheses tested in 37 cultures. *Behavioral and Brain Sciences, 12*, 1–49.

Cash, T. F., & Henry, P. E. (1995). Women's body images: The results of a national survey in the U.S.A. *Sex Roles, 33*(1–2), 19–28. doi:10.1007/BF01547933

Clark, L., & Tiggemann, M. (2008). Sociocultural and individual psychological predictors of body image in young girls: A prospective study. *Developmental Psychology, 44*, 1124–1134.

Dohnt, H. K., & Tiggemann, M. (2005). Peer influences on body dissatisfaction and dieting awareness in young girls. *British Journal of Developmental Psychology, 23,* 103–116.

Fallon, E. A., Harris, B. S., & Johnson, P. (2014). Prevalence of body dissatisfaction among a United States adult sample. *Eating Behaviors, 15*(1), 151–158. doi:10.1016/j.eatbeh.2013.11.007

Ferguson, C. J. (2013). In the eye of the beholder: Thin-ideal media affects some but not most viewers in a meta-analytic review of body dissatisfaction in women and men. *Psychology of Popular Media Culture, 2*(1), 20–37.

Ferguson, C. J., Munoz, M. E., Contreras, C., & Velasquez, K. (2011). Mirror, mirror on the wall: Peer competition, television influences and body image dissatisfaction. *Journal of Social and Clinical Psychology, 30*(5), 458–483.

Ferguson, C. J., Munoz, M. E., Garza, A., & Galindo, M. (2014). Concurrent and prospective analyses of peer, television and social media influences on body dissatisfaction, eating disorder symptoms and life satisfaction in adolescent girls. *Journal of Youth and Adolescence, 43*(1), 1–14.

Ferguson, C. J., Winegard, B., & Winegard, B. M. (2011). Who is the fairest one of all? How evolution guides peer and media influences on female body dissatisfaction. *Review of General Psychology, 15*(1), 11–28.

Festinger, L. (1954). A theory of social comparison processes. *Human Relations, 7,* 117–140. doi:10.1177/001872675400700202

Gangestad, S., Garver-Apgar, C., Simpson, J., & Cousins, A. (2007). Changes in women's mate preferences across the ovulatory cycle. *Journal of Personality and Social Psychology, 92*(1), 151–163.

Grabe, S., Ward, L., & Hyde, J. (2008). The role of the media in body image concerns among women: A meta-analysis of experimental and correlational studies. *Psychological Bulletin, 134*(3), 460–476.

Hayes, S., & Tantleff-Dunn, S. (2010). Am I too fat to be a princess? Examining the effects of popular children's media on young girls' body image. *British Journal of Developmental Psychology, 28*(2), 413–426. doi:10.1348/026151009X424240

Hoek, H. W., & van Hoeken, D. (2003). Review of the prevalence and incidence of eating disorders. *International Journal of Eating Disorders, 34,* 383–396.

Holmstrom, A. (2004). The effects of media on body image: A meta-analysis. *Journal of Broadcasting and Electronic Media, 48,* 186–217.

Jones, D. C., Vigfusdottir, T. H., & Lee, Y. (2004). Body image and the appearance culture among adolescent girls and boys: An examination of friend conversations, peer criticism, appearance magazines, and the internalization of appearance ideals. *Journal of Adolescent Research, 19,* 323–339.

Lilienfeld, S., Lynn, S., Ruscio, J., & Beyerstein, B. (2009). Mythbusting in introductory psychology courses: The whys and the hows. In S. A. Meyers & J. R. Stowell (Eds.), *Essays from e-xcellence in teaching* (Vol. 9). Retrieved February 6, 2012, from http://teachpsych.org/ebooks/eit2009/index.php

Lindner, D., Tantleff-Dunn, S., & Jentsch, F. (2012). Social comparison and the "circle of objectification." *Sex Roles, 67*(3–4), 222–235. doi:10.1007/s11199-012-0175-x

McCabe, M. P., Ricciardelli, L. A. (2005). A prospective study of pressures from parents, peers, and the media on extreme weight change behaviors among adolescent boys and girls. *Behavior Research and Therapy, 43,* 653–668.

Menzel, J. E., Schaefer, L. M., Burke, N. L., Mayhew, L. L., Brannick, M. T., & Thompson, J. K. (2010). Appearance-related teasing, body dissatisfaction, and disordered eating: A meta-analysis. *Body Image, 7,* 261–270.

Myers, T. A., Ridolfi, D. R., Crowther, J. H., & Ciesla, J. A. (2012). The impact of appearance-focused social comparisons on body image disturbance in the naturalistic environment: The roles of thin-ideal internalization and feminist beliefs. *Body Image, 9*(3), 342–351. doi:10.1016/j.bodyim.2012.03.005

Owen, P. R., & Laurel-Seller, E. (2000). Weight and shape ideals: Thin is dangerously in. *Journal of Applied Social Psychology, 30*(5), 979–990. doi:10.1111/j.1559-1816.2000.tb02506.x

Paxton, S. J., Schutz, H. K., Wertheim, E. H., & Muir, S. L. (1999). Friendship clique and peer influences on body image concerns, dietary restraint, extreme weight loss behaviours, and binge eating in adolescent girls. *Journal of Abnormal Psychology, 108,* 255–266.

Roberts, A., & Good, E. (2010). Media images and female body dissatisfaction: The moderating effects of the Five-Factor traits. *Eating Behaviors, 11*(4), 211–216. doi:10.1016/j.eatbeh.2010.04.002

Shroff, H., & Thompson, J. (2006). Peer influences, body-image satisfaction, eating dysfunction and self-esteem in adolescent girls. *Journal of Health Psychology, 11*(4), 533–551.

Taylor, C., Sharpe, T., Shisslak, C., Bryson, S., Estes, L. S., Gray, N., . . . Killen, J. D. (1998). Factors associated with weight concerns in adolescent girls. *International Journal of Eating Disorders, 24*, 31–42.

Tiggemann, M. (2014). The status of media effects on body image research: Commentary on articles in the themed issue on body image and media. *Media Psychology, 17*(2), 127–133.

Vartanian, L. R., & Dey, S. (2013). Self-concept clarity, thin-ideal internalization, and appearance-related social comparison as predictors of body dissatisfaction. *Body Image, 10*(4), 495–500. doi:10.1016/j.bodyim.2013.05.004

Veldhuis, J., Konijn, E. A., & Seidell, J. C. (2014). Negotiated media effects. Peer feedback modifies effects of media's thin-body ideal on adolescent girls. *Appetite, 73*, 172–182. doi:10.1016/j.appet.2013.10.023

Want, S. C. (2009). Meta-analytic moderators of experimental exposure to media portrayals of women on female appearance satisfaction: Social comparisons as automatic processes. *Body Image, 6*, 257–269.

Media and Teen
Sexual Behavior

n the United States the issue of teen sexuality is an issue
with significant moral valence. Even though a majority
of adults were not abstinent as teens, adults nonetheless
worry over the sexual behavior of their own children
once they become teens. This is somewhat different than many
European countries that consider sexuality to be less controversial (Ferguson & Konijn, in press). Thus, in the United States, the
morality of sexuality is often blurred by concerns about public health. This is not to say that there are no legitimate public
health concerns regarding teen sexuality. Far from it; sexually
transmitted diseases (STDs) and unexpected pregnancies are
issues of considerable import. However, in the United States, it is
not uncommon to see merely the act of having sex presented as
a negative public health outcome, whether such sexual behavior
is "protected" or "unprotected," resulting in public discourses on
teen sexuality that can be confused (Elliott, 2010). Given these

widespread concerns about teen sexuality, it should not be surprising that many would look to the media as a possible source for potentially negative influences on teen morality. Especially when parents often view their teens as asexual (Elliott, 2010), it may be particularly tempting to "blame" media for any discrepancies between parents' views of their children as asexual and their children's actual behavior. But what impact does the media actually have on teenage sexual behavior? As we see, the answer is more complex and nuanced than some may believe!

WHAT DO WE MEAN BY "SEXY MEDIA"?

As with a lot of terms in media psychology, we're discussing an area that appears to have conceptual meaning and yet can be awfully gray, fluid, and changing with societal standards. First, it's important to note we're not discussing pornography, which is considered in a separate chapter. Rather, this chapter is about mainstream media, whether television, music, music videos, books, and so on, that contain sexual themes. But here too, exactly what this means changes over time. For instance, in the 1950s, Elvis Presley was considered to be "sexy media," with controversy over his wiggling hips when he danced, potentially sending his youthful fans into mobs of orgasmic irresponsibility. And in the 1980s, as we mentioned in Chapter 1, even Cyndi Lauper's song "She Bop" was considered so controversial, because of masturbation references, that it made it into congressional hearings as part of the "Filthy Fifteen." But both of these artists are considered perfectly acceptable by contemporary society.

So "sexy media" is any media that contains any sexual themes, just to different degrees. That's a fairly wide swath, but that's pretty much the way the field looks at it. It's less categorical than it is continuous. So a sitcom like the 1980s *Golden Girls* might be "sexy media" in a mild sense, to the degree the show discusses the sex lives of the women and includes some sexual language. By contrast, the current show *Game of Thrones*, with full frontal nudity and explicit sex scenes, would be at the opposite end of the continuum.

CONCERNS ABOUT SEXY MEDIA

Obviously, people enjoy sexy media or it wouldn't be so popular. But, as adults, we like to enjoy it ourselves while simultaneously trying to shield our children from it. Given our perceptions of children, even teens, as innocent asexual angels, it is common to see advocacy groups portray children as helpless, hapless victims of sexy media. Thus, we hear a lot about children being *bombarded* (e.g., Childers & Brown, 2011; Commercial Free Childhood, 2014) or even just *exposed to* sexy media, as if teens were themselves not part of the motivational process in which they are so exposed. At the same time, concerns about sexual and other potentially offensive content such as violence or profanity in the media seem to be decreasing over time (Skynews, 2014). Most concerns that remain regard *shielding* children from such exposure.

Just how popular is sex in the media? Popular! This shouldn't be too surprising given that sex is such an integral part of our lives and identities. But what exactly is meant by "sexy media" is unclear. Are we talking about explicit sex and skimpy clothes? Or is a married couple referring to their sex life in passing or in a joke still "sexy media?" Most pertinent studies of "sexy media" include any reference at all to sex as "sexy media," so with that standard it's not surprising to find that sexy media is incredibly common.

The content analysis by The Kaiser Family Foundation (Kunkle et al., 2003) provides both a sense of the commonality of sexy media as well as difficulties in defining the term. This report, by an organization that tends to be a bit alarmist about media in my opinion, reported that 70% of television shows had sexual content. This sounds dramatic until you understand that they defined sexual content as *any* sexual content, such as merely mentioning sex in a conversation. This is not quite the same thing as explicit sexual behavior in television shows, although this distinction is not always made clear in press releases to the general public. Do I believe that 70% of television shows *mention* sex at some point? Sure. Is this the same thing as kids being "bombarded" by explicit sexuality? I'm not so sure.

Pardun, L'Engle, and Brown (2005) used a similarly broad definition of sexual content to include things like *implied* nudity (?) or partial nudity, kissing, discussions of crushes or romantic fantasies, coverage of topics such as abortion, masturbation, and so on. Using survey methodology, the authors found about 11% of media that teens actually consume contain any form of sexual content. Given the broad definition that they used and this relatively low response rate, these results seem somewhat less alarming than claims teens are "bombarded" with sexy media.

So "sexy media" certainly exists and is common, but it's also a remarkably broad category that includes any form of media that in any way mention, visually suggest, or show sex. With that kind of definition, it's not surprising that it's relatively common!

This prevalence of sexy media no doubt reflects a general trend in society toward greater openness regarding sexuality. Remember, in the 1950s it was considered taboo to picture even a married couple sleeping (let alone engaged in any physical activity) in the same bed together. This was also a time when people talked less openly about sex, and there were taboos and even laws against a variety of sexual expressions we now take for granted, whether homosexuality or interracial marriage (previous bans on which were intended to prevent sexual mixing and, thus, racial purity). As our culture has become more open about sexuality, that has naturally been reflected in our media. In many ways this is a good thing, and I imagine few people want to return to the 1950s. But does it come with a price regarding the well-being of our youth?

128

THE IMPACT OF SEXY MEDIA ON TEEN SEXUALITY

As I noted earlier, it's important to understand that teen sexuality and sexuality in general is a moral issue in the United States. During a friendly debate on video games, my colleague from the Netherlands, Elly Konijn, pointed out that Europeans tend to be less worried about sexual behaviors than Americans, so long as "safe sex" is practiced. Europeans worry less about sex as a moral issue, although health issues such as STDs are still a concern of course. Advocates of the "harm" position often point out, however, that sexual behavior is an obvious precursor to health-related outcomes such as STDs and pregnancy. That is true, of course, although some conflation of sexual behavior and negative outcomes such as STDs and pregnancy remain a problem for the field. That is to say, simply engaging in sexual behavior is often treated as a negative outcome whether such sexual behavior is "safe sex" or risky. This, again, may reflect American attitudes toward sexuality, particularly where teens are involved.

Perhaps not surprisingly, teens and their parents seem to differ with respect to their perceptions of media influences on sexual behavior (Werner-Wilson, Fitzharris, & Morrissey, 2004). Teens generally do not view media as a primary source of information regarding their sexuality. Of course, they may simply be unaware of unconscious influences. By contrast, parents do worry about media influences on their children. There again, however, this could be explained by a natural, parental fear of losing control over one's teens (teens generally stop listening to their parents) and a tendency to blame these changes on external forces rather than maturation.

Science has sought to answer the question of whether media really has an impact or not. However, it's important to note that there are several limitations that influence almost all studies in this field. First, it is clearly not possible to do experiments in which sexual behavior is the outcome (although imagine how

129

easy it would be to get participants!). No institutional review board would allow such a study to pass muster. So, we're mainly limited to correlational studies, whether short-term or longitudinal. Most of these are survey format in nature, and here lies the second problem. Sexual behavior is an awkward topic to discuss, even in anonymous surveys. Some people may feel societal pressure to underreport their sexual behavior. Thus, the "true" responses one gets may come mainly from a subsegment of the population that doesn't care too much about societal prohibitions, and this could drive up correlations if that group tends to like sexy media more as well. On the other hand it's possible to see what is also called "mischievous responding." Mischievous responding occurs when some respondents purposefully give extreme but untrue answers in order to be silly or funny, or purposefully sabotage the study. Such responding can cause spurious positive results (Robinson-Cimpian, 2014). For example, let's say you have a survey of teen sexuality and, on it, you include an item "I sometimes have sex with trees." Some portion of respondents will say "yes" to this even though (one hopes) they are not really having sex with trees. Given that such extreme, mischievous responders will also probably exaggerate their exposure to media sex, just to be silly there too, you'll get a correlation between media exposure and tree sex that is, of course, nonsense.

This issue of mischievous responding is far from a trivial one. Very few surveys test for it, which means that many of the correlations we take for granted on many topics may be due to either mischievous or unreliable responding. Some estimates suggest that, with teen surveys, nearly 20% of responses may be mischievous (Fan et al., 2002). In fairness to teens, it's unlikely the numbers get much better with adult respondents. Indeed, in one recent survey of clinicians I conducted (clinicians mind you, people with advanced degrees who ought to take mental health issues seriously), approximately 10% of responses proved to be mischievous or unreliable. Robinson-Cimpian (2014) points to several specific examples in which published research results were later found to be due to mischievous responding, leading to retractions. For example, in one large study of youth, 253 of them reported to have used an artificial limb for a year or more, but follow-up interviews in person revealed that only two actually had an artificial limb (Fan et al., 2006). In another study that had to be retracted (Miller, Fan, Christensen, Grotevant, & Van Dulmen, 2000), scholars initially found correlations between being adopted and a host of negative outcomes, such as substance abuse and risky behaviors. However, 19% of those who reported being adopted in fact were not, and when these individuals were removed from the dataset, the correlations vanished, and the article had to be retracted. In fairness to the authors, it was they themselves who discovered the error and used it as a platform to investigate mischievous responding in adolescent samples (e.g., Fan et al., 2006).

So with that rather large caveat about unreliable responding—large because so few surveys test for mischievous responding—let's have a look at the data, most of which does indeed rely on adolescent self-report. Such studies typically ask teens to report on the media they consume (some surveys ask the teens themselves to report how sexy it is!) and also self-report on a host of outcomes, including the initiation of sexuality, risky sex behaviors such as unprotected sex, and pregnancy (that's right, survey studies don't actually find out whether teens really had a pregnancy by using medical records; they just ask).

That all having been said, many surveys do indeed find evidence for small correlations, typically in the range of $r = .1$ to $r = .2$ (or about 1% to 4% shared variance) between exposure to sexy media and sexual-behavior–related outcomes (e.g., Brown, Childers, & Waszak, 1990; Fisher et al., 2009; Ward & Friedman, 2006). However, other studies have found no evidence for correlational effects (e.g., Nikken, & de Graaf, 2013; Peterson, Moore, & Furstenberg, 1991; Roberts, 1993). Still others have found inconsistent results (e.g., Somers & Tynan, 2006). Thus, to answer the question, is there a correlation between sexy media and sexual behavior in the teens years, the answer is . . . sort of? Many studies find it, but some do not, and, even when found, the relationship appears to be very small. Knowing how much sexy media a teen watches would give you about a 1% to 4% accuracy better than chance when predicting who might engage in sexual behavior (with 100% being perfect predictive accuracy). That's not much.

To further complicate this picture, if we are to assume that correlational relationships exist, it remains unclear whether watching sexy media causes one to engage in more sexual behaviors, or being more inclined toward sexuality makes you more likely to watch sexy media. Indeed, some research suggests that teens' exposure to sexy media isn't accidental, and more sexually precocious teens are more likely to seek out sexy media (Hawk, Vanswesenbeeck, de Graaf & Bakker, 2006). So perhaps teens who are already inclined toward sexual behavior are the ones watching sexy media, something we call the decline effect.

To try to untangle that, several studies have attempted to employ longitudinal analyses in which children are tracked over time. Longitudinal designs are still correlational (although some rare longitudinal experiments do exist) and thus can't be used to determine causality. However, they can help tease out a temporal order between variables. If, for instance, watching sexy media predicts later sexuality, but being sexually active doesn't predict later sexy media viewing, that presents a good argument that watching sexy media at least comes first in the developmental sequence, although of course an unmeasured third variable could still be driving the relationship.

Three such longitudinal studies are most notable. The first two were conducted by the same research group. Collins and colleagues (2004) followed a large group of adolescents over the course of 1 year and found that watching sexy television (recall the issue about definitions though—whether the shows merely mentioned sex or actually depicted sexual behavior) predicted the initiation of sexual behaviors by 1 year later. The same research group later found that watching sexy television even predicted teen pregnancy (Chandra et al., 2008). Brown and colleagues (2006) found similar results for sexy media predicting later adolescent sexual behavior. Thus, three longitudinal studies finding basically the same thing. Case closed? Well, no.

First, the findings of Chandra et al. (2008) displayed something unusual. The authors considered both general television viewing and viewing of sexy TV. Not surprisingly, those two variables were entered into regression equations together. When the authors did this, sexy TV predicted more sexual teen pregnancy later. But general television viewing predicted *less* teen pregnancy later. This is about the time you should hear screeching brakes. The two television variables were highly correlated . . . how can they predict the same outcome behavior in *opposite* directions? And aren't we told all the time how general television bombards teens with sexual messages? If so, how can general television viewing (which just means total time viewing TV, not excluding sexy TV) be protective of teen pregnancy if it's full of sexual messages? The answer to this problem is a phenomenon called *multicollinearity*. Basically, it is a statistical no-no to enter two highly correlated variables into the same regression equation, as you can get all kinds of weird and spurious results. The phenomenon is sometimes called a *bouncing beta* phenomenon, in which the results for two correlated variables essentially bounce away from each other in opposing directions in ways that are spurious. Deciding to check for this, I asked the authors to rerun their analyses, this time entering the media variables alone rather than together. When run this way, sexy media no longer predicted teen pregnancy! So it appears that this result was, indeed, a statistical artifact (Robin Beckman, personal communication, June 2015).

Other scholars haven't had much luck when they've directly asked for this dataset. Steinberg and Monahan (2011a) also requested the dataset from the same authors and were denied. However, they were successful in getting the Brown et al. (2006) dataset, which they reanalyzed using a technique called *propensity score matching*, which does a more robust job in controlling for other factors that may explain any relationship between two variables. Or put another way, propensity score matching is one technique to test whether a correlation may be spurious. Reanalyzing the Brown et al. (2006) dataset led Steinberg and Monahan (2011a) to conclude that viewing sexy media, in fact, had no relationship with later sexual behavior. The observed relationship was due entirely to other factors that Brown et al. (2006) had not adequately controlled in their own analysis. This set off a somewhat acrimonious exchange between the three research groups (Brown, 2011; Collins, Martino, & Elliott, 2011; Sternberg & Monahan, 2011b). Thus, we are still left with conflicting findings, even from the same datasets!

SHOULD PARENTS RESTRICT SEXY MEDIA?

What, then, should we be telling parents? Should they be restricting sexy media, and if so, does that really mean *all* sexy media, including just people talking about sex? Good luck with that! But assuming it were possible, how much would it help? A few studies have examined this issue and the results have been . . . guess what? . . . inconsistent. For example, one study by Bersamin and colleagues (2008) found that parental restriction of sexual media was correlated with later initiation of oral and vaginal sex. As with previous results, these are correlational; it may very well be that more-restrictive parents are simply more involved in their children's lives, and parental involvement is generally a good thing. It still might be worth suggesting to parents that monitoring and restricting exposure is worthwhile, even though a more recent study found essentially the exact opposite effect (Nikken & de Graaf, 2013), with parental restriction associated with no impact in boys and *earlier* initiation of sex in girls.

My best guess, based on rather limited data, is that the picture is complex. For instance, in a further study, although direct exposure to sexy media was not related to sexual behavior, parental efforts to restrict such media (even, apparently, if unsuccessful) were predictive of less sexual behavior (Parkes, Wight, Hunt, Henderson, & Sargent, 2013). This lends credence to the idea that parental involvement is a key variable rather than media exposure per se. And it likely depends on exactly what is being said between parents and children, how messages about sexuality are being communicated. Simply telling parents to take away the television set and leave it at that is probably not the most constructive thing.

So what should we be telling parents? If you've been reading all the chapters to this point, you'll probably see that a common thread in media psychology has begun to emerge: A significant gulf often exists between what scholars say and the actual data available to support the claims made. As with most areas of media psychology, results linking sexy media to sexual behavior are inconsistent, and, where they do exist, there is reason to believe they may be due to other variables or even simple mischievous responding. Thus, messages to the general public regarding sexy media should be cautious. At worst, the effects are small, increasing the risks of sexual behavior by 1% to 4%. Our messages of alarm should be tempered accordingly. Certainly, we should encourage parents to be involved in their children's media lives, but the current data do not indicate that an urgent public health crisis is imminent. Indeed, despite the plethora of sexy media, kids have initiated sex later in recent years, and there have been consistent reductions in teen pregnancy (childstats.gov, 2014). Overcommunicating the risk of "harm" prematurely risks distracting people from other, more pressing concerns (such as poverty, educational disparities, or mental health) and damaging the credibility of the research field (Steinberg & Monahan, 2011b).

REFERENCES

Bersamin, M., Todd, M., Fisher, D. A., Hill, D. L., Grube, J. W., & Walker, S. (2008). Parenting practices and adolescent sexual behavior: A longitudinal study. *Journal of Marriage and Family, 70*(1), 97–112. doi:10.1111/j.1741-3737.2007.00464.x

Brown, J., L'Engle, K. L., Pardun, C. J., Guo, G., Kenneavy, K., & Jackson, C. (2006). Sexy media matter: Exposure to sexual content in music, movies, television, and magazines predicts black and white adolescents' sexual behavior. *Pediatrics, 117,* 1018–1027.

Brown, J. D. (2011). The media do matter: Comment on Steinberg and Monahan (2011). *Developmental Psychology, 47*(2), 580–581. doi:10.1037/a0022553

Brown, J. D., Childers, K. W., & Waszak, C. S. (1990). Television and adolescent sexuality. *Journal of Adolescent Health Care, 11*(1), 62–70.

Chandra, A., Martino, S. C., Collins, R. L., Elliott, M. N., Berry, S. H., Kanouse, D. E., & Miu, A. (2008). Does watching sex on television predict teen pregnancy? Findings from a national longitudinal survey of youth. *Pediatrics, 122*(5), 1047–1054. doi:10.1542/peds.2007-3066

Childers, K., & Brown, J. (2011). *Sex on TV: Do all kids see the same show?* Retrieved from http://www.medialit.org/reading-room/sex-tv-do-all-kids-see-same-show

Childstats.gov. (2014). *America's children: Key national indicators of well-being, 2010.* Retrieved July 16, 2014, from http://www.childstats.gov

Collins, R. L., Elliott, M. N., Berry, S. H., Kanouse, D. E., Kunkel, D., Hunter, S. B., & Miu, A. (2004). Watching sex on television predicts adolescent initiation of sexual behavior. *Pediatrics, 114,* e280–e289.

Collins, R. L., Martino, S. C., & Elliott, M. N. (2011). Propensity scoring and the relationship between sexual media and adolescent sexual behavior: Comment on Steinberg and Monahan (2011). *Developmental Psychology, 47,* 577–579. doi:10.1037/a0022564

Commercial Free Childhood. (2014). *Sexualizing childhood.* Retrieved from http://www.commercialfreechildhood.org/sites/default/files/sexualization.pdf

Elliott, S. (2010). Parents' constructions of teen sexuality: Sex panics, contradictory discourses, and social inequality. *Symbolic Interaction, 33*(2), 191–212. doi:10.1525/si.2010.33.2.191

Fan, X., Miller, B. C., Christensen, M., Park, K.-E., Grotevant, H. D., van Dulmen, M., . . . Bayley, B. (2002). Questionnaire and interview inconsistencies exaggerated differences between adopted and non-adopted adolescents in a national sample. *Adoption Quarterly, 6,* 7–27. doi:10.1300/J145v06n02_02

Fan, X., Miller, B. C., Park, K.-E., Winward, B. W., Christensen, M., Grotevant, H. D., & Tai, R. H. (2006). An exploratory study about inaccuracy and invalidity in adolescent self-report surveys. *Field Methods, 18*, 223–244. doi:10.1177/152822X06289161

Ferguson, C. J., & Konijn, E. A. (in press). She said/he said: A peaceful debate on video game violence. *Psychology of Popular Media Culture.*

Fisher, D. A., Hill, D. L., Grube, J. W., Bersamin, M. M., Walker, S., & Gruber, E. L. (2009). Televised sexual content and parental mediation: Influences on adolescent sexuality. *Media Psychology, 12*(2), 121–147. doi:10.1080/15213260902849901

Hawk, S., Vanswesenbeeck, H., de Graaf, I., & Bakker, F. (2006). Adolescents' contact with sexuality in mainstream media: A selection-based perspective. *Journal of Sex Research, 43*, 352–363.

Kunkel, D., Biely, E., Eyal, K., Finnerty, K., Bieley, E., & Donnerstein, E. (2005). *Sex on TV 4: A Kaiser Family Foundation report.* Menlo Park, CA: Kaiser Family Foundation.

Miller, B. C., Fan, X., Christensen, M., Grotevant, H. D., & Van Dulmen, M. (2000). Comparisons of adopted and nonadopted adolescents in a large, nationally representative sample. *Child Development, 71*, 1458–1473. doi:10.1111/1467-8624.00239

Nikken, P., & de Graaf, H. (2013). Reciprocal relationships between friends' and parental mediation of adolescents' media use and their sexual attitudes and behavior. *Journal of Youth and Adolescence, 42*(11), 1696–1707. doi:10.1007/s10964-012-9873-5

Pardun, C. J., L'Engle, K., & Brown, J. D. (2005). Linking exposure to outcomes: Early adolescents' consumption of sexual content in six media. *Mass Communication & Society, 8*(2), 75–91. doi:10.1207/s15327825mcs0802_1

Parkes, A., Wight, D., Hunt, K., Henderson, M., & Sargent, J. (2013). Are sexual media exposure, parental restrictions on media use and co-viewing TV and DVDs with parents and friends associated with teenagers' early sexual behaviour? *Journal of Adolescence, 36*(6), 1121–1133. doi:10.1016/j.adolescence.2013.08.019

Peterson, J. L., Moore, K. A., & Furstenberg, F. F. (1991). Television viewing and early initiation of sexual intercourse: Is there a link? *Journal of Homosexuality, 21*(1–2), 93–118.

Roberts, D. F. (1993). Adolescents and the media: From "Leave It to Beaver" to "Beverly Hills 90210." *Teachers College Record, 94*, 629–644.

Robinson-Cimpian, J. P. (2014). Inaccurate estimation of disparities due to mischievous responders: Several suggestions to assess conclusions. *Educational Researcher, 43,* 171–185.

Skynews. (2014). *Viewers less worried by sex on television.* Retrieved from https://uk.news.yahoo.com/viewers-less-worried-sex-television-125223038.html#Ca890mC

Somers, C., & Tynan, J. (2006). Consumption of sexual dialogue and content on television and adolescent sexual outcomes: Multiethnic findings. *Adolescence, 41*(161), 15–38.

Steinberg, L., & Monahan, K. C. (2011a). Adolescents' exposure to sexy media does not hasten the initiation of sexual intercourse. *Developmental Psychology, 47*(2), 562–576. doi:10.1037/a0020613

Steinberg, L., & Monahan, K. C. (2011b). Premature dissemination of advice undermines our credibility as scientists: Reply to Brown (2011) and to Collins, Martino, and Elliott (2011). *Developmental Psychology, 47*(2), 582–584. doi:10.1037/a0022562

Ward, L., & Friedman, K. (2006). Using TV as a guide: Associations between television viewing and adolescents' sexual attitudes and behavior. *Journal of Research on Adolescence, 16*(1), 133–156. doi:10.1111/j.1532-7795.2006.00125.x

Werner-Wilson, R., Fitzharris, J., & Morrissey, K. M. (2004). Adolescent and parent perceptions of media influence on adolescent sexuality. *Adolescence, 39*(154), 303–313.

Race and the Media

The 2010 U.S. Census indicated that ours is a diverse nation. Although approximately 72% of individuals identified as "White alone," substantial minorities identified themselves with other races, particularly "Black" (12.6%), "Asian" (4.8%), or other races, as well as 2.9% who identified as biracial. The U.S. government considers Hispanic ethnicity as separate from race, and found that 16.3% identified as Hispanic or Latino. Census data also indicates that approximately 12% to 13% of our population are foreign-born. Other census data has indicated that non-White births (including children identified as biracial) now represent the majority of births. How well is our media representing our nation's racial diversity?

Arguably, cultural discussions of race and ethnicity fall across two related lines. First, race-related discussions and conflict may occur between two or more racial groups in a particular country where there is a historical record of conflict or oppression involving those groups. These conflicts may be between Caucasian,

African, and Native Americans living within the United States, for instance, or Causasian and indigenous populations in Australia or New Zealand, lighter-skinned and Mestizo populations in Mexico, Hutus and Tutsis in Rwanda, or among the Roma and various dominant populations of European countries. These types of racial conflicts appear more the norm than the exception, and can create strains between groups now trying to live in harmony under a single, national identity. For instance, as I write this, racial tension in the United States between Whites and Blacks has been stirred due to recent high-profile cases in which Black men have been allegedly fired upon or otherwise mistreated while unarmed or surrendering to White police officers, such as in Ferguson, Missouri.

Another issue that stirs up racial conflict is that of immigration of new racial groups into a country. Such new groups may be seen as straining a country's resources or diluting its cultural identity, whether fairly or not. Members of the preexisting culture may also worry about security concerns. Following the terrorist attacks of 9/11 and subsequent Islamist jihadi attacks in England, Spain, Russia, and elsewhere, concerns over immigration and illegal immigration in particular have been heightened in many nations, particularly involving Middle Eastern, Southeast Asian, or North African groups immigrating to European or North American nations. Public Agenda (2005) polls demonstrate that American attitudes toward immigration tend to harden following terrorist strikes. This reaction is hardly unique to Americans and demonstrates ongoing strain between members of different cultural units. Terror management theory (Greenberg, Solomon, & Pyszczynski, 1997) predicts that cultures are generally hostile to one another because different cultures adopt differing beliefs about religion and culture to help us overcome "death terror" (our fear of death). By adopting particular beliefs, we hope something of ourselves will survive beyond death. Other cultures with different ideas threaten this and attract our hostility.

When one particular ethnic or racial group has numerical and social dominance within a particular nation or culture, it is arguably not surprising to see media cater to the dominant group. The largest numerical group has the greatest appeal to advertisers, will provide more numbers for ratings, and may contribute more individuals who are writers and producers of media, thus perpetuating the cycle (Breuer, Festl, & Quandt, 2012). Racial and ethnic minorities may be represented only seldom in mainstream media, and when they are represented, they may be portrayed along narrow lines that reflect the stereotypes and prejudices of the dominant group.

As we've seen throughout the book thus far, it has become common in academic circles to discuss the media as a tool of socialization, in which persons behave in a manner consistent with models they view on television. Essentially, monkey see, monkey do, or what is sometimes referred to as the hypodermic needle model. Adopting such an approach raises concerns about the degree to which portrayals of ethnic minorities may influence viewer perceptions of those minority groups. Can negative portrayals of ethnic or racial minorities promote stereotypes and prejudices and, by contrast, can positive portrayals help promote social change? Or do media portrayals, and changes to the same, merely reflect prevailing social attitudes or demographic changes in society? If we argue that media portrayals of minority groups have become both more diverse and more positive, did media lead this charge or simply follow along in the wake of a changing society?

These are, of course, macro-level issues. On a more individualistic level, there is also the issue of how portrayals of minority ethnicities and races influence members of those groups as well. What is it like to grow up in a media landscape in which individuals in the media, in the main, do not look like you or hold your cultural values? Or when your ethnic or racial group is portrayed (or religious affiliation, such as in the case of Jewish or Muslim individuals), those portrayals are mainly negative?

Before examining these debate questions, it is important to clarify the meaning of two terms, *stereotype* and *prejudice*. "Stereotype" is here defined as a description of a group (ethnic, gender,

141

religious, etc.) wherein it is suggested that most or all members of that group share a particular trait or set of traits. Stereotypes are thus used to prejudge members of that group rather than to evaluate them on their individual characteristics. Although stereotypes are generally considered a negative phenomenon, the traits themselves may either be positive or negative. Examples thus range from positive stereotypes such as "all Asian people are good at math" to negative stereotypes such as "all Irish people are alcoholics." It is possible that stereotypes may, at times, be based on actual group differences but tend to be overgeneralized and used to make judgments about members of the group in the absence of supporting evidence for that individual. Perhaps the "classic" (if that is the right word) is the assumption that Asian Americans are relatively recent immigrants to the United States. Thus, many Asian Americans may endure the repeat question "Where are you from?" which, although perhaps intended politely, implies a differentness that tacitly excludes Asian Americans from American culture. For many Asian Americans who were born and raised in the United States and do not speak Asian languages or identify particularly with Asian culture (at least no more than Caucasian Americans do with their various European heritages), this may come across as excluding.

Admittedly, some negative stereotypes may have some basis in reality. For example, men are stereotyped as aggressive and/or violent in comparison to women. Indeed, men are responsible for 85% of violent crimes and tend also to dominate aggressive or extreme sports (Heimer, 2000). However, using this stereotype to judge individual men is unlikely to be reliable, as many men (indeed likely the majority) do not fit this stereotype of being violent or harmful.

By contrast, the term "prejudice" is here used to indicate a stereotype which is specifically intended to portray a group of individuals in an unfairly unfavorable light. Prejudice may often be used to promote a hostile social agenda such as racism, sexism, or religious bigotry. Examples include the 19th-century European notion of the "White man's burden," justifying the imposition of Western rule and culture on non-White people; discussions of Jewish conspiracies to rule the world (or interestingly enough, the media) that promote anti-Semitism; or portrayals of women as weak-willed and irrational (or men as dumb, immoral oafs) that promote sexism. The essence of prejudice is that the belief is not only negative but "unfair," that is, not based on any observable, independent reality. For example, unlike the stereotype of men as aggressive, which has some empirical basis (although as a stereotype is overgeneralized), the prejudice that individuals from non-European cultures are less intelligent than Europeans has no basis in empirical fact.

DOES THE MEDIA PROMOTE UNFAIR STEREOTYPES?

As discussed earlier, mass media has incentives to cater most to the dominant and most lucrative group of individuals within a culture. This produces one facet of the concept of *privilege,* in which members of the dominant group enjoy the privilege of seeing themselves represented in media often and generally favorably, a privilege not enjoyed by disadvantaged groups. Certainly, the media tends to give groups of people in ways that are largely consistent with the broader society's view of those groups. As such, the media may give a public face to the biases, concerns, and worries of the general social group from whom the media expects to extract its funding. The social concerns of a particular era may thus be reflected in the prevailing themes in the media. For example, during the Reagan era of the 1980s, when Cold War tension had reached a new peak, Russians were frequently portrayed in the media as authoritarian, aggressive, and technologically advanced. Examples of this include movies such as *Red Dawn,* in which the Warsaw Pact nations successfully invade the United States; *Rocky IV,* which features the tagline "Get ready for the next world war"; and television miniseries such as *The Day After* and *Amerika*. These examples from the Cold War indeed exemplify how stereotypes can be both accurate (in part at least) and inaccurate. By and large, the Soviet Union did have a history of authoritarianism and aggression, but, by the end of the Cold War, it proved to be economically and technologically struggling.

In this case, media portrayals, while certainly stereotypical, also reflected general concerns of U.S. society. In effect, they told the story that Americans wanted to hear, that plucky America would always manage to overcome a powerful, technologically advanced Soviet Union.

Such portrayals of Russians as amoral, ruthless, uncaring machines undoubtedly were unfair to the majority of Russians, regular people leading regular lives. However, these media portrayals can be understood as an outcropping of realistic group conflict theory (Sherif, Harvey, White, Hood, & Sherif, 1961), wherein prejudice can arise from situations in which groups are in conflict over limited resources. The struggle for world dominance between the West and the East can thus be seen as a source of prejudice.

Very often prejudice and stereotypical representations come at the expense of disadvantaged minorities, with the media reinforcing the stereotypes of the dominant majority. Perhaps a prime example is the silent film *Birth of a Nation* (1915, directed by D. W. Griffith), which portrays a virtuous South ransacked by African American Union soldiers during the Civil War and Reconstruction, until heroic Ku Klux Klansmen ride to the rescue. Such a narrative is absurd to modern sensibilities, but it reflects the racial tensions and prejudice toward African Americans at the time. We now consider media portrayals of several ethnic minorities.

First, despite the fact that Latinos are the fastest growing minority and (in part owing to biethnic marriages) likely to become a dominant ethnic group in the future, they generally remain underrepresented in the media. For example, during the 2013 TV season, there were almost no lead Latino characters on

TV, and only about 3% (for males) to 9.5% (for females) of supporting characters were Latino. This is approximately half of the proportion of Latinos in the U.S. population (Negron-Muntaner, Abbas, Figueroa, & Robson, 2014). Although it is possible that part of this discrepancy may be explained by television characters that are of ambiguous ancestry (meaning that the proportions of characters that are clearly identified as one ethnicity or another may not add up to 100%), it appears that the television media is underfocused on Latino characters. Many academics who study media presentations of ethnic minorities suggest that Latinos are more often presented as criminals of low income, functioning in less prestigious jobs, and tending to speak with thick accents more often than White characters. Thus the portrayal of Latinos on television tends to be more negative than for Whites.

Many scholars express concern that these negative portrayals of Latinos can promote negative stereotypes and that, by contrast, more positive portrayals could question those stereotypes (Mastro & Tukachinski, 2011). As is often the case for media psychology, effects are small, suggesting that people's opinions are generally entrenched and not easily shaped by media effects. Nonetheless, media portrayals can be part of an important larger discussion. Research suggests that Latinos themselves are naturally aware of these stereotypical portrayals but reasonably resistant to internalizing them (Rivadeneyra, 2006). Further, Hispanic ethnic identity may be protective against other sorts of media effects, for instance disinclined to accept media portrayals of Latinos as criminal or undereducated (Schooler & Daniels, 2014).

Few issues in media portrayals of ethnic minorities have been as controversial as the portrayal of African Americans. Although there have been improvements in recent years, negative portrayals of African Americans in mainstream media remain an issue, and some scholars express concern that this could negatively impact the racial identity of African American youth (Martin, 2008). Although awareness of these issues has increased, real effort to challenge the dialogue on African American race in mainstream media has been slow (Littlefield, 2008).

An interesting corollary to these results regarding portrayals of African Americans in U.S. media is a study of the portrayal of African Americans in media consumed in South Korea, a culture where people have relatively little direct exposure to people of African heritage (Tan, Dalisay, Zhang, Han, & Merchant, 2010). Results indicated that positive or negative portrayals of African Americans in U.S. media impacted the perceptions of African Americans among South Korean participants, but only if they believed the shows were realistic.

Other ethnic groups have expressed similar concerns, ranging from portrayals of Muslim women as passive and uneducated, to Russians as involved in criminal mafias, to Asians (people from India, Pakistan, the Koreas, etc.) as rude and relegated to careers at convenience stores. Common to all of these concerns is that these stereotypes are being used as part of a hostile movement to deny ethnic minorities the ability to integrate fully as equal members of American (or European) society.

One further corollary to this is that what constitutes a negative portrayal or stereotype can itself be subjective. Many people of a particular ethnicity may purposefully satire prejudiced depictions of their group as a means of asserting control over the stereotypes and mocking them. Similarly, ethnic minorities may incorporate racist language or depictions in their own art. For instance, is it acceptable for Black rap artists to use the n-word in their music? Even members of the ethnic group in question may differ on what is acceptable and what is offensive. For example, one individual may find George Lopez's portrayal of Mexican Americans as negative and prejudicial, whereas another may find the stereotypical depictions as playful or even empowering (see Rivadeneyra, 2006, for an expanded discussion of this particular example).

So how prevalent are negative depictions of ethnic minorities? Given the subjective nature of interpreting art, it may depend on whom you ask. For instance, as I write this, a new show, *Black-ish*, has become a hit comedy. It has invited some comparisons to the popular 1980s sitcom *The Cosby Show*, which featured an African American family but which, in general, did not make their racial identity a primary driver of the show (e.g., Whitaker, 2014). By contrast, *Black-ish* is very much about incorporating Black racial identity into a White-dominated culture and facing implicit and explicit stereotyping and racism from that culture. Does *Black-ish* promote racial stereotypes or challenge them? (I would argue challenge, but not everyone seems to agree. See for example, Donald Trump's comments in *The Telegram* [2014], but then again, perhaps Trump's views on race aren't exactly the most crucial.) Academic discussions of mass media and race may themselves be less than entirely reliable. Academics (and here this article risks its own stereotype, although see Redding, 2001, for a discussion of the self-selection of individuals into academia) tend to be liberal and arguably biased toward sometimes hysteria-prone critiques of the "dangers" of popular culture. By contrast, media executives may be insensitive to the perceptions of media portrayals and more focused on profit. The viewing public likely vary widely in their tastes regarding what is offensive and what is not regarding ethnic minority portrayals. For example, even children's cartoons can be viewed either as promoting strong positive images of ethnic minorities (and females) or as promoting gender and ethnic prejudice.

Given the history of racial oppression of African Americans, as well as long-standing prejudices toward immigrant groups such as Latinos, it's not surprising that most of the focus would be on these groups. However, some Caucasian subgroups also complain that media portrayals of their ethnicities are stereotyped or prejudicial. Perhaps the most obvious example is the portrayal of Italian Americans as loud, rude, and Mafia connected. Authors such as Messina (2004) note that a historical connection with the Mafia really does exist (just as it does for other ethnicities, however), but that this connection does not define Italian Americans. Messina argues that despite being generally identified as White Americans, Italian Americans nonetheless are stigmatized by media portrayals of them as obnoxious criminals. Jewish Americans are another Caucasian subgroup often subjected to stereotypical and anti-Semitic portrayals in the media. In some cases,

147

comedic shows such as *Seinfeld* and *Will and Grace* purposefully played on Jewish stereotypes for laughs, leading to debates about whether such self-mocking satires of racial prejudice are offensive or empowering. Even the "banned" episode of *Family Guy*, in which the lead (cartoon) character sings a song in which he references the Jews of Palestine as responsible for the death of Christ, raises arguments over whether the comment is genuinely anti-Semitic or intended as parody.

The immediate, direct effects of such media depictions, either positive or negative, appear to be small. Therefore, as in general with media effects, it behooves the scholar to be cautious in language and not overemphasize the power of media effects. At the same time, media, especially mass media, can be part of a larger societal dialogue on issues such as prejudice, racism, sexism, and so on. Constructive campaigns to bring change in mass media depictions can be part of a larger effort toward social change that can benefit all members of society, whatever the direct effects of mass media may or may not be.

ARGUMENTS IN SUPPORT OF MEDIA PORTRAYALS AS REFLECTIVE OF REAL DIFFERENCES

The obvious counterargument to the issue of stereotypical depictions of ethnic minorities in media is that such depictions may represent actual group differences. At least on the surface, this may appear to be something of a fair argument. If we grant that culture is important in shaping people's identities and behaviors, then of course people who come from different cultural groups will vary in certain identifiable ways, both positive and negative. To use an extreme example, few would argue that the depictions of Nazi war criminals, such as seen in *Schindler's List*, constitute an unfair portrayal of Nazis as bigots and murderers. In this case,

Nazis have a verified record of committed atrocities (despite the claims of Holocaust deniers), and thus their portrayal in the media as vicious war criminals has been earned through their collective group behavior. Although it may be true that a few members of the Nazi party may have been decent, compassionate individuals (for example, perhaps Albert Speer's public disavowal of his Nazi past redeemed him somewhat), it is difficult to imagine that the common portrayals of Nazis in the media represents a prejudice toward Nazis. On the other hand, the argument could be made that depicting most Germans as heartless and vile Nazis is an unfair stereotype, even if such a depiction had real roots in the events surrounding World War II.

So it's entirely plausible that some real group differences may exist, and that it wouldn't necessarily be unreasonable to see them appear in mass media. Indeed, the alternative may be the Disneyfication of race, in which characters of different ethnicities appear together with identical personas, with the influence of culture removed altogether. Such portrayals are positive in the sense of portraying a utopia of color-blind racial harmony, but at the cost of cultural sterilization.

The issue, however, is when racial or ethnic identity and stereotypes of the same become the dominant trait of media portrayals of characters from those backgrounds. For instance, ethnic minority characters are constantly portrayed as conforming to racial stereotypes, whereas characters from the dominant ethnicity are given greater freedom to grow into multiple character roles with fuller personalities. A good example of this is the concept of the Magic Minority, ethnic minority characters defined primarily by their culture's exotic religious beliefs. Native American and Asian characters, in particular, are often defined in this way, whereas Caucasian characters are seldom defined by their Christianity. This set of circumstances obviously contributes to the privilege of the dominant group, in which all minority characters in mass media are defined through the lens of the dominant group's stereotypes, whereas the dominant group does not have to endure portrayals of minority groups' stereotypes of them,

149

even if such stereotypes exist. Thus, as a whole, media representations of race or ethnicity are unfair and disparaging of certain groups more than others.

It should be noted that it is possible that these stereotypes, although initially based on some kernel of reality, may harden in the public consciousness and prove immutable even after the social circumstances that gave rise to them have changed. This is essentially the argument that Messina makes in regard to Italians—namely, that there may be some historical truth to the Italian Mafioso stereotype, but the Italian Syndicate has long since diminished in stature and so few Italians have any connection with the Mafia in current times that the stereotype has devolved into a full prejudice. That perhaps is one serious risk of "tolerating" stereotypes and leaving them unchallenged; what begins as a neutral observation may become distorted over time and eventually used to oppress groups of people.

Another risk, perhaps, comes when relatively neutral observations of group differences are assigned value labels by other cultures that are then used to judge them negatively. For instance, as noted earlier (Ferguson, 2004), Arab women are often portrayed as submissive and oppressed by their Arab husbands. This stereotype may have its origins in actual cultural differences between Arab and White Americans but may have been misinterpreted unfavorably by the mainstream American culture. Specifically, Arab women tend to address conflict with their husbands in a more indirect and subtle manner than is common for White women. Thus, what is, in effect, diplomacy may be construed as passivity by another culture. Indeed, Arab women often view themselves as the familial decision makers and diplomacy merely a part of convincing the husband to agree to (or trick into thinking he came up with) a course of action that the wife has already set upon. This is not to say that male oppression and domestic violence are not issues for Arab women (as indeed honor killings and female circumcision make clear), but rather that these cultural issues are often more complex than is commonly perceived by other cultures (e.g., many honor killings and female circumcisions are initiated by family matriarchs as well as by male family members). Naturally, male oppression and violence against women is also an issue for Whites.

Finally, it should be noted that it is possible that negative stereotypes may indeed be based on actual group differences. However, were the media to portray only these negative differences and fail to portray positive differences, it would be an unfair and prejudicial portrayal of immigrant groups. Thus, the argument that media stereotypes of immigrants are based on actual group differences can be considered nonprejudicial only if the media is presenting the cultural group in a well-rounded fashion. For example, in regard to Latinos, does the media also portray the remarkable faith, cultural pride, and strong family ties that are common among Latinos, or are only the social difficulties faced by Latino immigrants presented? In the absence of quantified data (and few studies examine the frequency of *positive* stereotypes in the media), this issue unfortunately remains subjective.

CONCLUSIONS

It is clear that evidence suggests that media portrayals of ethnic minorities continue to be problematic. Although improvements have occurred in recent years, minority groups tend to be portrayed in light of dominant-group stereotypes that promote negative impressions of minority groups. Although the current chapter focuses on Western media and, particularly, racial and ethnic tensions specific to the United States, it is unlikely that this state of affairs differs in other regions or cultures where cross-ethnic strife occurs.

It is probably best to understand media portrayals in the context of broader societal issues surrounding race. Media tends to reflect the interests of dominant cultural units. Discussions of race and ethnicity and social justice are likely to change both the dominant culture's views and media portrayals of race. Mass media is just one landscape in which such discussions occur, yet it may be a positive venue for such discussions. However, it is likely simplistic to assert that media is a dominant driver of attitudes toward race but is rather part of a far more complicated milieu. Efforts to change cultural discussions of race and the depictions of ethnic minorities will likely bear the greatest fruit to the degree that they focus on positive messages and the benefit of racial and ethnic equality for all members of the cultural community.

REFERENCES

Breuer, J., Festl, R., & Quandt, T. (2012). Digital war: An empirical analysis of narrative elements in military first-person shooters. *Journal of Gaming & Virtual Worlds, 4,* 225–237.

Ferguson, C. (2004). Arab Americans: Acculturation and prejudice in an era of international conflict. In C. Negy (Ed.), *Cross-cultural psychotherapy: Toward a critical understanding of diverse client populations* (pp. 265–280). Reno, NV: Bent Tree Press.

Greenberg, J., Solomon, S., & Pyszczynski, T. (1997). Terror management theory of self-esteem and cultural world-views: Empirical assessments and conceptual refinements. In M. P. Zanna (Ed.), *Advances in Experimental Social Psychology, 29,* 61–139.

Heimer, K. (2000). *Changes in the gender gap in crime and women's economic marginalization.* Retrieved from https://www.ncjrs.gov/criminal_ justice2000/vol_1/02i.pdf

Littlefield, M. (2008). The media as a system of racialization: Exploring images of African American women and the new racism. *American Behavioral Scientist, 51*(5), 675–685. doi:10.1177/ 0002764207307747

Martin, A. C. (2008). Television media as a potential negative factor in the racial identity development of African American youth. *Academic Psychiatry, 32*(4), 338–342. doi:10.1176/appi.ap.32.4.338

Mastro, D., & Tukachinski, R. (2011). The influence of exemplar versus prototype-based media primes on racial/ethnic evaluations. *Journal of Communication, 61,* 916–937.

Messina, E. (2004). Psychological perspectives on the stigmatization of Italian Americans in the American media. In R. Marchesani & M. Stern (Eds.), *Saints and rogues: Conflicts and convergence in psychotherapy* (pp. 87–121). New York, NY: Haworth.

Negron-Muntaner, F., with Abbas, C., Figueroa, L., & Robson, S. (2014). *The Latino media gap: A report on the state of Latinos in U.S. media.* Retrieved from http://www.columbia.edu/cu/cser/downloads/Latino_Media_Gap_Report.pdf

Public Agenda. (2005). *Immigration: Bills and proposals.* Retrieved from http://www.publicagenda.org/issues/major_proposals_detail.cfm?issue_type=immigration&list=1

Redding, R. (2001). Sociopolitical diversity in psychology. *American Psychologist, 56,* 205–215.

Rivadeneyra, R. (2006). Do you see what I see? Latino Americans' perceptions of the images on television. *Journal of Adolescent Research, 21,* 393–414.

Schooler, D., & Daniels, E. A. (2014). "I am not a skinny toothpick and proud of it": Latina adolescents' ethnic identity and responses to mainstream media images. *Body Image, 11*(1), 11–18. doi:10.1016/j.bodyim.2013.09.001

Sherif, M., Harvey, O. J., White, B. J., Hood, W. R., & Sherif, C. W. (1961). *Intergroup conflict and cooperation: The Robbers Cave experiment* (Vol. 10). Norman, OK: University Book Exchange.

Tan, A., Dalisay, F., Zhang, Y., Han, E., & Merchant, M. M. (2010). A cognitive processing model of information source use and stereotyping: African-American stereotypes in South Korea. *Journal of Broadcasting & Electronic Media, 54*(4), 569–587. doi:10.1080/08838151.2010.5198

The Telegram. (2014). Donald Trump: *Black-ish* is "racism at the highest level." Retrieved from http://www.herkimertelegram.com/article/ZZ/20141002/NEWS/310029997/10063/ENTERTAINMENT

United States Census Bureau. (2014). *2010 census data.* Retrieved from http://www.census.gov/2010census/data

Whitaker, M. (2014). Blackness, 'Black-ish' and 'The Cosby Show': How Cliff Huxtable changed American culture. *Time.com.* Retrieved from http://time.com/3388134/black-ish-cosby-show-cliff-huxtable-american-culture/#3388134/black-ish-cosby-show-cliff-huxtable-american-culture

Crime in the News

n May 2007, 3-year-old Madeleine McCann disappeared from a Portuguese tourism resort. Madeleine's parents, British nationals, stated that they left Madeleine and her two young siblings in an unlocked resort villa while they dined with friends a short distance away and checked on them regularly. The resort was in a low-crime area, so the parents judged their actions to be of low risk. Nonetheless, around 10 p.m., Madeleine's mother went to check on the children and found Madeleine was missing from her bed, with an open bedroom window suggesting an outside intruder. The parents called the Portuguese police and a search was begun for Madeleine. When she did not turn up in the immediate area, police concluded she may have been abducted, or that other foul play was involved. This began a frenzy of international news media attention that arguably would come to damage everyone involved in the case.

At initial stages the news media proved to be useful for the investigation itself, and both the McCanns and the Portuguese police made use of the news media to search for Madeleine. As we discuss later in the chapter, the news media may have focused on Madeleine because of certain features of the missing girl herself: a pretty, female, White, Westerner from a privileged background (both McCanns are doctors). Some expressed concern that the initial news media blast was handled poorly, such as the Portuguese police releasing too many details to news media (BBC News, 2007).

Initially, the investigation narrowed in on Robert Murat, a 33-year-old British/Portuguese man. Murat was a nearby resident who had a habit of inserting himself into the investigation as a translator, a role that seemed to thrill him. Investigators are aware that criminal perpetrators sometimes seek to inject themselves into a case in a way that is less common for innocent people. One journalist noticed this and began to comment on it (CBC News, 2007). Nonetheless, the investigation failed to find evidence that Murat was responsible for Madeleine's disappearance.

Several celebrities, such as Virgin's Richard Branson and author J. K. Rowling, answered the call of Madeleine's parents to help publicize the case (Smit, Tweedie, & Edwards, 2007). Even Pope Benedict visited the parents to wish them well. Madeleine's parents set up a website where people could send in any information they might have on their daughter's disappearance (McCann & McCann, 2007). However, by September, the Portuguese investigation narrowed in on the McCanns themselves, and they were publically named as suspects. This, too, is not uncommon, as foul play involving children is most often perpetrated by family members. Despite this, and somewhat strangely, the parents went home to England without resistance from the Portuguese authorities with whom they were (perhaps understandably) no longer cooperating.

By this point the news media began to turn on the McCanns. Some news outlets reported that Madeleine's blood had been found in the trunk of a rental car used by the parents, although the reliability of those reports was questioned (Sturcke & Orr, 2007). By 2008 the McCanns were officially exonerated by Portuguese police, who had apparently misinterpreted DNA evidence in concluding that Madeleine's blood had been found in the trunk of the rental car. The case remains unsolved as of this writing.

The McCann case demonstrates some of the risks of news media involvement in criminal cases. This case ultimately devolved from a cooperative investigation into considerable acrimony, finger pointing, criticism, and controversy among the family, Portuguese police, British police, and news media. This acrimony undoubtedly burned through considerable time and resources that might have been spent on searching for Madeleine. This case also highlights the media circus that can follow certain high-profile cases. Many reasonably asked why there was so much international news media attention on this particular missing girl, tragic though the case was, when many other children were missing worldwide. Some worried that the news media proved to be too powerful in shaping public opinion on the case, and that this came at a cost to the investigation. News media coverage of the case shifted rapidly from sympathetic coverage of the McCanns to microscrutiny of their actions once they were named as suspects (Platell, 2007). Madeleine's mother, Kate McCann, in particular, was mercilessly scrutinized for any sign that her behavior was inconsistent with a grieving parent (e.g., Brown, 2007). Thus, the McCann case highlights several issues of focus for this chapter:

- How do news media come to highlight certain stories but not others?
- To what extent do news media report information inaccurately or accurately?
- What effect do news media reports have on the beliefs of viewers?

In this chapter, we concentrate particularly on the way news media represent crime, as this is both a big focus of news media

157

itself as well as of research on the influence of news media. However, the general principles discussed here undoubtedly extend to other areas of coverage as well.

How Does the News Media Frame a Story?

As we enter this discussion it is important to understand some basic mechanisms of news media. News media serve to purvey information to the general public. But they are not a public service or part of the government. This is good, of course, for government-owned news media would likely be little more than propaganda! But to earn income, news media must maintain viewers or subscribers or, in the Internet age, see page clicks or clickthroughs to advertisements. Put simply, news media, just as with fictional media, is dependent for survival on ratings, sales, and viewership. As a result, news media do not simply present unvarnished information but must select the information that viewers/subscribers/readers will want to have and frame that information in such a way as to maximize their own profits. Accuracy and caution can easily take a backseat to sensationalism, reporting wild rumors as "news" and taking an "if it bleeds it leads" mentality that prioritizes horrible news over good but mundane news. If some people are hurt by this cycle, well, that is the cost of business.

Thus, with news arenas such as politics, stories may focus on rumors, scandals, and microexaminations of every mumbling a politician makes, with a readiness to blow any careless word into a scandal. I can only imagine how difficult it must be when any stupid thing one says can be blown onto the front page. On the issue of crime, news media often focus on "sensational" crime, particularly violent, shocking crimes, with a preference for bizarre crimes (the "zombie" face-eating assault of Rudy Eugene on a homeless man in 2012 comes to mind), or those with exceptionally sympathetic victims (Surette, 2007). Given that the majority of people do not have first-hand knowledge about crime trends or incident rates, news media can be a powerful force for our information on and beliefs about crime and other topics outside our immediate sphere of expertise (Dorfman & Schiraldi, 2001).

Regarding crime reporting, the American Bar Association's Juvenile Justice Center, the Juvenile Law Center and National Council on Crime and Delinquency, noted several issues with news reports of violent crimes (Dorfman & Schiraldi, 2001), most of which will probably not come as a surprise:

- Violent crimes are disproportionably represented in news stories.
- Coverage of crime stories has increased over time, while actual crime rates have fallen.
- Unusual crimes get more coverage than "typical" crimes. This includes interracial crimes in which victims are White, even though most violence occurs within racial groups.
- African Americans in particular are overrepresented as perpetrators of crime and underrepresented as crime victims.
- Youth are oftentimes represented as perpetrators of crime, even though youth make up a minority of crime perpetrators and youth violence has been declining.

The authors concluded that the selection of crime-related news stories perpetuates potentially false beliefs about crime, particularly the involvement of minorities and youth. Although the authors recommend a more balanced approach to crime reporting, this, again, may be difficult to attain when the public tends to reward reporting certain types of stories more than others.

Missing White Woman Syndrome (MWWS) is defined as the news media tendency to focus on stories in which victims are women or girls who are White, affluent, physically attractive, and apparently morally upstanding. There have been a number of such cases in which pretty faces of unfortunate crime victims have been splashed across the news media: Polly Klaas, Madeleine McCann, Laci Peterson, Elizabeth Smart, and Natalee Holloway, all White women or girls who disappeared or were murdered (of those listed only Elizabeth Smart was later found alive). The

159

issue is not that these women and girls don't deserve to have their tragic cases brought to national or international attention, but rather it is that cases involving minority women or girls, men and boys in general, as well as the unattractive, do not appear to warrant similar news media attention. MWWS not surprisingly taps into issues related to race, gender, social class, and society values. For example, consider the contrasting cases of Laci Peterson and LaToyia Figueroa, two missing pregnant women, one of whom received international news media attention and the other few people have ever heard of despite similarities in their cases.

CASE STUDY 1

Laci Peterson and LaToyia Figueroa

The missing-person cases of Laci Peterson and LaToyia Figueroa are similar in many regards. Laci Peterson, 8 months pregnant, went missing December 23, 2002, from Modesto, California. Her dog was found wandering the neighborhood that day, still wearing a leash, and her things were found inside the family home. Laci's husband, Scott, reported returning home from fishing only to find her missing. A search of the neighborhood ensued but failed to find any sign of the missing woman. In April 2003, the decomposing body of an 8-month old fetus was found; the next day the badly damaged and decomposing body of an adult woman was found. These were later identified as Laci Peterson and her unborn son. Soon after, Laci's husband, who had been conducting an ongoing extramarital fair at the time of the murder, was arrested for the deaths. He was convicted and sentenced to death by lethal injection.

LaToyia Figueroa was a woman of mixed African American and Hispanic descent who vanished in August 2005. Like Laci Peterson, LaToyia Figueroa was pregnant, 5 months, at

---

(continued)

(*continued*)

> the time of her disappearance. She was later found strangled
> to death. Soon after, the father of her unborn child, Stephen
> Poaches, was arrested and later convicted for the death of
> LaToyia and her unborn child. He is alleged to have been moti-
> vated by her refusal to get an abortion. As such, the circum-
> stances of the two cases bear a striking resemblance. However,
> LaToyia Figueroa's disappearance and death received almost
> no media coverage until similarities between the cases were
> noted in relation to MWWS. Unlike Peterson, Figueroa was of
> non-White descent, was not affluent, and was a single mother,
> unmarried to the father of her unborn child. Discrepancies in
> coverage between cases such as these raise serious questions
> regarding how we measure the "value" of victims of crime.

The phenomenon of MWWS is complex though. Which women or girls are ultimately picked by news media for intense coverage? It is apparent that race is one factor, but on the other hand, although most cases involving non-White female victims seem to be of little interest to news media, most White female victims of violent crime don't receive much news media coverage either. So, although race is part of it, there's obviously more at play. Attractiveness also seems to play a role: Women who seem to receive lots of media attention tend to be pretty, or cute if they are little girls. Social class also appears to be an issue, with most women who receive such news media attention being affluent. Few come from blue-collar or low-income backgrounds (see Jewkes, 2004). Most also tend to come across as "morally upstanding" citizens with relatively few skeletons in their closets. By contrast, women who are single moms, or who have a history of legal problems such as drug abuse or prostitution, are less likely to receive much coverage. Even younger girls with a history of legal, drug, or other behavioral problems don't seem to get much MWWS coverage.

Arguably, MWWS may reflect our society's fascination with "damsels in distress" (Robinson, 2005). This may help explain why pretty, "innocent"-appearing victims are particularly likely to be the focus of MWWS. Some scholars would argue that our fascination with their deaths or kidnappings stems from our own desire to protect innocence, particularly as represented by the "ideal" female. When these protective efforts fail, we experience distress or anger. Women who come from different backgrounds, or who appear to be less "innocent," as well as men in general, just don't tap into our "damsel in distress" narrative. It may be the case that, as our culture becomes more racially integrated and sensitive, we may see MWWS extended to women and girls of other ethnicities. However, I suspect social class, physical attractiveness, and perceived "innocence" will remain critical factors as long as they are central to the "damsel in distress" narrative.

How Accurately Does the News Media Report on Crime?

Because of our fascination with violence, news media tend to overwhelmingly focus on violent crimes. As we've discussed, this is a likely consequence of ratings and subscription battles and the need to attract audiences via the most thrilling or sensationalistic news available. Granny Potts's kitty being rescued from a tree by the local fire department isn't going to do it. You may observe news media in relatively quiet cities reaching farther and farther afield to other cities hours away for salacious crime stories when things are uneventful locally! All this bad news on crime could arguably give people the wrong impression that violent crime is worse than ever. And even though news media do sometimes report on declining crime statistics, the constant, daily reporting of crime has an erosive, cumulative effect on viewers' outlook.

Because of this, it may be easy for regular viewers of nightly news to overestimate crime both locally and nationally. Research for decades has indicated that many Americans believe crime is on the rise despite long-term decreasing trends (Doob, Marinos,

& Varma, 1995; Jones, 2010). It may be tempting for both news media and politicians to focus on short-term data suggesting increasing crime rather than on broader trends (Niskanen, 1994). Rare crimes, in particular, may fluctuate rapidly from year to year, allowing for dramatic claims. For example, if City A has 10 homicides one year, then 13 homicides the next year, a politician can claim that "homicides in our city have risen 30% in the last year," which sounds dramatic until one understands the data underlying the statistics. A change of three or so victims in either direction in a city of, say, 200,000 is fairly negligible (except to those victims!), and likely due to normal fluctuations rather than any particular societal influence.

To some degree public misperception of crime rates is the responsibility of news media, which tend to focus on salacious crimes. At the same time, there are also limitations to the way that people process information that is at play. As I mentioned, in fairness, news media do tend to report declining trends in crime as published by the Federal Bureau of Investigation (1951–2012). These occasional bits of data may get lost in the constant stream of bad news, however. Further, news media increasingly give air time to hyperbolic pundits who often expound upon "crises" of violence without being burdened by facts. As one example, throughout the 1990s, it was very common to hear pundits claim that juvenile crime was a "national crisis" (e.g., Coordinating Council on Juvenile Justice and Delinquency Prevention, 1996), even as juvenile crime rates began to fall. During that time, a supposed epidemic of female juvenile violence got particular attention (Alder & Worrall, 2004). Ultimately these crises on youth violence proved to be ephemeral, as youth violence, male or female, was declining, not rising.

Hyperbolic claims about impending doom make for great news stories though, much better than arguing that things may not be such a big deal. News media may often turn to "experts" (who may, in fact, have little relevant expertise) to add credibility to crisis news stories. Discussions by these talking heads may be combined with shocking footage of anecdotal crimes

163

to add emotional salience to the "crisis" in question. For instance, during the coverage of the 2012 Sandy Hook shooting, in which a young man killed over two dozen children and adults at an elementary school, claims of the effects of violent video games mixed hyperbolic pundits, footage of the shooting, and cherry-picked examples of violent video games to create an impression of impending crisis. Ultimately, however, it turned out the shooter was a bigger fan of nonviolent games like *Dance Dance Revolution* than he was of violent games (State's Attorney for the Judicial District of Dansbury, 2013). Through this process, scholars have noted that news media is one important contributor to the development and maintenance of crime-related moral panics (Gauntlett, 2005; see Figure 2.1 in Chapter 2, p. 41).

Scholars have understood for some time that societies have a tendency to form panics over moral issues and identify "folk devils" responsible for perceived social ills (Cohen, 1972; Gauntlett, 2005). Moral panic as a phenomenon is well understood within criminology but unfortunately doesn't get much attention in psychological science (arguably, by being ignorant of moral panics, psychologists may be at risk of promoting them). Cyclical patterns of moral panic following the advent of new media, from the Waltz to dime novels, to movies, to jazz and rock and roll, to comic books, to television, to *Dungeons and Dragons*, to *Harry Potter*, have been well discussed (Gauntlett, 2005; Kutner & Olson, 2008).

Generally, societal moral panics begin within the society itself. Very often they may be promoted by older adults who occupy the power structures of society (politics, news media, scientific communities, etc.), but who are becoming increasingly alienated from youth culture (and in some cases may be frustrated in their relations with their own youth!). Concerns about youth and their naughty behavior can then spread to sensationalist news reporting (for instance, "warning" parents about everything from rainbow sex parties to self-destructive behavior like the "choking game," none of which emerged as a real trend in youth), with calls for research to support the burgeoning panic. By contrast, with their "if it bleeds it leads" mentality, news media tend to ignore data that would question the moral panic.

This pattern can result in real problems for the quality of science produced during a time of moral panic. Science can often be made to act as a mechanism for translating moral repugnance into moral regulation (Critcher, 2009). Society itself may promote this through news media outlets choosing to cover only research that promotes the panic (Thompson, 2008). Being human, scientists may themselves experience *researcher expectancy effects*, in which their own moral repugnance of certain things may cause them to produce research or make public statements supportive of moral panics, even if the data is less than solid (Slovic, Finucane, Peters, & MacGregor, 2002).

The Follow-Through Failure Effect

CASE STUDY 2

Handless in Miami

In the late 1990s, a case was reported in the local Miami news that was bizarre and disturbing. As reported, a man and a woman were driven to the Florida Everglades in an unmarked van. The couple was subdued, possibly through the use of drugs, although reports on how the couple came to be kidnapped were sketchy at best. Once in a secluded area of the Everglades, an unknown suspect or suspects proceeded to kill the man and assault the woman. The woman managed to escape from the van, but not before both of her hands had been chopped off. She managed to run to Alligator Alley, the

(*continued*)

165

(*continued*)

> only major road passing through the Everglades at that point and hail a passing motorist. Fortunately, the motorist pulled over, rendered assistance to the woman and called the police. The woman survived, but her male companion was found dead in the van by police. At the time of the report, the suspects were unknown and many details of the crime remained uncertain.
>
> Given the bizarre circumstances and brutal nature of the crime, it initially received considerable local attention in the media. Few new details emerged in subsequent days however, and eventually the case vanished altogether, along with the numerous cases that are partially reported in the news, but for which the final circumstances are not made available to the public.

Some cases that news media follow capture the public's attention from start to finish, such as the 1995 O. J. Simpson trial. But many are more local and may fade quickly from public attention and news media coverage. In such cases, the viewing public may learn the initial details of a crime but never find out how the investigation turns out.

One possible outcome of this is that the public may think a higher number of criminal cases go unsolved than actually do. If news media report the occurrence of a crime but not its resolution, the public may be left with the impression of numerous unpunished criminals in their midst.

A second issue occurs when news media cover the initial identification of a suspect in a criminal investigation. Particularly controversial are "perp walks," when police haul a suspect out into public, often in handcuffs where they can be photographed by news media, typically when transporting the suspect. Naturally a suspect being hauled out of a police station in cuffs looks guilty. But in many cases, the investigation may ultimately shift to other suspects or result in a dismissal of charges or not-guilty verdict. If the news media fails to cover the outcomes, the initial suspect's colleagues and neighbors may be unaware of the exoneration, and the individual may have to live under a continued cloud of suspicion. Case study 3, regarding Richard Jewell, a security guard erroneously suspected in a bombing case, while being a classic "trial by media" case, also has elements of the follow-through failure effect.

Trial by Media

CASE STUDY 3

The Olympic Park Bombing

During the 1996 Summer Olympics in Atlanta, Georgia, a bomb was planted in a popular congregation area known as Olympic Park on July 27. During the evening, security guard Richard Jewell discovered the bomb and alerted the Georgia Bureau of Investigation. Jewell assisted in evacuating the crowd, but the bomb went off before everyone could be cleared to safety. The bomb consisted of several pipe bombs with nails to create shrapnel. One woman died from a shrapnel wound, and 111 others were wounded during the blast.

Jewell was originally considered a hero for moving people away from the blast area, risking his own life. Soon, however, the FBI began investigating the possibility that Jewell had planted the bomb so that he could enjoy the limelight looking like a hero. It is speculated that the FBI leaked a "lone bomber" profile to the media, implying that Jewell fit this profile. Jewell then became the target of intense media scrutiny, most of which was negative, identifying him as a suspect in the bombing. Psychologists commented to the media that

(*continued*)

(*continued*)

Jewell fit the FBI profile, and it was alleged that Jewell was a failed police officer who craved attention (Lehrer, 1996). Media camped out near his residence for weeks, reporting on any details that implied his guilt, such as when search warrants were filed on his home. Ultimately Jewell was cleared in the crime, which later was found to have been committed by Eric Rudolph, an antigovernment militant. Although the media did report the arrest of Eric Rudolph, a highly visible exoneration or apology to Jewell was not forthcoming from the media. Arguably, as attention focused on Rudolph, Jewell's guilt or innocence was simply ignored, allowing many to continue to speculate that Jewell might have been guilty.

Jewell sued several news outlets, including CNN, NBC, and the *New York Post*, and settled out of court (Weber, 2007). A lawsuit against the *Atlanta Journal-Constitution*, which arguably started the media firestorm, remains pending with Jewell's estate. Jewell died of natural causes in August 2007.

This case demonstrates the phenomenon of "trial by media," in which the media may selectively report information implying a suspect's guilt and fail to adequately report on exonerating information. Unfortunately, uninformed or misguided "experts" oftentimes add to this phenomenon by making ill-advised comments to the media.

When suspects show up in news media accounts, it is often easy to come to a snap decision that they must be guilty. After all, why else would they have been arrested or put on trial? People seem to like to follow bad guys as well. It may make us feel morally superior to look down on those who have done things worse than ourselves. Given that news media are likely aware of this, they may tend to highlight aspects of a case that suggest a suspect may indeed be guilty. For instance, an article in *The Lancet* medical journal highlighted a case in which journalists may have selectively interpreted ambiguous statistics to claim that a British surgeon was incompetent in treating breast cancer patients (Wright, Bradley, Sheldon, & Liford, 2006). Many experts appear to have disagreed with the journalists' interpretations of the statistics. However, as journalists essentially control the news flow, they can control what side of a story the public gets to hear. This is the phenomenon of *trial by media*, in which a suspect's guilt is implied through selective media coverage. The problem, particularly for high-profile cases, is that intensive news coverage will likely be viewed by the pool of potential jurors, possibly tainting their opinions before a trial actually begins. This news coverage can actually harm a defendant's right to a fair trial, so it is not a small issue! The Casey Anthony trial in central Florida, regarding a young woman accused of murdering her daughter, is one such example. The case received intense national news coverage, and a jury had to be selected from across the state (from Tampa rather than Orlando, where the crime actually occurred) to try to get a neutral panel. Given the heinous nature of a child's murder and some apparently odd behavior on Anthony's part (she was portrayed as a partyer indifferent to her daughter's death), many people assumed she was guilty. When the jury ultimately acquitted her, they rushed out of town apparently in fear that they might face the wrath of people who believed Anthony was guilty! Whether she did or did not in fact murder her child (and I will allow the reader to look up the case and make up his or her own mind), despite her acquittal, it is unlikely Anthony will ever be able to live a normal life.

The issue of trial-by-media pits press freedoms enshrined in the Constitution against a defendant's right to a fair trial. This is not an easy issue for courts to resolve. Courts do have some tools in hand to try to ensure a fair trial. For instance, courts may issue *gag rules* or a *gag order* to prevent people involved in a case from speaking to the media, or to exclude news media from trial proceedings or from obtaining other details of a criminal investigation. These tools and their restrictions on a free press have always been controversial however (e.g., *Nebraska Press Association v. Stuart*, 1976; *Sheppard v. Maxwell*, 1966).

For example, in the *Sheppard v. Maxwell* case, the Supreme Court found that pretrial media coverage, which portrayed a criminal defendant as guilty, damaged his right to a fair trial. Sam Sheppard was a physician accused of bludgeoning to death his pregnant wife. Handling of his case was a textbook example of trial by jury. News media covered the case intensely, and he was subjected to a public, 3-day inquest that was covered by news media. Names of the jurors during the trial were publicized, and they began receiving calls about the case. The jurors were also not sequestered or shielded from the media scrutiny, and several admitted having heard pretrial coverage of the case. Reporters were positioned near the defendant during the trial, preventing him from having private counsel with his attorney. The Supreme Court found that this scenario precluded the defendant's right to a fair trial (*Sheppard v. Maxwell*, 1966). Thus, although Sheppard was initially convicted, this conviction was later overturned. However, he spent 10 years in jail before his retrial and subsequent acquittal.

The *Nebraska Press Association v. Stuart* case addressed a court order limiting pretrial press coverage of a brutal multiple murder to ensure a fair trial for the defendant. In this case, the Supreme Court ruled that the pretrial gag order violated the First Amendment and was impermissible. The problem with the court order in the Nebraska case was that rather than shielding the jury from the media, the court ordered a "prior restraint"; that is, the court ordered the media not to report certain information about the case at all. The bar for "prior restraint" or outright censorship of the media is very high and was not met in this case, as the trial judge did not adequately consider alternate methods to ensure a fair trial.

What Effects Do the News Media Have on Viewers?

One thing that scholars have often wondered about is whether people's beliefs about news events might be influenced by news media. If you watch a lot of news shows that feature violent crimes, do you begin to think that the world is a scarier place?

One theory, called the *cultivation hypothesis* (Gerbner & Gross, 1976), suggests that media viewers can indeed develop beliefs about the world based on their exposure to media. Put somewhat simplistically, if you watch a lot of media involving crime, you may begin to believe that such crimes are commonplace. A lot of attention focuses particularly on news media since, unlike, say, fictional crime shows, news media is supposed to inform viewers about actual real-life events.

There indeed seems to be some research to indicate that exposure to news shows can influence perceptions of real-life crime. Exposure to negative events on the news does seem to increase people's concerns about becoming victims of those events (Daly & Chasteen, 1997). For instance, about the time I've written this, much of the United States wrestled with anxiety about an outbreak of the often-fatal Ebola virus, although only a handful of people were infected in the United States (thousands, however, died in Africa). The cultivation effects appear to be short lived, with recent news events exerting the greatest influence on beliefs about the world in viewers (McCombs & Gilbert, 1986) and effects on beliefs about crime most pronounced among those already prone to irrationally panic about remote events (McNaughton-Cassill, 2000). This is an important point—cultivation effects appear to interact with viewers' preexisting mental state, with only some viewers heavily influenced. We can see this with crime stories, as people living in lower socioeconomic status urban environments, women, and prior-crime victims being particularly prone to cultivation effects (Smolej & Kivivouri, 2006).

Coverage of rare but spectacular crimes such as the Columbine massacre in 1999, in which two student shooters killed 12 students, a teacher, and themselves, may be instrumental in perpetuating "moral panics" about crime that are out of proportion with real risks. For instance, the Columbine massacre may have sparked fears of a new breed of juvenile "superpredator" that never materialized (Muschert, 2007). Note that even the word "superpredator" appears to have been chosen to instill maximal fear in news consumers. Just as news media exaggerated the likelihood of a wave of juvenile superpredators, news media often whip up fears about violent films or video games that can't be supported by actual data (Grimes, Anderson, & Bergen, 2007). Fears about waves of female juvenile offenders, serial murders, and child abductions by strangers may also be inflamed in a similar manner, despite criminological data that such crimes are relatively rare. The cultivation effects of the news media may be strongest when erroneous beliefs are exploited by politicians, special interest groups, or even social scientists who wish to enforce a particular moral agenda on the wider populace (Ferguson, 2008). In other words, cultivation effects may be less owing to passive viewer effects than to the active efforts of special interest groups to sell a particular moral message. Many groups may seize upon the vulnerabilities of children, in particular, to stoke fears in adults and parents (Grimes, Anderson, & Bergen, 2007). Note that these risk factors overlap so that a person with all of these (an urban, unemployed, female former crime victim) is most likely to be influenced by crime-related news in regard to fear of crime.

Cultivation theory has sometimes been controversial though, and some critics have questioned its central premise that viewing media leads to beliefs about crime. For example, individuals who are already particularly concerned about crime may be more inclined to seek out news shows that cover crime (Griffin, 2012). Consider shows like *To Catch a Predator* that focus on adults who prey on children. Watching such shows may lead to beliefs that sexual predators are widespread (sexual abuse of children has actually been declining along with most crimes). However, people who are particularly concerned about sexual abuse of children may be particularly inclined to watch that show. Other scholarship has suggested that cultivation effects of some sort may occur, but they may not be quite the predictable effects scholars had expected (Hetsroni, 2014). Thus, as with many issues in media psychology, the influence of news media on viewer attitudes is likely a complex one.

REFERENCES

Alder, C., & Worrall, A. (2004). *Girls' violence: Myths and realities.* Albany, NY: SUNY Press.

BBC News. (2007, June 17). *Madeleine evidence "may be lost."* BBC News Channel. Retrieved June 2, 2008, from http://news.bbc.co.uk/1/hi/uk/6761669.stm

Brown, P. (2007, October 24). Open letter to Kate McCann. *The Daily Profiler.* Retrieved June 4, 2008, from http://patbrownprofiling.blogspot.com/2007/10/criminal-profiling-topic-of-day-open.html

CBC News. (2007, May 15). Police release suspect in Madeleine disappearance. *CBC News.* Retrieved June 2, 2008, from http://www.cbc.ca/world/story/2007/05/15/murat-madeleine-070515.html

Cohen, S. (1972). *Folk devils and moral panics.* London, UK: MacGibbon and Kee.

Coordinating Council on Juvenile Justice and Delinquency Prevention. (1996). *Combating violence and delinquency: The National Juvenile Justice Action Plan full report.* Washington, DC: National Criminal Justice Reference Service. Retrieved June 9, 2008, from http://www.ncjrs.gov/txtfiles/jjplanfr.txt

Critcher, R. (2009). Widening the focus: Moral panics as moral regulation. *British Journal of Criminology, 49,* 17–34.

Daly, K., & Chasteen, A. (1997). Crime news, crime fears and women's everyday lives. In M. Fineman & M. McCluskey (Eds.), *Feminism, media and the law* (pp. 235–248). New York, NY: Oxford University Press.

Doob, A., Marinos, V., & Varma, K. (1995). *Youth crime and the youth justice system in Canada: A research perspective.* Toronto, Ontario: University of Toronto Press.

Dorfman, L., & Schiraldi, V. (2001). *Off balance: Youth, race and crime in the news.* Retrieved June 4, 2008, from http://www.building-blocksforyouth.org/media/exec.html

Federal Bureau of Investigation. (1951–2012). *Uniform crime reports.* Washington, DC: U.S. Government Printing Office.

Ferguson, C. J. (2008). Media violence effects: Confirmed truth, or just another X-File? *Journal of Forensic Psychology Practice, 9*(2), 103–126.

Gauntlett, D. (2005). *Moving experiences: Understanding television's influences and effects.* Luton, UK: John Libbey.

Gerbner, G., & Gross, L. (1976). Living with television: The violence profile. *Journal of Communication, 26*, 172–199.

Griffin, E. (2012). *A first look at communication theory*. New York, NY: McGraw-Hill.

Grimes, T., Anderson, J., & Bergen, L. (2007). *Media violence and aggression: Science and ideology*. Thousand Oaks, CA: Sage.

Hetsroni, A. (2014). Ceiling effect in cultivation: General TV viewing, genre-specific viewing, and estimates of health concerns. *Journal of Media Psychology: Theories, Methods, and Applications, 26*(1), 10–18. doi:10.1027/1864-1105/a000099

Jewkes, Y. (2004). *Media and crime*. Thousand Oaks, CA: Sage.

Jones, J. (2010). Americans still perceive crime as on the rise. *Gallup*. Retrieved from http://www.gallup.com/poll/144827/Americans-Perceive-Crime-Rise.aspx

Kutner, L., & Olson, C. (2008). *Grand theft childhood: The surprising truth about violent video games and what parents can do*. New York, NY: Simon & Schuster.

Lehrer, J. (1996). Olympic Park: Another victim. *Newshour with Jim Lehrer*. Retrieved June 10, 2008, from http://www.pbs.org/newshour/bb/sports/jewell_10-28.html

McCann, K., & McCann, G. (2007). *Find Madeleine*. Retrieved June 2, 2008, from http://www.bringmadeleinehome.com/

McCombs, M., & Gilbert, S. (1986). News influence on our pictures of the world. In J. Byrant & D. Zillman (Eds.), *Perspectives on media effects* (pp. 1–15). Hillsdale, NJ: Lawrence Erlbaum.

McNaughton-Cassill, M. (2000). The news media and psychological distress. *Anxiety, Stress and Coping, 14*, 193–211.

Muschert, G. (2007). The Columbine victims and the myth of the juvenile superpredator. *Youth Violence and Juvenile Justice, 5*, 351–366.

Nebraska Press Association v. Stuart. (1976). 427 U.S. 539.

Niskanen, W. (1994). *Crime, police and root causes*. The Cato Institute. Retrieved June 6, 2008, from http://www.cato.org/pubs/pas/pa-218.html

Platell, A. (2007, October 22). Kate McCann does not deserve this public savaging. *The Daily Mail*. Retrieved June 4, 2008, from http://www.dailymail.co.uk/debate/columnists/article-488659/Kate-McCann-does-deserve-public-savaging.html#comments

Robinson, E. (2005, June 10). (White) women we love. *Washington Post*. Retrieved June 5, 2008, from http://www.washingtonpost.com/wp-dyn/content/article/2005/06/09/AR2005060901729.html

Sheppard v. Maxwell. (1966). 384 U.S. 333.

Slovic, P., Finucane, M., Peters, E., & MacGregor, D. G. (2002). Rational actors or rational fools: Implications of the affect heuristic for behavioral economics. *Journal of Socio-Economics, 31*(4), 329–342. doi:10.1016/S1053-5357(02)00174-9

Smit, M., Tweedie, N., & Edwards, R. (2007, May 12). Mark Maddy's birthday with renewed search. *The Telegraph.* Retrieved June 2, 2008, from http://www.telegraph.co.uk/news/worldnews/1551341/%27Mark-Maddy%27s-birthday-with-renewed-search%27.html

Smolej, M., & Kivivouri, J. (2006). The relation between crime news and fear of violence. *Journal of Scandinavian Studies in Criminology and Crime Prevention, 7*, 211–217.

State's Attorney for the Judicial District of Dansbury. (2013). *Report of the State's Attorney for the Judicial District of Danbury on the shootings at Sandy Hook Elementary School and 36 Yogananda Street, Newtown, Connecticut on December 14, 2012.* Danbury, CT: Office of the State's Attorney Judicial District of Danbury.

Sturcke, J., & Orr, J. (2007, September 7). Kate McCann "fears Madeleine killing charge over blood traces in car." *The Guardian.* Retrieved June 2, 2008, from http://www.guardian.co.uk/uk/2007/sep/07/ukcrime.madeleinemccann

Surette, R. (2007). *Media crime and criminal justice: Images, realities and policies.* Belmont, CA: Wadsworth.

Thompson, K. (2008). The classic moral panic: Mods and rockers. In R. Heiner (Ed.), *Deviance across cultures* (pp. 60–68). New York, NY: Oxford University Press.

Weber, H. (2007, August 30). Former Olympic Park guard dies. *Washington Post.* Retrieved June 8, 2009, from http://www.washingtonpost.com/wp-dyn/content/article/2007/08/30/AR2007083000324.html

Wright, J., Bradley, C., Sheldon, T., & Liford, R. (2006). Trial by media: Dangers of misinterpretation of medical statistics. *The Lancet, 367*, 1139–1140.

Television/Movie
Violence Research

For many years, people have been concerned about the potential impact of television violence on children who enjoy popular action shows. I can remember during my own youth, for instance, people worrying that we children couldn't distinguish reality from fiction, and that we might shoot someone in the face and think they'd get right back up like the characters in Bugs Bunny cartoons did. Others worried that superhero shows like *Mighty Morphin Power Rangers* would teach us that violence was an acceptable way to handle conflict. In part, this concern seems to have occurred as the popularity of violence on television, introduced in the 1950s, appeared to coincide with a rise in violent crimes in the United States, lasting from the early 1970s through approximately 1993 (Federal Bureau of Investigation, 1951–2014). Beginning in the early 1960s, Albert Bandura published a series of experiments (e.g., Bandura, 1965; Bandura, Ross, & Ross, 1961, 1963) that suggested young children may be able to learn aggressive behavior by watching adults engage in such behavior on a film.

This argument of whether television (and, ultimately other media such as video games, which we discuss in the next chapter) violence causes aggression has been one of the longest and most bitter in the social sciences. In 2000, the American Psychological Association cosigned a joint declaration of health organizations (American Academy of Pediatrics, 2000) that stated that research studies on television and other media violence "point overwhelmingly to a causal connection between media violence and aggressive behavior in some children." Despite this, skeptical scholars (e.g., Felson, 1996; Freedman, 2002; Fischoff, 1999; Gauntlett, 1995; Grimes, Anderson, & Bergen, 2008; Moeller, 2005; Olson, 2004; Savage, 2004; Stipp & Milavsky, 1988; Trend, 2007) have questioned these claims, suggesting that the research was never as consistent or clear as sometimes claimed.

When a given theoretical paradigm is in vogue, it may be difficult for the scientific profession to objectively evaluate it (Ioannidis, 2005). Throughout the history of psychology, psychoanalysis and radical behaviorism, for instance, provide examples of dominant paradigms once considered "truth" in psychological science, only to crumble under the weight of new evidence. This is quite natural in science, of course, as the falsification of old theories is often painful and fraught with controversy (Kuhn, 1970). As Ioannidis (2005) notes, "Of course, investigators working in any field are likely to resist accepting that the whole field in which they have spent their careers is a 'null field.'" Given the heady claims made by television violence research, including that 3,500 studies have been conducted on television or other media violence with only 18 finding null effects (Cook, 2000), and that the effects of television violence on viewer aggression approximate those for smoking on lung cancer (Bushman & Anderson, 2001; Huesmann, 2007), and that television violence was a key factor in the 1970s to 1993 violent-crime increase (Bushman & Anderson,

2001; Centerwall, 1989), it is imperative that such claims be put to close and even skeptical scientific scrutiny.

EXAMINATION OF THE EVIDENCE: CLASSIC STUDIES FROM BOTH SIDES

The exact number of studies on television violence is not precisely known, but most reviews and meta-analyses find several hundred studies (typically between 200–300), including those that are unpublished (Bushman & Huesmann, 2006; Freedman, 2002; Paik & Comstock, 1994). This is an impressive array of studies; however, much debate remains on the consistency, strength, validity, and meaningfulness of these studies. For instance, it is well known that only a small fraction of these studies actually directly measure person-on-person aggression (Ferguson & Kilburn, 2009; Grimes, Anderson, & Bergen, 2008; Paik & Comstock, 1994; Savage & Yancey, 2008). Given that several hundred studies, whether published or unpublished, of television violence have been conducted, it is difficult for any review to give a comprehensive summary. However, a number of those articles often cited by both advocates of the causal position (e.g., Anderson et al., 2003; Bushman & Huesmann, 2006; Huesmann, 2007; Huesmann & Taylor, 2003; Wood, Wong, & Chachere, 1991) and the skeptics' position (e.g., Anderson, 2008; Freedman, 1984, 2002; Gauntlett, 1995; Kaplan & Singer, 1976; Moeller, 2005; Savage, 2004, 2008) are discussed here. Thus, although discussions of the meaningfulness and validity of these seminal articles differ, there is general agreement these articles are indicative of the research both supportive and unsupportive of television violence effects. These articles are presented below by date of publication.

Feshbach and Singer (1971) conducted a field experiment of boys living in several residential facilities. The boys were randomly assigned to watch either nonviolent or violent programs for a 6-week period. Those who watched violent television were

179

actually less likely to behave aggressively than were the boys who watched nonviolent television, suggesting a kind of cathartic effect. But, as with the case of many television studies, it's not clear that the television shows were clearly matched so that they were as exciting, despite the presence or absence of violent content. Much later, Feshbach and Tangney (2008) published a report that indicated that exposure to television violence correlated with reduced aggressiveness in some boys but not others. However, these correlations were small in size and based on bivariate correlations. Were other factors controlled, it is possible that these aggression-reduction effects may have disappeared.

Huesmann and colleagues have published two longitudinal studies of television violence, the first beginning in the 1960s (Lefkowitz, Eron, Walder, & Huesmann, 1972, 1977; Huesmann, 1986), and the second beginning in the 1970s (Huesmann, Moise-Titus, Podolski, & Eron, 2003). The first longitudinal study focused on peer-nominated aggression as an outcome variable. Some scholars (e.g., Freedman, 1984; Gauntlett, 1995; Savage, 2004) have specifically criticized this measure as it includes a number of items that appear related to naughty behavior but not aggressiveness. The entire measure is presented in Table 11.1. Only two of 10 items are directly related to physical aggression. It is also possible that a peer-nominated measure of any negative outcome may function more as a popularity contest than a valid measure of aggression. In later stages of the longitudinal analysis, children were asked to report retrospectively on peers who they were no longer in contact with. Indeed, peer-nominated aggression has been found to have weak validity coefficients (Henry & Metropolitan Area Child Study Research Group, 2006). Small correlations in the range of .2 to .3 were found between television violence viewing and peer-nominated aggression, although these studies have been criticized for poor controls of other variables (Savage, 2004). The final follow-up (Huesmann, 1986) examining links between television violence–viewing preference and later adult criminality was discussed briefly in a theoretical article. The relationship between childhood television violence

TABLE 11.1   ITEMS FROM THE LEFKOWITZ, ERON, WALDER, AND HUESMANN MEASURE OF AGGRESSION

1. Who does not obey the teacher?
2. Who often says, "Give me that?"
3. Who gives dirty looks or sticks out their tongue at other children?
4. Who makes up stories and lies to get other children into trouble?
5. Who does things that bother others?
6. Who starts a fight over nothing?
7. Who pushes or shoves other children?
8. Who is always getting into trouble?
9. Who says mean things?
10. Who takes other children's things without asking?

Source: Lefkowitz, Eron, Walder, and Huesmann (1977).

preference and adult criminality was described by the author as "weakly correlated" (Huesmann et al., 2003, p. 203) and may have been due to three outlier cases (Savage, 2004). Aside from criticizing the outcome measure and statistical controls, critics have noted that the predictor variable was *preference* for violent television rather than exposure (Freedman, 2002; Savage, 2004). It is thus possible this study conflated what essentially is a personality variable with an exposure variable.

The Huesmann et al. (2003) longitudinal study attempted to correct some of the criticisms of the earlier studies by more carefully examining television violence exposure and controls for "third" variables. Childhood aggression was still measured using the controversial peer-nomination scale. Adult aggression was measured using a composite score of several well-validated measures (e.g., the Minnesota Multiphasic Personality Inventory, the Conflict Tactics Scale, and the National Youth Survey) and several measures created by the authors that have not been subjected to well-controlled validity studies. Correlations between childhood television violence exposure and adult aggression were in the range of $r = .15$ to .2. Although the authors controlled for

181

several parental and environmental "third" variables, the authors curiously appear to have controlled for only one at a time. Thus it is possible, had all control variables been included in a multiple regression together, the relationship between early television violence exposure and adult aggression may have been less than reported.

One study by Friedrich and Stein (1973) examined whether children who watch violent programs (such as *Batman* or *Superman*) are more interpersonally aggressive. The authors included five measures of aggression (including one composite of two of the basic aggression measures) and provided a number of separate analyses. Generally, the results did not support the hypothesis that exposure to violent programs increased the various aggressive outcomes, including hitting other children, verbal aggression, or fantasy aggression. The only significant finding was an interaction between initial aggressiveness and violent programs. Had a Bonferonni correction for multiple analyses been used, this finding would not have been significant, although Bonferonni corrections remain controversial. However, once gender was controlled in the analysis, this interaction was no longer significant. Thus, overall, results from this study do not support a link between watching violent television and aggression.

One important study by Belson (1978) examined the correlation between television violence viewing and aggressive behavior. The Belson study is unusual in its use of probability sampling, which represents a strength of this study. Belson concluded that television violence viewing was correlated with a higher number of aggressive acts. Belson also examined the relationship between antisocial attitudes and aggressive personality and found little correlation with television viewing. Some reviews (Comstock, 2008) have interpreted this as ruling out the "reverse" hypothesis, that aggressive personality leads to increased viewing of television violence. However, the data might also be interpreted as indicating television violence exposure does not correlate with the increases in aggressive or antisocial personality normally linked with increased aggression. Had positive correlations between these temperamental variables and television violence been found, they might simply have been interpreted as further evidence of causal effects on anti-social traits rather than support for the "reverse" hypothesis. Other scholars have noted that these variables were not used adequately as controls in examining correlations between television violence exposure and aggressive behavior (Savage, 2004), nor were other variables such as family violence controlled (Ferguson, 2009). Other scholars have suggested that the Belson study is far less con-clusive than often reported in reviews. For instance, Moeller (2005) notes that only one of 20 of Belson's major hypotheses were ulti-mately supported unequivocally in the data. Thus, interpreta-tion of the Belson study (like, perhaps, all others) differs greatly depending upon the a priori view of the reader.

Milavsky and colleagues (Milavsky, Kessler, Stipp, & Rubens, 1982; Milavsky, Stipp, Kessler, & Rubens, 1982) reported on a 3-year longitudinal study of television violence effects on youth aggression and delinquency. The authors examined both elemen-tary school children and teenage boys, and controlled for initial (Time 1) aggression and several other relevant control variables, such as socioeconomic status and family environment variables. Outcome measures included a similar measure of aggression as used by Lefkowitz, Eron, Walder, and Huesmann (1977), although in this case physically aggressive items were weighted higher. Onset of delinquency provided the outcome variable for the teen-age sample. Exposure to television violence was not related to aggressive behavior or onset of delinquency. Overall, the authors concluded that television violence did not contribute to aggressive behavior in young viewers. However, this study has been criticized on several grounds. First, the aggression measure used arguably suffers from some of the same potential weaknesses as that of Lefkowitz et al. (1977). Second, the analytic strategy, while gener-ally sophisticated, may have lacked sufficient power to detect very small cumulative effects (Cook, Kendzierski, & Thomas, 1983).

In another very ambitious project, Huesmann and Eron (1986) examined the effects of television violence exposure cross-culturally, including boys and girls in the United States,

Australia, Finland, Israel (both a city sample and a kibbutz sample), and Poland. A Dutch group exited the study early and published their results in a separate manuscript (Wiegman & Kuttschreuter, 1992) apparently because of methodological and interpretive differences. The authors examined whether television viewing habits predicted aggressive behaviors in children at a later age (3 years later) while controlling for trait aggression. Out of all six countries (including the Dutch), statistically significant results based on the original model (direct effects of television violence on aggression) were found only for American girls. In no other case were significant results reported for television violence exposure and later aggression. Given that the authors did not control error due to multiple comparisons using Bonferonni corrections, it is possible even this one finding may have been spurious. However, the authors developed an additional measure in which they compiled television viewing habits with a personality measure ("identification with aggressive characters") that was used only for the boys but not the girls. This latter personality characteristic is highly correlated with aggressive personality, and, as a result, aggressive personality can no longer be teased out from television viewing habits in this study (Savage, 2004), presenting a considerable confound and resulting in a lack of standardized outcome assessment across the various countries. With this personality measure combined with television viewing now substituting for television viewing habits alone (which was the actual study hypothesis), the end results were mixed, with some groups showing weak effects and others (such as the Dutch and Australians, children on the Israeli kibbutz, and girls in Poland and Finland) still showing no effects. Although Huesmann and Eron (1986) interpreted the results as supportive of the link between television violence and aggression cross-nationally, the Dutch authors came to the opposite conclusion (Wiegman & Kuttschreuter, 1992). Thus, effects from this study are mixed, at best, arguably leaning in favor of null effects. Furthermore, this study did not control for potential "third" variables such as family, peer, or mental health influences.

Josephson (1987) conducted an experimental study of violent television exposure on 396 young boys. The boys, in second or third grade, were randomly assigned to watch violent or nonviolent television. Teachers rated the boys' subsequent aggression. Results suggested that the impact of television violence dependended on how aggressive boys were at the beginning of the study. Nonaggressive boys actually *reduced* in aggression following the violent program as did boys watching the nonviolent program. However, more aggressive boys became yet more aggressive still after watching the violent program. These results suggest that response to television violence is not consistent across viewers but rather is dependent on where the viewer starts from.

CRITICISMS OF THE "CLASSIC" STUDIES

Criticisms of the classic studies fall into several categories discussed in the following sections. It is important to note that many of these criticisms apply to studies both supportive of causal effects and those that have found null effects. Furthermore, it is important to note that these problems have been identified not only for specific studies but also as problems that are largely endemic to the field (Ferguson, 2009; Freedman, 2002; Savage, 2004).

Difficulties in Measuring Aggression and Violence

For a while now, scholars have understood that measuring aggression in a satisfactory manner is actually quite difficult (Benjamin, 1985; Elson, Mohseni, Breuer, Scharkow, & Quandt, 2014; Giancola & Chermack, 1998; Ritter & Eslea, 2005; Tedeschi & Quigley, 1996, 2000).

Aggression is typically defined as behaviors that are intended to harm or attain dominance over another entity who wishes to avoid that behavior. In essence, lack of consent on the part of the "victim" is typically built into most definitions. Granted, definitions of aggression can be moralistic, and it's not clear that aggression is always a bad thing in moderate amounts. However, such definitions would exclude rough but consenting activities such as play fighting, sports, "Cops and Robbers," wrestling, and so on, wherein both individuals are having fun and "playing by the rules." So a child who watches a kung fu show and begins to playact kung fu with a friend who is also having fun is not behaving aggressively. If the other child asks them to stop but they don't, it may very well be considered aggressive!

Consider the famous (or infamous, depending on how you look at it) Milgram studies (Milgram, 1963). These studies let participants think they were causing real physical injuries to the "learner" who repeatedly asked, indeed even begged, to be released from the electric shocks. Granted, everything was pretend; no shocks were delivered. However, such an aversive procedure has since been considered largely unethical, given that participants might come to see themselves as awful people for giving these shocks (see Baumrind, 1964). As a consequence of these ethical discussions, it has become harder to measure aggression in the laboratory. We can't have people beat each other up, of course. So how do we get at aggression, but in such a way as not to risk participants believing they are awful people for behaving the way they do in the lab?

Part of the issue with aggression measures has revolved around their lack of standardization, which plays into a larger "questionable researcher practice" debate that has been going on in psychology in a larger context. Put simply, methods in psychology have often been so fluid that it is possible for scholars to pick and choose from among multiple possible outcomes that best fit their hypotheses. If that's the case, what scholars are doing isn't really science but merely adding numbers to their opinions. It has been observed that many aggression measures used in television violence research have been developed ad hoc for a specific study, are used differently between different groups within a single study, allow for multiple outcome measures from which study authors may pick and choose, or are used inconsistently across studies, even sometimes by individual authors

(Ferguson, 2009; Freedman, 2002; Gauntlett, 1995; Savage, 2004). For instance, Huesmann and Eron (1986), upon finding few significant effects for direct television violence exposure, then employed a combined personality by television exposure variable, which was used for boys but not for girls.

Similarly, it has been observed that the "noise burst" version of the Taylor Competitive Reaction Time Test (TCRTT) has been used inconsistently across studies, sometimes by individual authors (Ferguson & Rueda, 2009). The TCRTT, in particular, allows for multiple potential outcomes from which study authors can pick and choose. When different authors (or sometimes even the same author) use different outcomes across studies, this raises the potential that study authors are allowed to pick and choose (whether consciously or not) from among those outcomes that best support their a priori hypotheses. Thus it should not be surprising that meta-analysis has revealed that these forms of unstandardized measures tend to result in much higher effect size estimates in television violence research than for effects seen with more rigidly standardized assessments (Ferguson & Kilburn, 2009).

Many aggression measures don't measure physical aggression at all. As examples, some studies tried to measure aggression by asking children if they wanted to pop a balloon (Mussen & Rutherford, 1961); asking college students if they would like to have a graduate-student confederate who had just insulted them as an instructor in a future course (Berkowitz, 1965); puffing up a blood-pressure cuff on a person's arm (Zillman & Weaver, 2007); and examining the time it took children to "seek help" from an adult after watching two young children argue on a videotape (Molitor & Hirsch, 1994). Other studies measure aggression through how much hot spicy sauce or chilly water people may ask another person to tolerate (Tedeschi & Quigley, 1996; Ritter & Eslea, 2005). These may be a little better than some of the others, but of course gangs don't fight it out with buckets of ice water or sandwiches loaded with Tabasco sauce.

Many other measures involve things such as filling in the missing letters of words, completing the endings of stories, interpreting the actions of people or animals in stories, and so on

(Freedman, 2002; Gauntlett, 1995). Clearly, many of these behaviors are far removed from the kinds of criminal assaults society is most interested in, yet caution in generalizing from these measures to real-world acts has been in short supply. Instead, it is quite common to find media scholars directly generalizing media violence studies to violent crime in the United States and elsewhere (Bushman & Anderson, 2001; Cantor & Wilson, 2003; Huesmann, Moise, & Podolski, 1997).

Laboratory measures of aggression, beyond the straightforward validity problems and typically poor standardization, may further have the problem of demand characteristics. Put simply, participants may be able to guess that, after viewing a violent television program and given control of an electroshock machine (or some other outcome with less evident validity), they are expected to give additional shocks to the opponent or learner. Much like the children in Bandura's studies, the responses of experimental participants may have more to do with pleasing the experimenter than behaving aggressively. This may be particularly true when the participants are psychology undergraduate students (as tends to be the case in the majority of studies), who may be well informed on Milgram's and Bandura's studies, and may even know very well the attitudes of the experimenter/professor about television violence. It may not be surprising that television violence effects seen for "adults" (who tend to be college students) are considerably higher than for children, contrary to the expectations of brain plasticity (Ferguson & Kilburn, 2009; Paik & Comstock, 1994).

Failure to Control for "Third" Variables

One issue that has plagued correlational studies of television violence has been the failure of many such studies to adequately control for "third" variables that might explain any correlational relationship between television violence and aggression. As the old adage goes, "correlation does not prove causation," and when there are good reasons to think a particular variable might explain a correlation, it is important to control for that variable to see if any relationship remains. For example, boys both watch more violent television and are more aggressive than girls. Thus controlling for gender is essential. So too, children with more aggressive personalities or more difficult family backgrounds may be drawn to more violent television; thus controlling for these variables too may be informative.

Prior to the 2000s, correlational studies that attempted to control for many of these potential confounds were in surprisingly short supply, and reliance on bivariate correlations was common (Freedman, 2002; Gauntlett, 1995; Savage, 2004). Indeed Savage (2004, p. 113) stated of such correlational studies that "these studies should not be weighted heavily in an assessment of the evidence even though there are so many of them" owing to this absence of controls. In fairness, this critique is true for correlational studies that both did and did not find correlational relationships. Several more recent analyses have attempted to use better controls with Johnson, Cohen, Smailes, Kasen, and Brook (2002) being the most impressive of them. Huesmann et al. (2003), as noted earlier, despite measuring a number of control variables, controlled for only one at a time. Many did reduce the size of effect between television violence exposure and adult aggressiveness, raising the possibility that including all control variables together might have eliminated the relationship altogether.

Some recent analyses have implemented such controls (Ferguson, San Miguel, & Hartley, 2009; Fikkers, Piotrowski, Weeda, Vossen, & Valkenburg, 2013; Ybarra et al., 2008). These studies generally indicate that, with other controls in place, the impact of television violence on youth aggression is minimal.

Effect Sizes Are Too Small for Practical Significance

One other issue that has often come up is whether the effects seen in media research, even if taken at face value (i.e., ignoring systematic flaws), are large enough to conclude television violence has a meaningful impact on aggression. The effect sizes are usually measured using correlational coefficients with $r = .00$, meaning no effect at all, and $r = 1.00$, indicating a perfect correlation. Effect size estimates for television violence research range from a low of approximately $r = .04$ (Savage & Yancey, 2008) to a high of $r = .31$ (Paik & Comstock, 1994). That's actually a wide range of effect size estimates. Perhaps not surprisingly, when people wish to emphasize the potential importance of television violence research, the effect size estimate for Paik and Comstock is typically used and others ignored.

However, in understanding these results, two things must be noted. First, most meta-analyses consider only what are called *bivariate* correlations, that is the correlation between two variables without anything else controlled. However, most scholars now understand that controlled effect sizes are often more important than bivariate effect sizes (Savage, 2008). For instance, boys both watch more violent television and are more aggressive than girls. Thus, we might expect to see a correlation between television violence and aggression that is simply a gender effect; therefore, controlling for gender is critical. The Savage and Yancey (2008) meta-analysis is one of very few to consider controlled rather than bivariate effect sizes. When they do so, they find the correlation between television violence and aggression to be near to zero. Second, the $r = .31$ statistic often cited is misleading, as Paik and Comstock (1994) note themselves that the majority of studies included in this statistic do not include an outcome measure related to interpersonal aggression. For instance, when the analysis is limited to a tiny minority of studies that directly measure interpersonal violence, the effect size estimate is a far lower $r = .10$, closer to the results of Savage and Yancey (2008) even without using controlled effect sizes. Thus, when we're looking at the types of effects that are most interesting to society, namely the impact of television violence on societal violence and aggression, even with the flaws in the research, the results are quite small. Indeed, as shown in Table 11.2, the effect size for television violence on outcome measures related to violent crime tend to be among the smallest in criminal justice literature.

TABLE 11.2 EFFECT SIZES IN CRIMINAL JUSTICE RESEARCH

Relationship	Effect Size (r)
Video game sales and youth violence rates in United States[a]	–.95
Genetic influences on antisocial behavior[b,c]	.64 to .75
Self-control and perceptions of criminal opportunity on crime[d]	.58
Protective effect of community institutions on neighborhood crime[d]	.39
Cruelty to animals and later violence toward people[e]	.37
Firearms ownership on crime[d]	.35
Incarceration use as a deterrent on crime[d]	.33
Religiosity and crime[d]	–.29
Psychopathy on criminal recidivism in juveniles	.26
Negative family environment on crime[d]	.26
Peer group on crime[d]	.25
Poverty on crime[d]	.25
Exposure to child abuse and aggressive behavior in young men[g]	.23
Television violence on violent crime	.02 to .10

[a] Ferguson (2010a). [b] Rhee and Waldman (2002). [c] Ferguson (2010b).
[d] Pratt and Cullen (2005). [e] Merz-Perez, Heide, and Silverman (2001).
[f] Douglas, Epstein, and Poythress (2008). [g] Nicholas and Rasmussen (2006).

WHERE HAVE ALL THE VIOLENT PEOPLE GONE?

Prior to the 2000s, media violence researchers commonly referred to violent crime rates in the United States and elsewhere as one source of evidence that television violence directly contributed to violent crime. Although no researcher said television violence was the only cause of violent crime, estimates ranged as high as 10%, a significant percentage of violent crime allegedly attributable directly to the effects of television violence. Bushman and Anderson (2001) link the "explosion" of media violence with the "explosion" of real-life violence, implying that violent crime only exploded when the first generation of youth exposed to heavy diets of television violence became adults. Centerwall (1992, p. 5), writing in the prestigious *Journal of the American Medical Association*, claimed "It is concluded that the introduction of television in the 1950s caused a subsequent doubling of the homicide rate, i.e., long-term childhood exposure to television is a causal factor behind approximately one half of the homicides committed in the United States, or approximately 10,000 homicides annually. Although the data are not as well developed for other forms of violence, they indicate that exposure to television is also a causal factor behind a major proportion—perhaps one half of rapes, assaults, and other forms of interpersonal violence in the United States." Centerwall also claimed that the introduction of television caused similar spikes in violent crime in Canada and South Africa. Seldom reported is evidence that the introduction of television on the island of St. Helena was met with a decrease in aggressiveness among children, not an increase (Charlton, Panting, Davie, Coles, & Whitmarsh, 2000). Nor did Centerwall's proposed relationship between the introduction of television and societal violence hold for European countries such as France, Germany, or Italy, as well as Japan (Zimring & Hawkins, 1997). Speaking on violent crime rates, Anderson (1997, p. 176) stated "Although changes in U.S. society undoubtedly have many origins, it is probably not a coincidence that dramatic increases in exposure to violent media within the U.S. have been paralleled by an increase in the willingness to blame others for our individual problems and to pursue forceful resolution strategies for these problems, in both legal and illegal ways (i.e. lawsuits and assaults)." Statements such as these suggest that television violence researchers took violent crime rates very seriously prior to 2001. Since 2001, statements regarding violent crime rates in the

United States and other societies have virtually vanished from papers on the topic of media violence.

The reason for this is apparent in violent crime statistics themselves. Since a peak in approximately 1993, violent crime rates in the United States and most other industrialized nations have plummeted to 50-year lows (Federal Bureau of Investigation, 1951–2014; van Dijk, van Kesteren, & Smit, 2007), roughly the original rates seen in the 1960s before the "explosion" of violent crime described by Bushman and Anderson (2001). By contrast I am not aware of any scholars arguing that television violence has declined in the same period. I am concerned that media scholars commonly referred to violent crime rates as one source of evidence for the television violence hypothesis so long as societal violence rates were increasing, but have not been intellectually curious about falling violent crime rates since. Indeed, it is increasingly clear that television violence has not caused any increase in violence, as the violence increase of the 1970s through 1993 has all but evaporated (and continues to trend downward as of this writing, despite many bad economic years).

One argument against considering falling violent crime rates as evidence against the television violence hypothesis is a curious reversal of the "third variable" argument, namely that other variables may be accounting for the decline in violent crime, even if television violence increases aggression. This argument fails on two counts. First, even if this argument is taken at face value, it is a retreat to what skeptics have been saying all along—that the impact of television violence on violent behaviors is of trivial importance, and it is other variables we should be considering. Second, this argument is a retreat to an unfalsifiable position— that television violence hypotheses need not show consistency with real-world data on violent crime. This argument also might appear less hypocritical had many of the same scholars not referred to violent crime rates as important evidence in the past, essentially opening the door to counterarguments now that violence rates are declining precipitously.

Figure 11.1 presents an overlap of trends in media violence (movie violence specifically) across the 20th century, alongside societal homicide rates. From this it's not hard to see why people may have made the wrong assumptions about media violence and societal violence. For over two decades, from the 1970s through 1993, increasing media violence consumption appeared to correlate with increased homicides in society. However, this data failed to consider that, in the early part of the century, media violence consumption correlated with *lower* societal violence, a relationship that returned after 1993. In other words, much of the emotional appeal of the media violence/societal violence

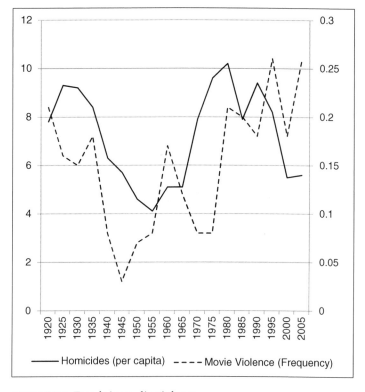

FIGURE 11.1 Trends in media violence.
Source: Ferguson (2015).

argument was based on an ecological fallacy—an observed correlation in society that was due simply to chance, not any real relationship.

As noted earlier, similar trends are seen for violent crime arrests and homicide data in the United States and most other developed nations. Looking at the plateau of violence occurring between 1973 and 1993, it is not difficult to understand how scholars such as Anderson (1997) viewed an apparent correlation with the introduction of television and soaring violence rates in society as "not a coincidence." Of course, now we have a longer view, and it is becoming apparent that a coincidence is exactly the relationship between television's introduction and the peak in violent crime between the late 1960s and early 1990s. Indeed, it appears time to rescind claims that the introduction of television led to crime increases between the late 1960s and early 1990s.

I note that these declines in violent crime are not small. For example, the victimization rate by youthful offenders in 2014 is at roughly 11% of the rate in 1993. These are considerable declines in violence in the United States. Although most media scholars have been largely silent or dismissive of such data, I would argue that these data present a significant challenge to the importance of the television violence hypothesis. Indeed, had crime rates remained steady, or declined slightly, it would remain reasonable to argue that television violence continued to exert an important impact on societal violence despite more positive changes in other realms. However, this precipitous decline in violence in United States society simply does not add up with claims that television violence is a substantial contributor to societal violence. This societal data on violent crime would be akin to finding lower lung-cancer rates among smokers. No theory that is such a poor match to a real-world phenomenon should be allowed to survive, yet I argue this is exactly what has occurred with television violence research.

It's important to note that there is also evidence that, at least for movie violence, the release of popular violent movies tends to be associated with immediate *declines* in violence (Dahl &

DellaVigna, 2009), and despite some worrying over the possibility that movie violence has increased in recent decades, there is no evidence that such an increase is associated with increases in societal violence (Markey, French, & Markey, 2015). Some suggest that whatever impact violent television or movies may have on immediate thoughts or attitudes, such media still may decrease aggression simply by keeping people busy, something called *routine activities theory*. In essence, violent movies or television keep more aggressive people off the streets, as long as it takes to watch the media at least, thereby reducing opportunities for crime.

CONCLUSIONS

It is important to note that the debate about television violence (like video game violence as we discuss in the next chapter) has focused on *general* effects, that is, the notion that television violence has predictable overall effects on just about all viewers in a particular direction. Perhaps some viewers are more influenced than others, but the effects are all generally the same, predictable and automatic. It is this approach to understanding television violence, morally valenced as it is, that, by now, has largely failed to garner good empirical support.

This does not mean that television has no impact on us at all, merely that such influences are difficult to predict. It remains possible that television, both violent and nonviolent, may have very different influences on different individuals. The influences may be viewer driven rather than content driven in many circumstances. In other words, we may seek out certain media on purpose to get a particular emotional reaction, watching comedies when we're feeling down, for instance. And any television influences are, overall, likely to be short term and minor, not long term and profound. And most critically, I suspect that effects are idiosyncratic, differing from one person to the next.

For instance, I sometimes joke (although it is true) that *I do* notice myself getting angry sometimes when I watch television. However, it is mainly shows like *Full House* that make me angry, because I think they are terrible. So I can be emotionally influenced by television, just not in the way the "classic" studies would have predicted. As a field, we have probably gotten too focused on moral issues such as sex and violence rather than on a more sophisticated analysis of how media and individual consumers interact. So long as the field remains rooted in content-based moral issues rather than consumer-based interaction analyses, we will probably never have a clear understanding of what media effects do or do not exist.

REFERENCES

American Academy of Pediatrics. (2000). *Joint statement on the impact of entertainment violence on children.* Retrieved May 10, 2010, from http://www.aap.org/advocacy/releases/jstmtevc.htm

Anderson, C., Berkowitz, L., Donnerstein, E., Huesmann, L. R., Johnson, J., Linz, D., Malamuth, N., & Wartella, E. (2003). The influence of media violence on youth. *Psychological Science in the Public Interest, 4,* 81–110.

Anderson, C. A. (1997). Effects of violent movies and trait irritability on hostile feelings and aggressive thoughts. *Aggressive Behavior, 23,* 161–178.

Anderson, J. (2008). The production of media violence and aggression research. *American Behavioral Scientist, 51,* 1260–1279.

Bandura, A. (1965). Influence of models' reinforcement contingencies on the acquisition of imitative response. *Journal of Personality and Social Psychology, 1,* 589–595.

Bandura, A., Ross, D., & Ross, S. A. (1961). Transmission of aggression through imitation of aggressive models. *Journal of Abnormal and Social Psychology, 63,* 575–582.

Bandura, A., Ross, D., & Ross, S. A. (1963). Imitation of film-mediated aggressive models. *Journal of Abnormal and Social Psychology, 66,* 3–11.

Baumrind, D. (1964). Some thoughts on ethics of research: After reading Milgram's "Behavioral Study of Obedience." *American Psychologist, 19*(6), 421–423. doi:10.1037/h0040128

Belson, W. (1978). *Television violence and the adolescent boy.* Westmead, UK: Saxon House.

Benjamin, L. T. (1985). Defining aggression: An exercise for classroom discussion. *Teaching of Psychology, 12*(1), 40–42. doi:10.1207/s1532 8023top1201_11

Berkowitz, L. (1965). Some aspects of observed aggression. *Journal of Personality and Social Psychology, 2,* 359–369.

Bushman, B., & Anderson, C. (2001). Media violence and the American public. *American Psychologist, 56,* 477–489.

Bushman, B. J., & Huesmann, L. R. (2006). Short-term and long-term effects of violent media on aggression in children and adults. *Archives of Pediatrics and Adolescent Medicine, 160*(4), 348–352.

Cantor, J., & Wilson, B. (2003). Media and violence: Intervention strategies for reducing aggression. *Media Psychology, 5*(4), 363–403. doi:10.1207/S1532785XMEP0504_03

Centerwall, B. (1989). Exposure to television as a risk factor for violence. *American Journal of Epidemiology, 129,* 643–652.

Centerwall, B. (1992). Television and violence: The scale of the problem and where to go from here. *Journal of the American Medical Association, 267*(22). Retrieved June 12, 2010, from http://webs.lanset.com/koba/centwall5.pdf

Charlton, T., Panting, C., Davie, R., Coles, D., & Whitmarsh, L. (2000). Children's playground behaviour across five years of broadcast television: A naturalistic study in a remote community. *Emotional & Behavioural Difficulties, 5*(4), 4–12.

Comstock, G. (2008). A sociological perspective on television violence and aggression. *American Behavioral Scientist, 51*(8), 1184–1211. doi:10.1177/0002764207312009

Cook, D. (2000). *Testimony of the American Academy of Pediatrics on media violence before the U.S. Senate Commerce Committee.* Elk Grove Village, IL: American Academy of Pediatrics. Retrieved June 12, 2010, from http://www.aap.org/advocacy/releases/mediaviolencetestimony.pdf

Cook, T., Kendzierski, D., & Thomas, S. (1983). The implicit assumptions of television research: An analysis of the 1982 NIMH report on Television and Behavior. *Public Opinion Quarterly, 47*(2), 161–201. doi:10.1086/268779

Dahl, G., & DellaVigna, S. (2009). Does movie violence increase violent crime? *The Quarterly Journal of Economics, 124*(2), 677–734.

Douglas, K., Epstein, M., & Poythress, N. (2008). Criminal recidivism among juvenile offenders: Testing the incremental and predictive validity of three measures of psychopathic features. *Law and Human Behavior, 32*(5), 423–438. doi:10.1007/s10979-007-9114-8

Elson, M., Mohseni, M. R., Breuer, J., Scharkow, M., & Quandt, T. (2014). Press CRTT to measure aggressive behavior: The unstandardized use of the competitive reaction time task in aggression research. *Psychological Assessment, 26*(2), 419–432. doi:10.1037/a0035569

Federal Bureau of Investigation. (1951–2014). *Uniform crime reports.* Washington, DC: U.S. Government Printing Office.

Felson, R. B. (1996). Mass media effects on violent behavior. *Annual Review of Sociology, 22*, 103–128.

Ferguson, C. J. (2009). Media violence effects: Confirmed truth, or just another X-file? *Journal of Forensic Psychology Practice, 9*(2), 103–126.

Ferguson, C. J. (2010a). *Blazing Angels* or *Resident Evil?* Can violent video games be a force for good? *Review of General Psychology, 14*(2), 61–82.

Ferguson, C. J. (2010b). Genetic contributions to antisocial personality and behavior (APB): A meta-analytic review from an evolutionary perspective. *Journal of Social Psychology, 150*(2), 160–180.

Ferguson, C. J. (2015). Does movie or video game violence predict societal violence? It depends on what you look at and when—Revised. *Journal of Communication, 65*(1), 193–212. doi:10.1111/jcom.12142

Ferguson, C. J., & Kilburn, J. (2009). The public health risks of media violence: A meta-analytic review. *Journal of Pediatrics, 154*(5), 759–763.

Ferguson, C. J., & Rueda, S. M. (2009). Examining the validity of the Modified Taylor Competitive Reaction Time Test of aggression. *Journal of Experimental Criminology, 5*(2), 121–137.

Ferguson, C. J., San Miguel, C., & Hartley, R. D. (2009). A multivariate analysis of youth violence and aggression: The influence of family, peers, depression and media violence. *Journal of Pediatrics, 155*(6), 904–908.

Feshbach, S., & Singer, R. (1971). *Television and aggression.* San Francisco, CA: Jossey-Boss.

Feshbach, S., & Tangney, J. (2008). Television viewing and aggression: Some alternative perspectives. *Perspectives on Psychological Science, 3*(5), 387–389. doi:10.1111/j.1745-6924.2008.00086.x

Fikkers, K., Piotrowski, J., Weeda, W., Vossen, H., & Valkenburg, P. (2013). Double dose: High family conflict enhances the effect of media violence exposure on adolescents' aggression. *Societies, 3,* 280–292.

Fischoff, S. (1999). *Psychology's quixotic quest for the media-violence connection.* An invited address at the Annual Convention of the American Psychological Association, Boston, August 21, 1999. Retrieved May 11, 2010, from http://www.calstatela.edu/faculty/sfischo/violence.html

Freedman, J. (1984). Effect of television violence on aggressiveness. *Psychological Bulletin, 96*(2), 227–246. doi:10.1037/0033-2909.96.2.227

Freedman, J. (2002). *Media violence and its effect on aggression: Assessing the scientific evidence.* Toronto, Ontario: University of Toronto Press.

Friedrich, L., & Stein, A. (1973). Aggressive and prosocial television programs and the natural behavior of preschool children. *Monographs of the Society for Research in Child Development, 38,* 63.

Gauntlett, D. (1995). *Moving experiences: Understanding television's influences and effects.* Luton, UK: John Libbey.

Giancola, P., & Chermack, S. (1998). Construct validity of laboratory aggression paradigms: A response to Tedeschi and Quigley (1996). *Aggression and Violent Behavior, 3*(3), 237–253. doi:10.1016/S1359-1789(97)00004-9

Grimes, T., Anderson, J., & Bergen, L. (2008). *Media violence and aggression: Science and ideology.* Thousand Oaks, CA: Sage.

Henry, D., & Metropolitan Area Child Study Research Group. (2006). Associations between peer nominations, teacher ratings, self-reports, and observations of malicious and disruptive behavior. *Assessment, 13,* 241–252.

Huesmann, L. R. (1986). Psychological processes promoting the relation between exposure to media violence and aggressive behavior by the viewer. *Journal of Social Issues, 423,* 125–139.

Huesmann, L. R. (2007). The impact of electronic media violence: Scientific theory and research. *Journal of Adolescent Health, 41,* S6–S13.

Huesmann, L. R., & Eron, L. D. (Eds.). (1986). *Television and the aggressive child: A cross-national comparison.* Hillsdale, NJ: Lawrence Erlbaum.

Huesmann, L. R., Moise, J. F., & Podolski, C.-L. (1997). The effects of media violence on the development of antisocial behavior. In D. M. Stoff, J. Breiling, & J. D. Maser (Eds.), *Handbook of antisocial behavior* (pp. 181–193). Hoboken, NJ: John Wiley & Sons.

Huesmann, L. R., Moise-Titus, J. F., Podolski, C.-L., & Eron, L. D. (2003). Longitudinal relations between children's exposure to TV violence and their aggressive and violent behavior in young adulthood: 1977–1992. *Developmental Psychology, 39*(2), 201–221. doi:10.1037/0012-1649.39.2.201

Huesmann, L. R., & Taylor, L. (2003). The case against the case against media violence. In D. Gentile (Ed.), *Media violence and children: A complete guide for parents and professionals.* New York, NY: Praeger.

Ioannidis, J. P. (2005). Why most published research findings are false. *PLoS Medicine, 2,* e124. Retrieved June 14, 2010, from http://www.plosmedicine.org/article/info:doi/10.1371/journal.pmed.0020124

Johnson, J., Cohen, P., Smailes, E., Kasen, S., & Brook, J. (2002). Television viewing and aggressive behavior during adolescence and adulthood. *Science, 295,* 2468–2471.

Josephson, W. (1987). Television violence and children's aggression: Testing the priming, social script, and disinhibition predictions. *Journal of Personality and Social Psychology, 53*(5), 882–890. doi:10.1037/0022-3514.53.5.882

Kaplan, R., & Singer, R. (1976). Television violence and viewer aggression: A reexamination of the evidence. *Journal of Social Issues, 32*(4), 35–70.

Kuhn, T. (1970) *The structure of scientific revolutions.* Chicago, IL: University of Chicago Press.

Lefkowitz, M. M., Eron, L. D., Walder, L. O., & Huesmann, L. R. (1972). Television violence and child aggression: A follow-up study. In G. A. Comstock & E. A. Rubinstein (Eds.), *Television and social behavior. Television and adolescent aggressiveness* (Vol. 3, pp. 35–135). Washington, DC: U.S. Government Printing Office.

Lefkowitz, M. M., Eron, L. D., Walder, L. O., & Huesmann, L. R. (1977). *Growing up to be violent: A longitudinal study of the development of aggression.* New York, NY: Pergamon.

Markey, P. M., French, J. E., & Markey, C. N. (2015). Violent movies and severe acts of violence: Sensationalism versus science. *Human Communication Research, 41*(2), 155–173. doi:10.1111/hcre.12046

Merz-Perez, L., Heide, K., & Silverman, I. (2001). Childhood cruelty to animals and subsequent violence against humans. *International Journal of Offender Therapy and Comparative Criminology, 45*(5), 556–573. doi:10.1177/0306624X01455003

Milavsky, J. R., Kessler, R., Stipp, H., & Rubens, W. S. (1982). Television and aggression: Results of a panel study. In D. Pearl, L. Bouthilet, & J. Lazar (Eds.), *Television and behavior: Ten years of scientific progress and implications for the 80s. Technical reviews* (Vol. 2, pp. 138–157). Washington, DC: U.S. Government Printing Office.

Milavsky, J. R., Stipp, H. H., Kessler, R., & Rubens, W. S. (1982). *Television and aggression: A panel study.* New York, NY: Academic Press.

Milgram, S. (1963). Behavioral study of obedience. *Journal of Abnormal and Social Psychology, 67*(4), 371–378. doi:10.1037/h0040525

Moeller, T. (2005). How "unequivocal" is the evidence regarding television violence and children's aggression? *APS Observer, 18,* 6.

Molitor, F., & Hirsch, K. (1994). Children's toleration of real-life aggression after exposure to media violence: A replication of the Drabman and Thomas studies. *Child Study Journal, 24*(3), 191–207.

Mussen, P., & Rutherford, E. (1961). Effects of aggressive cartoons on children's aggressive play. *Journal of Abnormal and Social Psychology, 62,* 461–464.

Nicholas, K., & Rasmussen, E. (2006). Childhood abusive and supportive experiences, inter-parental violence, and parental alcohol use: Prediction of young adult depressive symptoms and aggression. *Journal of Family Violence, 21*(1), 43–61. doi:10.1007/s10896-005-9001-3

Olson, C. (2004). Media violence research and youth violence data: Why do they conflict? *Academic Psychiatry, 28,* 144–150.

Paik, H., & Comstock, G. (1994). The effects of television violence on anti-social behavior: A meta-analysis. *Communication Research, 21,* 516–546.

Pratt, T., & Cullen, C. (2005). Assessing macro-level predictors and theories of crime: A meta-analysis. In Michael Tomry (Ed.), *Crime and justice: A review of research* (Vol. 32, pp. 373–450). Chicago, IL: University of Chicago Press.

Rhee, S., & Waldman, I. (2002). Genetic and environmental influences on antisocial behavior: A meta-analysis of twin and adoption studies. *Psychological Bulletin, 128,* 490–529.

Ritter, D., & Eslea, M. (2005). Hot sauce, toy guns and graffiti: A critical account of current laboratory aggression paradigms. *Aggressive Behavior, 31,* 407–419.

Savage, J. (2004). Does viewing violent media really cause criminal violence? A methodological review. *Aggression and Violent Behavior, 10,* 99–128.

Savage, J. (2008). The role of exposure to media violence in the etiology of violent behavior: A criminologist weighs in. *American Behavioral Scientist, 51,* 1123–1136.

Savage, J., & Yancey, C. (2008). The effects of media violence exposure on criminal aggression: A meta-analysis. *Criminal Justice and Behavior, 35,* 772–791.

Stipp, H., & Milavsky, J. (1988). U.S. television programming's effects on aggressive behavior of children and adolescents. *Current Psychology: Research & Reviews, 7*(1), 76–92. doi:10.1007/BF02686665

Tedeschi, J., & Quigley, B. (1996). Limitations of laboratory paradigms for studying aggression. *Aggression & Violent Behavior, 2,* 163–177.

Tedeschi, J., & Quigley, B. (2000). A further comment on the construct validity of laboratory aggression paradigms: A response to Giancola and Chermack. *Aggression & Violent Behavior, 5,* 127–136.

Trend, D. (2007). *The myth of media violence: A critical introduction.* Malden, MA: Blackwell.

van Dijk, J., van Kesteren, J., & Smit, P. (2007). *Criminal victimization in international perspective.* The Hague, The Netherlands: United Nations Office on Drug and Crime.

Wiegman, O., & Kuttschreuter, M. (1992). A longitudinal study of the effects of television viewing on aggressive and prosocial behaviors. *British Journal of Social Psychology, 31,* 147–164.

Wood, W., Wong, F., & Chachere, J. (1991). Effects of media violence on viewers' aggression in unconstrained social interaction. *Psychological Bulletin, 109*(3), 371–383. doi:10.1037/0033-2909.109.3.371

Ybarra, M., Diener-West, M., Markow, D., Leaf, P., Hamburger, M., & Boxer, P. (2008). Linkages between internet and other media violence with seriously violent behavior by youth. *Pediatrics, 122*(5), 929–937.

Zillman, D., & Weaver, J. (2007). Aggressive personality traits in the effects of violent imagery on unprovoked impulsive aggression. *Journal of Research in Personality, 41*, 753–771.

Zimring, F., & Hawkins, G. (1997). *Crime is not the problem: Lethal violence in America.* New York, NY: Oxford University Press.

Video Game
Violence Research

n August 2013, an 8-year-old boy shot his grandmother shortly after reportedly playing the video game *Grand Theft Auto IV* (*GTA*). *GTA* is a violent shooter game that has gained notoriety for its sandbox-style allowance for players to engage in criminal actions, such as beating prostitutes or shooting police officers. The game has an Entertainment Software Ratings Board (ESRB) rating of "M," which is equivalent to a movie rating of "R." In a news release immediately following the shooting, investigating police opined that the child had intentionally shot his grandmother, potentially motivated by playing *GTA*. The police were quoted as claiming *GTA* "awards points to players for killing people" (Minton, 2013). However, the investigation ultimately revealed that the shooting was, in fact, accidental, and the boy thought the weapon was a toy gun (Campbell, 2013). Further, contrary to the police statement, *GTA* does not "award points" for killing, although its open-play style does not prevent such acts.

Although other similar tragedies have not been accidents, it is curious that investigators and news coverage leapt so quickly to focus on *GTA* rather than, say, why it was so easy for an 8-year-old to gain access to a loaded handgun, or what family and supervision issues may have been at play in the family. Why did the investigators assume so quickly that a shooting by a child was intentional murder rather than an accident? Why did investigators so quickly focus on the presence of a single video game in the house, seeming to forget the same game is in the homes of millions of children with no behavioral problems? This case, and others like it, tells us something about the way society reacts to new media.

Since the 1980s, when simple video games such as *Centipede* and *Pac-Man* became popular, video games have been accused by politicians of being a major contributor to societal violence (as noted by Cooper & Mackie, 1986). It may seem silly, even quaint, to suggest that *Pac-Man* is a violent video game (he eats ghosts after all!), but even in 2013 a scholar testified in court that *Pac-Man* could be considered a violent video game (Rushton, 2013). However, most focus today is on ultraviolent games such as *GTA*. Do these games cause, in part, societal violence and decreased empathy toward others, or are we experiencing a moral panic about media?

A HISTORY OF VIOLENT VIDEO GAME RESEARCH

It is not uncommon to hear claims that violent video games are a causal influence on real-life violence. Indeed, some scholars are so convinced that they claim anyone who disagrees with them must be "industry apologists" (Anderson, 2013) or even argue that news reporters should only report on their views, not the views of those who disagree with them (Prot & Gentile, 2014).

Others have claimed that the impact of video game violence on aggression is similar to the impact of smoking on lung cancer and other important effects (Huesmann, 2007). Strong words indeed! Does the research evidence really support this level of hyperbole?

Obviously, it depends on who you ask, but let's look at the evidence across time. During the early years of video game violence research, when games like *Centipede* and *Pac-Man* were considered violent video games, and even when the research had moved on to *Mortal Kombat* and such games in the 1990s, the research was inconsistent and most scholars acknowledged it as so (e.g., Dominick, 1984; Kirsh, 1998; van Schie & Wiegman, 1997). This changed in the early 2000s immediately following the tragic Columbine massacre in 1999, in which two teenagers who had played the shooter game *Doom* (which was recently included in the Smithsonian Institute's Art of Video Games Exhibit) killed 12 peers and a teacher before killing themselves. Although violent video game play was, by then, ubiquitous among boys (Griffiths & Hunt, 1995), a social narrative was created on the press among politicians (e.g., Senator Lieberman's comments on CNN, 1997) and among some scholars (e.g., Anderson, 2004) linking violent video games to mass shootings. This narrative created a false correlation by focusing on young shooters who had played violent games, and by ignoring those who didn't (such as the Virginia Tech shooter) and those older shooters for whom no evidence of a gaming connection emerged. That narrative seemed to catch on in the social science community because statements of absolute causal certitude about violent game effects became common among scholars even though the research evidence did not substantially change and, in fact, remained inconclusive (e.g., Anderson, 2004; Huesmann, 2007).

There is considerable risk in advocating for an extreme position if the data does not clearly support it, as many scholars and some professional groups did, including the American Psychological Association ([APA], 2005) and the American Academy of Pediatrics ([AAP], 2009). By taking such an extreme position, this could place scholars in the situation of needing to defend it rather than considering research evidence carefully and objectively. This failure to consider divergent evidence is clear from the failure of some scholars (e.g., Anderon, 2004) or groups like the APA and AAP to cite available disconfirmatory evidence. Making erroneous statements in such a way can damage the credibility of the field (Hall, Day, & Hall, 2011). Indeed, this is precisely what happened. In reviewing the evidence for the argument that video game violence leads to aggression, the U.S. Supreme Court has said (*Brown v. Entertainment Merchants Association*, 2011) that "These studies have been rejected by every court to consider them, and with good reason: They do not prove that violent video games *cause* minors to *act* aggressively (which would at least be a beginning). Instead, '[n]early all of the research is based on correlation, not evidence of causation, and most of the studies suffer from significant, admitted flaws in methodology.'" Most of the existing studies were with college students (who can typically guess the hypothesis and what they're supposed to do in a study), not with children, and aggression measures involved things such as giving a consenting opponent a burst of white noise or filling in the missing letters of words such that "kill" is more aggressive than "kiss."

In recent years, more research evidence has come to light suggesting that video game violence does not have a substantial influence on aggression or prosocial behavior (e.g., Ballard, Visser, & Jocoy, 2012; Charles, Baker, Hartman, Easton, & Kretzberger, 2013; Tear & Nielson, 2013) or youth violence (Ferguson, San Miguel, Garza, & Jerabeck, 2012; Kutner & Olson, 2008; von Salisch, Vogelgesang, Kristen, & Oppl, 2011). So exactly what research do we have?

1. Violent Video Games and Aggression. We have a relatively large pool of studies, over 100, that examine the issue of violent video games on "aggression," which may be measured by things ranging from filling in the missing letters of words (so that "kill" is more aggressive than "kiss" for instance)

to delivering nonpainful bursts of white noise. This pool of research has often been criticized, by the Supreme Court, among others, for considerable methodological weaknesses. These weaknesses include questions about the degree to which these aggression measures actually relate to real-world aggression (Adachi & Willoughby, 2011; Elson, Mohseni, Breuer, Scharkow, & Quandt, 2014); failure to adequately control for other important variables in correlational studies (Kutner & Olson, 2008); and mismatches between video games in experimental and control conditions in experiments (Adachi & Willoughby, 2011). Related to this last point, imagine comparing a game like *Modern Warfare 3* to *Tetris*. One is violent, the other is not, but they differ on so many other levels that it would be difficult to ascribe any differences to violent content. Or, put in the lingo of research methods classes, such experiments lack internal validity. Further, this pool of research has returned inconsistent results that, coupled with the methodological limitations of many of the studies, have been difficult to apply to the real world, as the Supreme Court correctly noted.

2. A much smaller pool of correlational studies has examined the impact of video games on real-world aggression and violence among youth. Like the first group of studies, results here are also inconsistent but generally weaker, with most studies finding that the predictive ability of video game violence on later aggression is negligible or weak (e.g., Ferguson et al., 2012; von Salisch et al., 2011; Willoughby, Adachi, & Good, 2012). Willoughby et al. (2012), for instance, found that with other factors controlled, violent video games predicted less than half a percent of the variance in youth aggression (or $r = .07$ for the statistically inclined), and even this may have been due to the competitive nature of some games rather than the violence (Adachi & Willoughby, 2013). A recent meta-analysis of studies of youth and video games suggested that video game influence on youth mental health was minimal, with published studies subject to publication bias (Ferguson, in press).

3. As video games have soared in popularity, particularly in the years after 1993, youth violence declined by almost 90% to levels not seen since the 1960s (childstats.gov, 2013). Although only one piece of evidence and correlational, not causal, this data conflicts with statements by politicians and scholars alike that "strong" video game violence influence would have an impact on violence in the real-world.

4. Data on mass shooters themselves have never returned information that they are particularly prone to consuming violent media. Almost all young males consume violent media, of course, so finding that a young shooter happened to play violent video games isn't as revealing as some imply, given that such behavior is normal for any young male, shooter or not. Further, when news media or politicians try to link video games to mass shootings, they do so by either ignoring or distorting the cases that don't fit this narrative, as with older shooters like William Spengler or even some younger ones like the Virginia Tech shooter, who did not play violent games. An examination of school shooters in 2002 by the U.S. Secret Service found little evidence they were inclined to consume unusual levels of violent media (aside from their own violent writings), and, in a recent criminological investigation of mass shooters, Fox and DeLateur (2014) specifically referred to efforts to link such shootings to video games a "myth."

Thus, taken together, data to link video games to real-world aggression and violence is inconsistent at best, and I would argue weak overall. This is not to say that there is no value in a debate or that some scholars couldn't make reasoned arguments for some types of negative effects. Rather, my concern is that too often the debate on video game violence has progressed through distortions of the research evidence.

Succinctly put, research is not conclusive in one direction or another. Indeed, one can selectively cite research to suggest that violent video games are either the devil's gift to society or a blessing to society (e.g., McGonigal, 2011). However, this is exactly the problem because too often scholars and even the APA (2005) have cited research to support a popular moralizing belief rather than a scientific position, and this has ultimately damaged the credibility of our field. In the next portion of this chapter, I would like to explore how this came to pass.

MEDIA AND MORAL PANICS

A Harris poll (2013) released soon after the tragic December 2012 Sandy Hook shooting in which a young man rumored to be a gamer killed 20 schoolchildren revealed that Americans are split on whether video games contribute to societal violence. However, this poll revealed that people less familiar with video games were more likely to think they were harmful. Elderly adults unfamiliar with the ESRB ratings were most prone to worrying about video games. Empirical research has also confirmed that lack of familiarity is associated with fear of video games (Ivory & Kalyanaraman, 2009). Put simply, lack of knowledge breeds fear.

These types of media-based moral panics are well documented (Gauntlett, 2005), and the source of these panics have ranged from books (such as Harry Potter), to comic books, to rock and roll. In many of these incidents, the scientific community added fuel to the moral panic. For instance, during fears about comic books during the 1950s, some psychiatrists testified before Congress that comic books caused not only delinquency but also homosexuality because, it was said, Batman and Robin were secretly gay (Kutner & Olson, 2008). The "Tipper Gore hearings" in the 1980s about music lyrics employed social scientist Dr. Joe Stuessy and psychiatrist Dr. Paul King, who expressed concerns over the behavioral effects of music by, for example, Van Halen and Cyndi Lauper (whose song "She Bop" was considered hypersexual because of its veiled reference to masturbation), songs now mainly considered harmless classics. These

211

fears seem laughable today, but we have difficulty recognizing when we enter the same cycle.

It's probably difficult to underestimate the influence that statements from the APA (2005) and AAP (2009) have had in fostering these types of moral panics, damaging the credibility of our field in the process. The incentives for scholars to do so are worth discussing. First, let me say, that scholars are certainly acting in good faith when communicating worries about media. But there are some social and cultural issues both within and outside the field that can lead to problematic statements by scholars. As Moral Panic Theory details (Gauntlett, 2005), the societal narrative on media can have considerable influence on the scientific community. Put simply, once society has made up its mind on an issue (e.g., "Video game violence is bad!"), society itself drives the science by selecting what studies get funded and get news attention, giving more attention to alarmist outcomes than less alarmist ones. After all, it's harder to get a grant arguing that something isn't a pressing social problem than to argue that it is. Politicians can get involved in this by calling for research while making very clear what they wish the outcomes of this research to be. For instance, in the weeks and months after the 2012 Newtown shooting, Senator Rockefeller called for research that would challenge the Supreme Court's opinion in *Brown v. Entertainment Merchants Association* and open avenues for further legislation. To quote Senator Rockefeller, "Recent court decisions demonstrate that some people still do not get it. They believe that violent video games are no more dangerous to young minds than classic literature or Saturday morning cartoons. Parents, pediatricians, and psychologists know better. These court decisions show we need to do more and explore ways Congress can lay additional groundwork on this issue. This report will be a critical resource in this process" (Terkel, 2012). By using such hostile wording in calling for a research report, Senator Rockefeller placed undo pressure on the scientific community to produce a particular desired result that can be distorting of the scientific process. This is particularly true when politicians control the budget of scientific organizations such as the Centers for Disease Control and Prevention (CDC) or the National Science Foundation (NSF).

Groups including the AAP and APA may also view worrying about media as being in their short-term interest. The APA represents psychologists as a profession, and identifying a "pressing issue" to solve may appear to be in their short-term interest, gaining political influence, public appreciation for the profession, and potential grant funding for members. As such, the APA's previous policy statement on video game violence has been found to be highly error prone (Ferguson, 2013), although in fairness to the APA, it should be noted that they have willingly published research critical of their past policy statement or suggested new approaches to conceptualizing the role of video games in society (e.g., Granic, Lobel, & Engels, 2013). This represents the recognition, on the part of the APA, that the committee that produced the early policy statement included only scholars who were invested in viewing video games as harmful. No skeptical scholars were invited. These invested scholars, in essence, reviewed their own work and declared it beyond further debate and simply ignored and failed to cite studies that challenged their view. This policy statement should not be mistaken for an objective report, nor should similar problematic policy statements such as that by the AAP (2009). Unfortunately, a new task force employed by the APA to review video game research just after the Sandy Hook massacre in 2012 wasn't much better, with the majority of members having staked out clear antigame positions in prior years.

WHERE CAN WE GO FROM HERE?

It may be frustrating to see the same simple premise "video game violence causes aggression" go back and forth so often with no conclusion. How do we get out of this cycle?

As I have indicated earlier, this cycle may be fed, in large part, by repetitive cycles of generational conflict in which older adults disparage newer media popular among youth (Przybylski, 2014). To some degree, some aspects of academic psychology have arguably made the mistake that Farley (2012), a well-regarded media scholar, calls the problem of big-V, little-v violence distortion. That is to say, society has questions about real acts of criminal violence (big-V), and we try to answer these questions with dubious laboratory studies measuring violence by such means as filling in the missing letters of words or giving consenting opponents bursts of nonharmful noise (little-v). As long as we stay in this mold, focused on violent video games as a moralistic issue, it will probably be difficult to escape this cycle.

Part of the problem has been the degree to which video games have been considered something other than an integral part of and reflection on society. That is to say, even scholars may begin with the premise that games, or at least violent games, are a corrupting influence on society . . . not a legitimate part of society, but rather damaging to it. This perspective seems to be both naïve and simply wrong. This is not to say that it's impossible for negative influences on society to exist, of course; however, my concern is that too often fields such as this begin with a premise, by separating media from society, and then selectively interpret evidence to fit a preexisting premise. Media is very much a product of society, and thus it is difficult to separate it from the cultural context of the society that creates it.

Some readers of this chapter may be students who will become the next generation of scholars. Some of you may do undergraduate research on the topic or are graduate students or media researchers examining media effects. Here, then, are some thoughts for how you might develop cutting-edge research programs that move beyond the old effects model.

1. **Conduct research returning the user, rather than the media, to the center of relationships and effects.** This is something that was lost long ago in media effects research, not just on video games but television too—the notion of the viewer as an active driver of the media experience, not

merely a passive victim, particularly true in an era in which we can create our own media or individualize our media experiences to a greater degree than ever before. Once we return the viewer/player to the forefront of the media experience, I believe we'll have a deeper understanding of the interaction between media and media consumer.

A big part of such a new research agenda might focus on a player's motivations for playing various video games (Przybylski, Weinstein, Murayama, Lynch, & Ryan, 2012) or examine how video games, including violent games, are used by people to improve their mood or reduce stress (Bowman & Tamborini, 2012). Other research may focus on qualitative designs to get a deeper perspective about gamers' experience in playing games (e.g., Colwell, 2007; Oswald, Prorock, & Murphy, 2014). Yet other research may look at how the cooperative play in both violent and nonviolent games can lead to prosocial outcomes and reduced aggression (Granic et al., 2013; Velez & Ewoldsen, 2013).

2. **A sociology of media violence perspective.** Increasingly, it is being recognized that the production of media violence research did not occur in a social vacuum but, in many ways, responded to larger political and social influences (Ferguson, 2013; Granic et al., 2013). A reasonable question, one that could be studied empirically, is why did the field progress the way it did, becoming, at times, almost quasi religious in the promotion of certain ideological views about media violence, even when data were weak and inconsistent? Research programs could examine scholars, clinicians, researchers, politicians, and the general public. What factors relate to a heavy interest in promoting fears about media violence? Are they related to political leanings, certain personality variables, pacifism, conventional thinking, age, experience with media, and so on? My colleague Andrew Przybylski (2014) has opened these doors, working primarily with the general public. But there's no reason that media scholars themselves or the scholarship they produce shouldn't become sources

of inquiry! Do scholars feel a boost in self-worth from complaining about popular culture, or is it easier to get grant funding by arguing something is a big problem versus arguing it is no big deal?

3. **Integrating video games into family life.** Another potentially interesting avenue for research might involve examining ways to more fully incorporate video gaming into family life. For instance, if parents are encouraged to play video games with their children, are there positive outcomes? Some of my own research has indicated that children who play violent games *with* their parents are more helpful and civically involved than children who either played alone mostly or didn't play at all (Ferguson & Garza, 2011). Does engagement work more effectively than media restriction? Does parental involvement in playing games reduce their fear of them? Some research by my colleague James Ivory (Ivory & Kalyanaraman, 2009) suggests people tend to be more afraid of violent video games as an abstract concept and less afraid of specific video games once they see them in action. Does promoting knowledge of the ESRB ratings for video games and other content controls change people's perceptions of video games? Does language promoting censorship or regulation of violent games help the image of psychology as a profession or harm it? There are a lot of interesting and important questions in this realm that could be answered through good research!

Ultimately, there are multiple views and answers to the debate on video game violence. In that way, it is impossible to be entirely unbiased, and we absolutely must begin to indicate this for all to hear. In future research, not just one, but all, of these positions on topics such as video game violence need to be given representation in research and in research conclusions. For video games, this includes the views of pro-videogamers, anti-videogamers, financially invested video game makers, actual video game players, and so forth. This is especially true in a document as important as an APA statement.

216

REFERENCES

Adachi, P. C., & Willoughby, T. (2011). The effect of video game competition and violence on aggressive behavior: Which characteristic has the greatest influence? *Psychology of Violence, 1*(4), 259–274. doi:10.1037/a0024908

Adachi, P. C., & Willoughby, T. (2013). Demolishing the competition: The longitudinal link between competitive video games, competitive gambling, and aggression. *Journal of Youth and Adolescence, 42*(7), 1090–1104. doi:10.1007/s10964-013-9952-2

American Academy of Pediatrics. (2009). Media violence policy statement. *Pediatrics, 124*(5), 1495–1503.

American Psychological Association. (2005). *Resolution on violence in video games and interactive media*. Retrieved from http://www.apa.org/about/policy/interactive-media.pdf

Anderson, C. (2004). An update on the effects of playing violent video games. *Journal of Adolescence, 27*, 113–122.

Anderson, C. (2013). Games, guns, and mass shootings in the US. *Bulletin of the International Society for Research on Aggression, 35*(1), 14–19. Retrieved from http://www.psychology.iastate.edu/faculty/caa/abstracts/2010-2014/13A.pdf

Ballard, M., Visser, K., & Jocoy, K. (2012). Social context and video game play: Impact on cardiovascular and affective responses. *Mass Communication and Society, 15*, 875–898. doi:10.1080/15205436.2011.632106

Bowman, N. D., & Tamborini, R. (2012). Task demand and mood repair: The intervention potential of computer games. *New Media & Society, 14*(8), 1339–1357. doi:10.1177/1461444812450426

Brown v. Entertainment Merchants Association. (2011, June 27). Retrieved from http://www.supremecourt.gov/opinions/10pdf/08-1448.pdf

Campbell, A. (2013, August 27). 8-year-old who shot grandmother, Marie Smothers, after playing *Grand Theft Auto* won't face charges. *Huffington Post*. Retrieved from http://www.huffingtonpost.com/2013/08/27/marie-smothers-grand-theft-auto_n_3821879.html

Charles, E. P., Baker, C. M., Hartman, K., Easton, B. P., & Kretzberger, C. (2013). Motion capture controls negate the violent video-game effect. *Computers in Human Behavior, 29*, 2519–2523. doi:10.1016/j.chb.2013.05.028

217

Childstats.gov. (2013). *America's children: Key national indicators of well-being, 2010.* Retrieved July 1, 2012, from http://www.childstats.gov

CNN. (1997). *Senator decries violent video games.* CNN. Retrieved July 5, 2011, from http://edition.cnn.com/ALLPOLITICS/1997/11/25/email/videos

Colwell, J. (2007). Needs met through computer game play among adolescents. *Personality and Individual Differences, 43*(8), 2072–2082. doi:10.1016/j.paid.2007.06.021

Cooper, J., & Mackie, D. (1986). Video games and aggression in children. *Journal of Applied Social Psychology, 16,* 726–744. doi:10.1111/j.1559-1816.1986.tb01755.x

Dominick, J. R. (1984). Videogames, television violence, and aggression in teenagers. *Journal of Communication, 34,* 136–147. doi:10.1111/j.1460-2466.1984.tb02165.x

Elson, M., Mohseni, M. R., Breuer, J., Scharkow, M., & Quandt, T. (2014). Press CRTT to measure aggressive behavior: The unstandardized use of the competitive reaction time task in aggression research. *Psychological Assessment, 26*(2), 419–432. doi:10.1037/a0035569

Farley, F. (2012, December 30). Bad, better, best. *Psychology Today.* Retrieved from http://www.psychologytoday.com/em/114563

Ferguson, C. J. (2013). Violent video games and the Supreme Court: Lessons for the scientific community in the wake of Brown v. EMA. *American Psychologist, 68,* 57–74.

Ferguson, C. J. (in press). Do angry birds make for angry children? A meta-analysis of video game influences on children's and adolescents' aggression, mental health, prosocial behavior and academic performance. *Perspectives on Psychological Science.*

Ferguson, C. J., & Garza, A. (2011). Call of (civic) duty: Action games and civic behavior in a large sample of youth. *Computers in Human Behavior, 27,* 770–775.

Ferguson, C. J., San Miguel, C., Garza, A., & Jerabeck, J. (2012). A longitudinal test of video game violence effects on dating violence, aggression, and bullying: A 3-year longitudinal study of adolescents. *Journal of Psychiatric Research, 46,* 141–146.

Fox, J. A., & DeLateur, M. J. (2014). Mass shootings in America: Moving beyond Newtown. *Homicide Studies: An Interdisciplinary & International Journal, 18*(1), 125–145. doi:10.1177/1088767913510297

Gauntlett, D. (2005). *Moving experiences: Understanding television's influences and effects.* Luton, UK: John Libbey.

Granic, I., Lobel, A., & Engels, R. (2013). The benefits of playing video games. *American Psychologist.* doi:10.1037/a0034857

Griffiths, M., & Hunt, N. (1995). Computer game playing in adolescence: Prevalence and demographic indicators. *Journal of Community and Applied Social Psychology, 5,* 189–193.

Hall, R., Day, T., & Hall, R. (2011). A plea for caution: Violent video games, the Supreme Court, and the role of science. *Mayo Clinic Proceedings, 86,* 315–321.

Harris Polls. (2013, February 27). *Majority of Americans see connection between video games and violent behavior in teens.* Retrieved from http://www.harrisinteractive.com/NewsRoom/HarrisPolls/ tabid/447/mid/1508/articleId/1160/ctl/ReadCustom%20Default/ Default.aspx

Huesmann, L. R. (2007). The impact of electronic media violence: Scientific theory and research. *Journal of Adolescent Health, 41,* S6–S13.

Ivory, J., & Kalyanaraman, S. (2009). Video games make people violent—well, maybe not that game: Effects of content and person abstraction on perceptions of violent video games' effects and support of censorship. *Communication Reports, 22,* 1–12. doi:10.1080/ 08934210902798536

Kirsh, S. (1998). Seeing the world through Mortal Kombat-colored glasses: Violent video games and the development of a short-term hostile attribution bias. *Childhood: A Global Journal of Child Research, 5*(2), 177–184. doi:10.1177/0907568298005002005

Kutner, L., & Olson, C. (2008). *Grand theft childhood: The surprising truth about violent video games and what parents can do.* New York, NY: Simon & Schuster.

McGonigal, J. (2011). *Reality is broken: Why games make us better and how they can change the world.* New York, NY: Penguin Press.

Minton, J. (2013, August 25). Investigators say shooter, 8, played violent video game. *The Advocate.* Retrieved from http://theadvocate .com/home/6860976-125/investigators-say-shooter-8-played

Oswald, C. A., Prorock, C., & Murphy, S. M. (2014). The perceived meaning of the video game experience: An exploratory study. *Psychology of Popular Media Culture, 3*(2), 110–126. doi:10.1037/a0033828

Prot, S., & Gentile, D. (2014). Applying risk and resilience models to predicting the effects of media violence on development. In J. Benson (Ed.), *Advances in child development and behavior* (Vol. 46, pp. 215–238). London, UK: Elsevier.

Przybylski, A. K. (2014). Who believes electronic games cause real world aggression? *Cyberpsychology, Behavior, and Social Networking, 17*(4), 228–234. doi:10.1089/cyber.2013.0245

Przybylski, A. K., Weinstein, N., Murayama, K., Lynch, M. F., & Ryan, R. M. (2012). The ideal self at play: The appeal of video games that let you be all you can be. *Psychological Science, 23*(1), 69–76. doi:10.1177/0956797611418676

Quandt, T., & Kroger, S. (2013). *Multiplayer: The social aspects of digital gaming.* Oxon, UK: Routledge.

Rushton, B. (2013, May 29). Backdooring it: Defense maneuvers around setback. *Illinois Times.* Retrieved from http://www.illinois-times.com/Springfield/article-11440-backdooring-it.html

Tear, M., & Nielson, M. (2013). Failure to demonstrate that playing violent video games diminishes prosocial behavior. *PLoS One, 8*, e68382.

Terkel, A. (2012, December 19). Video games targeted by Senate in wake of Sandy Hook shooting. *Huffington Post.* Retrieved from http://www.huffingtonpost.com/2012/12/19/video-games-sandy-hook_n_2330741.html?utm_hp_ref=technology&utm_hp_ref=technology

United States Secret Service and United States Department of Education. (2002). *The final report and findings of the Safe School Initiative: Implications for the prevention of school attacks in the United States.* Retrieved July 2, 2011, from http://www.secretservice.gov/ntac/ssi_final_report.pdf

van Schie, E., & Wiegman, O. (1997). Children and videogames: Leisure activities, aggression, social integration, and school performance. *Journal of Applied Social Psychology, 27*(13), 1175–1194.

Velez, J., & Ewoldsen, D. (2013). Helping behaviors during video game play. *Journal of Media Psychology, 25*, 190–200.

von Salisch, M., Vogelgesang, J., Kristen, A., & Oppl, C. (2011). Preference for violent electronic games and aggressive behavior among children: The beginning of the downward spiral? *Media Psychology, 14*, 233–258. doi:10.1080/15213269.2011.596468

Willoughby, T., Adachi, P. C., & Good, M. (2012). A longitudinal study of the association between violent video game play and aggression among adolescents. *Developmental Psychology.* doi:10.1037/a0026046

Pornography

ornography has been an incredibly complex part of the social fabric across history. Simultaneously consumed in mass amounts and reviled by exactly the same public that consumes it, pornography and its effects have probably been the most difficult of the media areas to separate good science from moral grandstanding. One theme that has run through this book is that it is tempting for scholars, even acting in good faith, to make moralistic statements based on weak data, or to allow their passions to influence the data they produce. This is just human nature. But probably nowhere is there a greater risk of this phenomenon, particularly in the United States, where there have been such dogged efforts to condemn pornography on public health as well as moral grounds. After all, who wants to be the person to stand up and defend pornography and immediately get labeled as a perv! But what effects does pornography have and where are things still unclear?

HISTORY OF PORNOGRAPHY

First, although the Internet may have ushered in a "golden age of porn" where even the most explicit pornography is readily available to anyone who wants it, it's important to understand that pornography is nothing new to history. People have always enjoyed consuming sexually explicit material. They have been limited across time mainly by the limits of technology or societal prohibitions against such material.

Naturally, our concepts of pornography are rooted within our own culture and perceptions of sexuality. Exactly what "porn" is arguably differs from one cultural context to another. For instance, we might view the nude image of women in *Playboy* magazine as "porn," yet an almost identical image hanging in a museum is "art," and nudity in the context of athletics in ancient Greece wasn't primarily sexual at all. For this chapter, pornography is defined as any media with sexual activity or nudity that is explicit and has sexual arousal as its main purpose. That having been said, exactly where the boundaries are between art and porn aren't always clear. As I mentioned, why are the nude images in *Playboy* "porn" but identical images in museums "art?" There are a few "real" movies in which actors have explicit sex . . . are these movies "art" rather than "porn" just because the dialogue is better?

There is another concept that also needs to be defined, *obscenity*. Obscenity is a legal term that involves material that is so prurient or disgusting that the majority of society would consider it in a negative light. Once again, the line between pornography and obscenity really isn't clear. Many people consider any pornography to be obscene, yet because consumption rates for most "typical" porn are so high, it's difficult to argue that most of society considers it in a negative light, even if they say so in public. There are some materials that are clearly obscene though. Pornography involving children, since children are obviously harmed in the making of such material, is clearly obscene. Some case law exists that has set general guidelines on obscene material. For instance, *Roth v. United States* (1957) ruled that material was obscene when it would be considered objectionable by an average person, using community standards, and where the media has only prurient, not artistic merit. *Miller v. California* (1973) provided further guidelines as to what materials were obscene. Under this ruling, any media that had undue interest in nudity, sex, or excretory functions, and no redeeming social value, were considered to be obscene. In the Miller case, the court specifically mentioned pornography, ruling that most pornography has First Amendment protections because any media that portrays adults engaged in consensual sexual activity would not be considered obscene by community standards based on its popular consumption.

As I've mentioned before, interest in sex, nudity, and viewing people having sex is not remotely new or a product of the modern age. Sculptures or mosaics that would be considered pornographic, even by modern sensibilities, have been found throughout archaeology, whether in the East, West, Africa or elsewhere. One well-known example from the otherwise conservative Hindu culture is the *Kama Sutra*. *Kama Sutra* is an Indian tome famous for its sexually explicit content (Burton, 1883).

The modern concept of pornography is likely a product of Victorian England (Sigel, 2002). During this very proper period of British history, England experienced a clear dichotomy between ideal moral behavior, which emphasized a kind of chasteness and moderation, and the often prurient interests of real people. But because of the moral standards of the day, legal efforts began to evolve to restrict people's access to pornography, presumably for their moral good.

Not surprisingly, photography and, later, moving pictures expanded the availability of pornography. No sooner was such technology available than it was applied toward porn! Initially most porn produced in this way was amateur, however, and distributing it commercially was forbidden. It wasn't legal to own porn in the United States in the early 20th century. But underground pornography proved to be remarkably popular.

Legally, things began to change in the United States by the mid-20th century. People began to bring First Amendment cases to the Supreme Court of the United States (SCOTUS). Of course, the First Amendment protected our ability to speak, even to say unpopular things, but did it protect our ability to consume smut? For the most part, SCOTUS ruled, it did. At first SCOTUS ruled that nude images were protected, but pornography involving explicit sex could still be censored. However, by the 1970s, even this began to change. After the film *Deep Throat* was released in 1972, New York's mayor ordered the theater where it was being shown closed down. The police also arrested one of the actors in the film, Harry Reems. Reems was initially convicted, but his conviction was overturned on appeal. Finally, under the *Miller v. California* ruling, films involving explicit sex were given First Amendment protections. Porn could now come out of the shadows and into living rooms. For a brief moment, porn producers even began to consider that pornography could be artistic. Such art-porn, of course, never really happened despite a few porn films with artistic pretentions.

By the 1980s, porn availability saw a considerable increase through the distribution of VHS tapes. With VHS, porn could be viewed in the home, not just in specialized theaters. This widespread availability of porn naturally alarmed antiporn crusaders, both social and religious conservatives, as well as feminists concerned about violence toward women. These groups were an unusual alliance, coming from the right and left sides of the political spectrum, but they came together in arguing for greater restrictions on pornography for society. Their concerns undoubtedly lead to President Ronald Reagan forming the Meese Commission to investigate the impact of pornography.

The Meese Commission

Regarding government efforts to investigate porn, we mostly hear about the somewhat infamous Meese Commission. However, in fact, two national commissions, one in the early 1970s and one in the early 1980s, attempted to provide the public with more definitive answers regarding the link between pornography exposure and negative outcomes. However, they came to very differing conclusions. The first, in 1970, found that consumption of pornography did not have any clear adverse effects. Naturally, this outcome was not what the antiporn movement had hoped for. When you don't get the government report you want, call for another one!

In the mid-1980s, President Reagan commissioned another government inquiry into the effects of pornography. This second effort has been called the Meese Commission, named after then Attorney General Edwin Meese. The thing about government commissions (just like APA and AAP councils and task forces, it seems) is you can often get the result you want by stacking the commission with people who have clear, a priori, hardline views one way or another. This is precisely what many felt had happened with the Meese Commission, which included such antipornography crusaders as Father Bruce Ritter (who later was involved in alleged sexual activity with male residents of a Christian youth shelter) and James Dobson of Focus on the Family (Wilcox, 1987). Thus, the Meese Commission was controversial before it even released its results owing to the perception the Commission was a rubber stamp for antiporn crusading (Hertzberg, 1986). Predictably, the Meese Commission concluded that pornography was associated with a host of dramatic negative outcomes (Attorney General's Commission on Pornography, 1986). According to the report, viewing pornography changes perceptions of "typical" sexual behavior, trivializes rape, promotes rape myths, and directly leads to male aggression toward women. Though the Meese Commission acknowledged that these effects were particularly prevalent for violent porn, these conclusions were generalized to include all pornographic material. The Commission clearly came out in support of greater restrictions to pornography access. However, it is worth noting that two members of the Commission, Becker and Levine, explicitly came out against the overall findings of the Commission (Linsey, 1998).

The Meese Commission was also controversial among academics who studied the impact of pornography. Some (e.g., Page, 1990) were supportive of the Meese Commission's findings; others were not so sure. For example, Linz, Donnerstein, and Penrod (1987) questioned whether viewing typical pornography could lead to sexualized violence, one of the findings of the Meese Commission. Linz et al. (1987) suggested that the Meese Commission had failed to clearly differentiate between nonviolent and violent porn. Further, as noted by Palys (1986), nonviolent pornography tends to depict few acts of sexualized aggression, but rather depicts egalitarian sexual relationships between males and females. Violent pornography, by contrast, is comparatively rare.

If the intent of the Meese Commission was to reduce pornography consumption, it obviously did not succeed. Some convenience stores did remove pornographic magazines from their shelves, but little else was done to stop the popularity of porn. By contrast, the Meese Commission itself has largely come to represent the ham-fisted way moral crusaders will sometimes try to make public health claims to support their moral agendas.

By the 1990s, attention shifted to the Internet. Internet porn raised all new concerns as porn became even easier to access by anyone, anytime, often for free. Even children might be able to access hard-core pornography. Until the advent of social media, pornography consumption quickly became the most popular activity on the Internet.

Out of concern about children accessing all this porn, the U.S. Congress tried to place restrictions on Internet porn. Their first effort in 1996, the Communications Decency Act, criminalized websites that did not adequately restrict pornography access to minors. This effort makes sense on the surface, of course. However, in 1997, SCOTUS decided that this act was too vague and too restrictive for adults. The Child Online Protection Act of 1998, which required commercial distributors of harmful material to restrict access to minors, was also struck down as unconstitutional by the Supreme Court. SCOTUS had particular concerns that regulating pornography access to minors, while understandable, would also inadvertently restrict adults' access to porn. For instance, some websites required a credit-card swipe to prove age, even if the pornography was legal. But some adults might not want their names to be associated with pornography use. Thus, asking them to swipe a credit card could inadvertently prevent them from having free and easy access to material they are constitutionally protected to having access to. Responding to these constitutional challenges in 2000, Congress enacted a watered down version of the Child Online Protection Act, retitled the Child Internet Protection Act (CIPA), which mandated that schools and libraries install software to block the viewing of pornographic Internet sites. No mandatory blocking is included on home computers, and adult library patrons could ask that blockers be removed. Why anyone would want to view porn in a public library is anyone's guess. Visitors to pornographic websites are required to state that they are of legal age but, by and large, they are taken at their word.

DOES PORNOGRAPHY INFLUENCE VIOLENCE TOWARD WOMEN?

Much of the debate over pornography's effects concerns how pornography may influence men's attitudes toward women, possibly resulting in increased violence toward women. Despite that most pornography is nonviolent (Palys, 1986), it's not hard to understand why this might be. Historically, porn audiences have been male dominated (although some recent data suggests more women are consuming porn), and pornographic material has emphasized male sexual fantasies. In such material, actresses can seem like mere objects of male sexual desire. Thus, it is not hard to see that people may worry that men viewing such material may come to view real-life women the same way. Again, such concerns assume an easy transportation of beliefs and behavior from media to real life.

Scientific examination of the issue of porn's influence on violence toward women really began in the 1970s and 1980s at the height of society's concerns, when pornography began to greatly expand. Such studies ran into one obvious problem: We might be particularly concerned about the exposure to porn among children. After all, childhood and adolescence are the most formative years when it comes to sexuality. But of course no experimental studies with younger populations can be conducted, as they would be not only unethical but illegal! So we've had to rely on experimental studies of college students as well as correlational survey studies of younger populations. As far as survey responses go, there's another obvious problem: Not everyone may be willing to be honest about porn consumption. Also, the very sensitive nature of the topic may result in more "mischievous responding," in which people do not take the survey seriously and give ridiculous responses that can result in false correlations. Thus, this is a particularly tricky issue to investigate, even for media psychology.

As with most areas of media psychology, the results obtained from the studies out there are difficult to use to make definitive conclusions. Results vary from study to study, as the interpretation of results vary from one scholar to the next. Some scholars certainly feel that pornography, whether violent or nonviolent, can be linked to violence toward women (Malamuth & Ceniti, 1986), whereas others feel that there are little substantial effects (Fisher & Grenier, 1994), or even that pornography may be responsible for an unprecedented decline in rape over the past few decades (D'Amato, 2006).

Thus, it is probably safest to say that, as with most other areas of media psychology, evidence for links between pornography and assaultive behavior toward women is inconsistent at best (Dwyer, 2008; Segal, 1994). As with other areas of media psychology, researchers have tried to make sense of competing research results by performing meta-analyses (e.g., Allen, D'Allesio, & Emmers-Sommer, 2000; Gunter, 2002; Hald, Malamuth, & Yuen, 2010; Oddone-Paolucci, Genuis, & Violato, 2000). However, aside from the general observation that violent pornography may have more negative effects than nonviolent porn, even the meta-analyses don't agree on whether the effects of pornography on male attitudes and violence toward women are consistent or of practical significance.

It's also clear that the way the research itself is conducted can influence outcomes. For instance, Malamuth and Ceniti (1986) studied male college students who self-reported likelihood of rape. The experiment included 42 subjects who were exposed to violent pornography, nonviolent pornography, or nonpornographic material. Participants were studied over a 4-week period and were exposed to the media 10 separate times. They were then administered a questionnaire testing anger toward females, a desire to hurt females, and rape proclivity. This study is curious for its particular disconnect between the abstract and conclusions of the study, and the actual results. For instance, the authors in the study abstract suggest that their results supported the hypothesis that pornography viewing could increase male proclivity toward rape, yet their actual results were nonsignificant. In fact, neither violent nor nonviolent pornography viewed over time increased men's anger toward women or willingness to rape them. This study demonstrates why it is important to read not only the abstract of a study but the results, and to understand that not all studies truly reveal what they claim to. As with many areas, do not assume that because you read something, it is therefore true!

Another example of a classic pornography study comes from Linz, Donnerstein, and Penrod (1988). They exposed 156 college males to either an R-rated "slasher" movie with sexualized violence, a sexy R-rated movie without violence, a nonviolent pornographic movie, or no movie at all. The college men then their anxiety, depression, and sympathy toward a rape victim. Those who watched the violent R-rated movie reported being less anxious and depressed. Results indicated that exposure to sexuality in movies didn't impact sympathy toward a rape victim, but exposure to violence had a small but significant impact on decreased sympathy toward a rape victim. They concluded that sexually violent movies might lead to acceptance of rape myths.

229

As an example from more skeptical scholars, Fisher and Grenier (1994) randomly exposed male college students to violent pornography, including scenes in which the women involved appeared to either enjoy or try to avoid the sex act in question, nonviolent pornography, and neutral media. The participants then filled out responses related to acceptance of rape myths, attitudes toward women, and overall acceptance of violence as a means of solving problems. The authors in this study concluded that none of the pornography conditions influenced the men's attitudes toward women or rape and that pornography research may, in fact, be difficult to replicate. A second study by one of the authors (Barak & Fisher, 1997) came to a similar conclusion.

These experimental studies are only a few examples, of course, from a much larger pool of studies. But they are pretty typical of what is out there. Again, a fairly common pattern emerges as with many areas of media effects. Studies by scholars who believe in effects tend to produce small but statistically significant results. Studies by more skeptical scholars have difficulty replicating those effects. The studies depend heavily on college students who may be able to figure out what they are supposed to do given the rather obvious nature of the study. The degree to which the "aggression" measures used in the studies actually inform us much about real-life violence toward women is unclear. Thus, some scholars have been quite critical in concluding that these studies are, overall, not very effective in informing us about violence toward women at all (Mould, 1988).

CORRELATIONAL STUDIES OF PORNOGRAPHY EFFECTS

It has obviously been difficult to construct good experimental data to inform us about pornography's effects. Experiments have, generally, been very artificial, both in the ways male participants are asked to consume porn and in the types of outcome measures employed. Effects have been small and inconsistent. And, given the obvious nature of many of the experiments, the small effect seen in some studies may have been the result of participants guessing what they were supposed to do. Further, most studies didn't involve researcher blinding, allowing researcher expectancy effects to also influence results. But perhaps the biggest inherent weaknesses were simply that, if we are really interested in violence toward women, it is both unethical and illegal to directly examine anything even remotely approximate to such behaviors in the lab.

With correlational research, such as with using surveys, we could potentially ask about more serious behaviors such as violence toward women. Thus, while correlational research can't be used to determine causality, at least we can use it to examine whether associations exist between pornography consumption and violence toward women.

But correlational research also comes with weaknesses. First, on surveys, even anonymous ones, many people lie. As discussed earlier in the book, some people may engage in mischievous responding, exaggerating outrageous negative behaviors to get a few laughs. Such mischievous responding has now been found to cause spurious correlations in other areas of research, and of course the same might apply to pornography research. Unfortunately, very few correlational studies examine for mischievous responding. On the other hand, many people may be quite reluctant to honestly report their pornography consumption, not to mention violent behaviors toward women, given the obvious social and/or legal pressures condemning such behaviors. Questionnaires that examine sexist attitudes or rape acceptance likewise tend to have obvious "right" answers, so statistical analyses may need to reply on very little variance based on flawed answers. Put simply, survey correlational data also must be taken with a serious grain of salt!

That having been said, results of correlational studies are perhaps even more varied than are experimental studies. Correlational studies do not agree on whether pornography consumption is associated with increased violence toward women, decreased violence toward women, or little effect at all. Survey results appear to vary depending on who is asked, how they are asked, or even which scholars are doing the asking! For instance, Garos, Beggan, Kluck, and Easton (2004) found that porn consumption was associated with less hostility toward women but was correlated with greater *benevolent sexism,* which tends to suggest that women are morally superior to men and need to be protected by men. By contrast, McKee (2007) found no evidence at all for a relationship between pornography consumption and hostility toward women.

Other studies have suggested that pornography consumption may be correlated with violence toward women (Malamuth, Addison, & Koss, 2000; Vega & Malamuth, 2007), although these studies relied mainly on college students. Again, given the social desirability and mischievous responding issues, it's not clear how these studies apply to real life (that goes for studies on both sides of the evidence, of course). Some studies have sought to answer whether sex offenders consumed pornography earlier or more often than nonoffenders. Some studies suggest that sex offenders have generally consumed pornography later and less often than nonoffenders (Becker & Stein, 1991; Goldstein & Kant, 1973; Kendall, 2006; Nutter & Kearns, 1993; Walker, 1970). However, once again, these studies are basically dependent upon self-report. Kingston, Federoff, Firestone, Curry, & Bradford (2008) studied child molesters and the influence of pornography on risk for recidivism. Their results revealed that use of pornography was not a significant predictor of recidivism for crime, in general, or for sex offenses, specifically. They did find, however, that exposure to pornography was associated with recidivism for nonsexual assault; these associations, however, were very weak. The authors concluded that there was little support for an influence of pornography on risk of sex offenders reoffending.

One issue of significant contention is whether pornography consumption in society correlates with rape rates and, if so, in which direction? One of the first studies to attempt to examine this, in the heyday of antiporn fear, was Baron and Straus (1984). The authors examined whether subscriptions to pornographic magazines correlated with rape rates in the United States and found a moderate correlation between these variables. So porn consumption and rape are correlated in society? Although correlational, this could be important data.

Then, a contemporary study by Scott (1985) found that only soft-core porn consumption (not involving explicit penetration) but not hard-core porn consumption (involving penetration) was associated with rape rates. This is a bit of a surprising finding, as we'd expect harder pornography to be associated with rape to a greater degree than softer pornography. Perhaps more curiously, circulation rates of neutral magazines (e.g., *Field and Stream*) also correlated with rape rates. This suggests that the observed correlation between pornography and rape rates in the 1970s and 1980s was an ecological fallacy. That is to say, an observed correlation between two variables in the real world is simply due to chance, not any causal relationship. That's why we have to be careful of correlational data!

More recently, both in the United States and other countries, data suggest that pornography consumption has been associated with decreased rape rates. These inverse correlations between the liberalization of porn and declining rape rates have been found for Denmark (Ben-Veniste, 1971; Kutchinsky, 1973), Japan (Abramson & Hayashi, 1984; Diamond & Uchiyama, 1999), Germany and Sweden (Kutchinsky, 1991), and the United States (Ferguson & Hartley, 2009). It is important to note, for instance, that rape rates in the United States today are at their lowest levels since 1960 (Bureau of Justice Statistics, 2006). Thus, the Internet explosion in pornography did not lead to an epidemic of violence toward women. However, it is also premature to say that pornography *caused* this massive decline in sexual violence that, we must remember, occurred while crime in general has been decreasing. Ecological fallacies are always a possibility!

OTHER OUTCOMES

Given the seriousness of violence toward women as an issue, it's not surprising that this discussion of pornography effects has overshadowed much else. But whether or not pornography influences violence toward women, it remains possible that pornography may influence other areas of our lives, such as the quality of our relationships, our attitudes toward sex, or other outcomes. Psychologist Phil Zimbardo has blamed pornography (and video games) for a general demise in men's economic and relational fortunes (Zimbardo & Duncan, 2012). Similar concerns are sometimes expressed in more scholarly works as well (e.g., Bloom & Hagedorn, 2015).

The reality is probably a bit less dramatic than that (but discussing subtle idiosyncratic effects is not a good way to sell books!). One thing that appears clear is that, perhaps owing to the Internet "Golden Age of Porn," porn use is increasing among both young men and women, and such use has lost much of its stigma (Willoughby, Carroll, Nelson, & Padilla-Walker, 2014).

First, let's look at research regarding how pornography consumption may influence our sexual and romantic relationships. As usual, the story is complex. One study from Croatia (Štulhofer, Buško, & Landripet, 2010) found small negative associations between consuming paraphilic pornography (S&M, bondage, bestiality, and violent porn) and decreased sexual satisfaction, but viewing mainstream pornography did not correlate with sexual satisfaction or sexual intimacy. A recent experimental study (Staley & Prause, 2013) suggested that viewing pornography, either alone or with a partner, increased excitement and desire to be close to one's romantic partner, but also brought on anxiety and guilt.

Clearer threats to relationship satisfaction due to pornography use appear when partners have different expectations about pornography use, and one partner's use of pornography involves deception (Zitzman & Butler, 2009). Men and women have a variety of expectations for what pornography use would mean in the context of a romantic relationship, whether it is acceptable or not (Olmstead, Negash, Pasley, & Fincham, 2013). When those expectations don't match well, and porn use is deceptive, this can result in damaged trust and intimacy and the view by the aggrieved partner that porn use is a kind of infidelity. Not surprisingly, research also reveals that problematic use of pornography (what is sometimes loosely called "porn addiction") is particularly damaging to relationship quality (Stewart & Szymanski, 2012). By contrast, honesty and mutual use of pornography predicted higher relationship quality among young women (Resch & Alderson, 2014).

There appear to be small correlations between pornography use and sexual experience as well. For instance, in one study of Swedish high school students, having more positive perceptions of pornography correlated with greater experience with sexual behaviors (Mattebo, Tydén, Häggström-Nordin, Nilsson, & Larsson, 2014). Viewing pornography, among teens, is also associated with beliefs that people tend to have more sex in real life and greater openness to a variety of sexual behaviors (Weber, Quiring, & Daschmann, 2012). Here again, it's difficult to apply causal conclusions to these data. It is reasonable to suggest that youth who are more sexually liberal may simply be more open to consuming pornography, as well as a variety of other sexual acts. As Bale (2011) recently observed, public health discussions of pornography are too often unidimensional and miss the nuances in both potential positive and negative influences of pornography.

Put simply, if pornography had considerable influences on our behavior that were definitively negative, the "Golden Age of Porn" that began with the Internet age should have ushered in considerable problems and chaos. It clearly did not and, if anything, aside from a general liberalizing trend regarding sex, things got better rather than worse on most issues regarding women's health and sexual health. This does not rule out the possibility that pornography may not have some specific negative effects on some specific users, particularly those prone toward problematic use. However, just as with most areas of media effects, the data on pornography suggests it is time that we move away from general discussions of frightening global effects to more nuanced discussions about how specific types of media, or pornography in this case, may interact with specific users' personalities and motivations that may vary widely from one individual to the next and in ways that are subtle and difficult to predict.

REFERENCES

Abramson, P., & Hayashi, H. (1984). Pornography in Japan: Cross-cultural and theoretical considerations. In N. Malamuth & E. Donnerstein (Eds.), *Pornography and sexual aggression.* Orlando, FL: Academic Press.

Allen, M., D'Alessio, D., & Emmers-Sommer, T. (2000). Reactions of criminal sexual offenders to pornography: A meta-analytic summary. In M. Roloff (Ed.), *Communication yearbook 22.* Thousand Oaks, CA: Sage.

Attorney General's Commission on Pornography. (1986). *Final report.* Washington, DC: Author.

Bale, C. (2011). Raunch or romance? Framing and interpreting the relationship between sexualized culture and young people's sexual health. *Sex Education, 11*(3), 303–313. doi:10.1080/14681811.2011.590088

Barak, A., & Fisher, W. A. (1997). Effects of interactive computer erotica on men's attitudes and behavior toward women: An experimental study. *Computers in Human Behavior, 13*(3), 353–369. doi:10.1016/S0747-5632(97)00014-9

Baron, L., & Straus, M. (1984). Sexual stratification, pornography, and rape in the United States. In N. M. Malamuth & E. Donnerstein (Eds.), *Pornography and sexual aggression.* New York, NY: Academic Press.

Becker, J., & Stein, R. (1991). Is sexual erotica associated with sexual deviance in adolescent males? *International Journal of Law and Psychiatry, 14,* 85–95.

Ben-Veniste, R. (1971). Pornography and sex crime: The Danish experience. *Technical reports of the Commission on Obscenity and Pornography* (Vol. 7). Washington, DC: U.S. Government Printing Office.

Bloom, Z. D., & Hagedorn, W. B. (2015). Male adolescents and contemporary pornography: Implications for marriage and family counselors. *Family Journal, 23*(1), 82–89. doi:10.1177/1066480714555672

Bureau of Justice Statistics. (2006). *National Crime Victimization Survey violent crime trends 1973–2005.* Retrived March 5, 2009, from http://www.ojp.usdoj.gov/bjs/glance/tables/viortrdtab.htm

Burton, R. (1883, translation). *Kama sutra.* Retrieved January 8, 2009, from http://www.indohistory.com/kamasutra.html

D'Amato, A. (2006). Porn up, rape down. *Public Law and Legal Theory Research Paper Series.* Retrieved March 3, 2009, from http://anthonydamato.law.northwestern.edu/Adobefiles/porn.pdf

Diamond, M., & Uchiyama, A. (1999). Pornography, rape and sex crimes in Japan. *International Journal of Law and Psychiatry, 22,* 1–22.

Dwyer, S. (2008). Pornography. In P. Livingstone & C. Plantinga (Eds.), *The Routledge companion to philosophy and film.* New York, NY: Routledge.

Ferguson, C. J., & Hartley, R. D. (2009). The pleasure is momentary . . . the expense damnable? The influence of pornography on rape and sexual assault. *Aggression and Violent Behavior, 14*(5), 323–329.

Fisher, W., & Grenier, G. (1994). Violent pornography, antiwoman thoughts and antiwoman acts: In search of reliable effects. *Journal of Sex Research, 31,* 23–38.

Garos, S., Beggan, J., Kluck, A., & Easton, A. (2004). Sexism and pornography use: Toward explaining past (null) results. *Journal of Psychology and Human Sexuality, 16,* 69–96.

Gentry, C. S. (1991). Pornography and rape: An empirical analysis. *Deviant Behavior, 12,* 277–288.

Goldstein, M. J., & Kant, H. S. (1973). *Pornography and sexual deviance: A report of the legal and behavioral institute.* Berkeley, CA: University of California Press.

Gunter, G. (2002). *Media sex: What are the issues?* Mahwah, NJ: Lawrence Erlbaum.

Hald, G. M., Malamuth, N. M., & Yuen, C. (2010). Pornography and attitudes supporting violence against women: Revisiting the relationship in nonexperimental studies. *Aggressive Behavior, 36*(1), 14–20. doi:10.1002/ab.20328

Hertzberg, H. (1986). Ed Meese and his pornography commission. *New Republic, 14*, 21–24.

Kendall, T. (2006). *Pornography rape and the internet.* Paper presented at the Law and Economics Seminar, Clemson University, Clemson, SC.

Kingston, D., Federoff, P., Firestone, P., Curry, S., & Bradford, J. (2008). Pornography use and sexual aggression: The impact of frequency and type of pornography use on recidivism among sexual offenders. *Aggressive Behavior, 34*, 1–11.

Kutchinsky, B. (1973). The effect of easy availability of pornography on the incidence of sex crimes: The Danish experience. *Journal of Social Issues, 29*, 163–181.

Kutchinsky, B. (1991). Pornography and rape: Theory and practice? Evidence from crime data in four countries where pornography is easily available. *International Journal of Law and Psychiatry, 14*, 47–64.

Linsey, W. (1998). The case against censorship of pornography. In R. Baird & S. Rosenbaum (Eds.), *Pornography: Private right or public menace.* Amherst, NY: Prometheus Books.

Linz, D., Donnerstein, E., & Penrod, S. (1987). The findings and recommendations of the Attorney General's Commission on Pornography: Do the psychological "facts" fit the political fury? *American Psychologist, 42*, 946–953.

Linz, D., Donnerstein, E., & Penrod, S. (1988). Effects of long-term exposure to violent and sexually degrading depictions of women. *Journal of Personality and Social Psychology, 55*, 758–768.

Malamuth, N., Addison, T., & Koss, M. (2000). Pornography and sexual aggression: Are there reliable effects and how might we understand them? *Annual Review of Sex Research, 11*, 26–91.

Malamuth, N., & Ceniti, J. (1986). Repeated exposure to violent and nonviolent pornography: Likelihood of raping ratings and laboratory aggression against women. *Aggressive Behavior, 12*, 129–137.

Mattebo, M., Tydén, T., Häggström-Nordin, E., Nilsson, K. W., & Larsson, M. (2014). Pornography and sexual experiences among high school students in Sweden. *Journal of Developmental and Behavioral Pediatrics, 35*(3), 179–188. doi:10.1097/DBP.0000000000000034

McKee, A. (2007). The relationship between attitudes towards women, consumption of pornography, and other demographic variables in a survey of 1,023 consumers of pornography. *International Journal of Sexual Health, 19,* 31–45.

Miller v. California, 413 U.S. 15 (1973).

Mould, D. (1988). A critical analysis of resent research of violent erotica. *Journal of Sex Research, 24,* 326–340.

Nutter, D., & Kearns, M. (1993). Patterns of exposure to sexually explicit material among sex offenders, child molesters, and controls. *Journal of Sex and Marital Therapy, 19,* 77–85.

Odone-Paolucci, E., Genuis, M., & Violato, C. (2000). A meta-analysis of the published research on the effects of pornography. In C. Violato, E. Oddone-Paolucci, & M. Genuis (Eds.), *The changing family and child development.* Aldershot, UK: Ashgate Publishing.

Olmstead, S. B., Negash, S., Pasley, K., & Fincham, F. D. (2013). Emerging adults' expectations for pornography use in the context of future committed romantic relationships: A qualitative study. *Archives of Sexual Behavior, 42*(4), 625–635. doi:10.1007/s10508-012-9986-7

Page, S. (1990). The turnaround on pornography research: Some implications for psychology and women. *Canadian Psychologist, 31,* 359–367.

Palys, T. (1986). Testing the common wisdom: The social content of video pornography. *Canadian Psychology, 27,* 22–35.

Reno v. American Civil Liberties Union, 521 U.S. 844 (1997).

Resch, M. N., & Alderson, K. G. (2014). Female partners of men who use pornography: Are honesty and mutual use associated with relationship satisfaction? *Journal of Sex & Marital Therapy, 40*(5), 410–424. doi:10.1080/0092623X.2012.751077

Roth v. United States, 354 U.S. 476 (1957).

Scott, J. (1985). *Violence and erotic material: The relationship between adult entertainment and rape.* Paper presented at the annual meeting for the American Academy for the Advancement of Science, Los Angeles, CA.

Segal, L. (1994). False promises—Anti-pornography feminism. In M. Evans (Ed.), *The woman question* (2nd ed.). Thousand Oaks, CA: Sage.

Sigel, L. (2002). *Governing pleasures: Pornography and social change in England, 1815–1914*. Piscataway, NJ: Rutgers University Press.

Staley, C., & Prause, N. (2013). Erotica viewing effects on intimate relationships and self/partner evaluations. *Archives of Sexual Behavior, 42*(4), 615–624. doi:10.1007/s10508-012-0034-4

Stewart, D. N., & Szymanski, D. M. (2012). Young adult women's reports of their male romantic partner's pornography use as a correlate of their self-esteem, relationship quality, and sexual satisfaction. *Sex Roles, 67*(5–6), 257–271. doi:10.1007/s11199-012-0164-0

Štulhofer, A., Buško, V., & Landripet, I. (2010). Pornography, sexual socialization, and satisfaction among young men. *Archives of Sexual Behavior, 39*(1), 168–178. doi:10.1007/s10508-008-9387-0

Vega, V., & Malamuth, N. (2007). Predicting sexual aggression: The role of pornography in the context of general and specific risk factors. *Aggressive Behavior, 33*, 1–14.

Walker, C. E. (1970). *Erotic stimuli and the aggressive sexual offender*. Technical report (Vol. 7). Washington, DC: U.S. Commission on Obscenity and Pornography.

Weber, M., Quiring, O., & Daschmann, G. (2012). Peers, parents and pornography: Exploring adolescents' exposure to sexually explicit material and its developmental correlates. *Sexuality & Culture: An Interdisciplinary Quarterly, 16*(4), 408–427. doi:10.1007/s12119-012-9132-7

Wilcox, B. L. (1987). Pornography, social science, and politics: When research and ideology collide. *American Psychologist, 42*, 941–943.

Willoughby, B. J., Carroll, J. S., Nelson, L. J., & Padilla-Walker, L. M. (2014). Associations between relational sexual behaviour, pornography use, and pornography acceptance among US college students. *Culture, Health & Sexuality, 16*(9), 1052–1069. doi:10.1080/13691058.2014.927075

Zimbardo, P. G., & Duncan, N. (2012). *The demise of guys: Why boys are struggling and what we can do about it*. New York, NY: TED Conferences.

Zitzman, S. T., & Butler, M. H. (2009). Wives' experience of husbands' pornography use and concomitant deception as an attachment threat in the adult pair-bond relationship. *Sexual Addiction & Compulsivity, 16*(3), 210–240. doi:10.1080/10720160903202679

14

Social Media

One of the most curious aspects of contemporary life is that so much of it can be conducted not in real life but rather in virtual worlds through interconnected computer systems. Today it is possible to order groceries or have food delivered, maintain friendships, debate politics, science, or religion, or meet and date potential romantic partners entirely on the web (one would imagine the marriage partners would eventually meet in real life but perhaps even this is only a recommendation!). This change in society is, in many ways, a real dramatic shift. Consider, in the previous chapter, what the Internet did to pornography, vastly increasing our exposure to it and essentially bringing it out into the sun. It's not hard to imagine that the Internet revolution that began in the 1990s must have revolutionized many other aspects of our society. But does this come at a price? In interacting so often in virtual space, have we lost something fundamentally valuable about the way we used to communicate in real space? Does all this time online fundamentally rewire our brains as some claim, making us narcissists or depressed? What concerns do we have or should we have regarding privacy in this new show-everything age?

As with most issues with media psychology, the travails of social media involve separating the hype from the truth. We've long since seen that all new media go through periods of moral panic. But this does not rule out the potential for some real concerns either. One of the curious things about social media is that, unlike some other previous forms of feared media such as rock music, rap, comic books, or video games, social media has been relatively effectively embraced even by older generations. For instance, data suggests that half of adults over 65 are online, and at least a third regularly use social media sites such as Facebook or Twitter (Leist, 2013). That's lower than the rate for younger people, of course, but nonetheless a significant number of older adults have become involved in social media, higher numbers of older adults than you typically find playing games like *Grand Theft Auto 5* or listening to gangsta rap. This leads me to posit two corollaries regarding the duration and intensity of moral panics surrounding new technology and media:

1. The degree and intensity of moral panics can be predicted by the degree to which they tap into existing moral concerns, such as sex, violence, or privacy.
2. The degree and intensity of moral panics are mitigated by the extent to which older adults embrace the new technology.

As we've discussed in previous chapters, moral panics tend to be driven in large part by the concerns of older generations rather than younger (Przybylski, 2014), and fears of new media are often reduced by direct exposure (Ivory & Kalyanaraman, 2009). Thus, older adults embracing social media may have done much to stifle some of the fears of social media. After all, following mass shootings, few people call for massive crackdowns on social media (despite that social media is well known to be involved in the recruitment of terrorists, for instance), but people are quick to blame video games. Moral panics are fundamentally about finding blame in media that older adults don't value, and many older adults do value social media!

Concerns about social media, though, tend to fall into two broad categories. First, there are privacy concerns. Are social media companies digging for information on us and then using that information to boost their own profits, potentially at our expense? What is called *data mining* is a big thing now in business, such as using our previous shopping habits to direct us toward more products we might be inclined to buy. See how Amazon, for instance, helpfully suggests lots of new items based on your previous buying history. But people are also sharing more information via social media now than was possible in the premedia past. At the extreme of this is sexting, in which individuals may share explicit photos, some of which then emerge into the public sphere. But we've also entered an age in which every off-hand comment can be immediately scrutinized by a kind of outrage machine, and a single misguided or offensive thought can derail lives or careers.

Second, people do worry about what impact social media has on our communication, socialization, and moods as individuals. Are we being fundamentally rewired, whether positively or negatively, by our interactions with social media? Is social media breeding a generation of narcissists? We first tackle the issues of privacy, then turn to potential impact on individuals.

PRIVACY CONCERNS

Somewhere around 2008, news outlets began to suggest that social media finally managed to outdistance pornography as the number one activity on the web (e.g., Goldsmith, 2008). Social media developed an unsurpassed ability for us to keep in touch with a wide variety of family, friends, and vaguely distant acquaintances we might otherwise forget. It also allows us to communicate almost any thought or interest we have instantly, giving ourselves the illusion that others distinctly care. But this sharing comes with risks, insofar as businesses, governments, hackers, and so on, may have unprecedented access to information that can be used to harm us. Many companies collect personal information on us and then share that information (for money) with other businesses, often without our consent (or consent buried in longer user agreements they know most folks won't read). Social media may also allow us to post private information that could fall into the wrong hands.

Not surprisingly, many people are worried that all this information on the Internet could be used against us. Examples of high-profile hackings that have obtained millions of credit card numbers, or revelations that government organizations such as the National Security Agency have been snooping through Americans' Internet transmissions and phone data, have not helped to assuage people's privacy concerns. Neither has awareness that Internet companies such as Facebook may use online data and behaviors without a user's knowledge, marketing that information to other companies.

As with many issues, privacy concerns appear to be generational. A recent poll by J.D. Power and Associates (see Coldewey, 2013) suggested that younger people are less concerned about privacy violations than are older adults. At the same time, however, younger people take more steps to ensure their privacy than do older adults. Perhaps it is the case that younger people feel more empowered to protect their privacy online (Baek, Kim, & Bae, 2014).

Many scholars (e.g., Chander, 2010) have expressed particular concern for youth living in the "fishbowl" of the Internet, where any indiscretion is enshrined for the rest of their lives. Fostering appropriate privacy concerns in youth is therefore important and appears to be best handled through constructive conversations rather than rule setting (Moscardelli & Divine, 2007). Privacy concern does decrease personal disclosures online, although many factors are involved, including the family and the youth's personality (it will surprise no one that narcissists tend to disclose more online; Liu, Ang, & Lwin, 2013).

The issues are not merely personal disclosures, of course, but also individuals providing dangerous information online. Although online child abuse predation is actually fairly rare, teaching children not to disclose their address or other personal information to strangers online is just as important as the same conversation applied to real life. However, youth are not the only social media users potentially at risk. As any Internet user knows, there are a whole host of phishing and other scams out there, not to mention viruses and Trojan horses.

Sexting

"Fing-fangled" smartphones come with a camera. Mix that with rambunctious, hormone-flooded youth (or adults for that matter, in fairness), and the result is fairly predictable. No longer burdened by clumsy Polaroids or having to have intimate photos developed by some stranger at a photo shop, camera and other digital phones have created an explosion of nude "selfies" (self-taken photos from one's camera phone). This is undoubtedly a technological revolution, not a revolution in naughtiness among youth (previous generations would have sexted too if they only had decent cell phones).

Sexting actually can refer both to sending explicit text messages as well as sending nude or explicit photographs but, with a few exceptions, most of the attention has been on the nude photographs. One interesting case involved a police officer who had been sending sexually explicit messages to his romantic partner on a city-issued phone. His supervisor searched the text messages, and when the police officer found out about this, sued. The case went to the Supreme Court asked whether workers had a reasonable expectation of privacy when sending personal messages on an employer-issued device (Turns out: nope. See Savage, 2010).

Most of the concern, however, surrounds the sending of explicit images. The big issue is that the images can get into the public sphere away from the intended audience (some applications like Snapchat try to prevent this by making images temporary). In 2014 this risk was highlighted when the online data accounts (such as iCloud) of dozens of celebrities, mainly women, were hacked, and private nude images were disseminated into the public. Also at issue is underage teens sexting, where the dissemination of nude teen images potentially violates child pornography laws.

The law has struggled to deal with what to do with teen sexting. Child pornography laws were designed to protect children from adult predators, not necessarily prosecute youthful indiscretions themselves. Here is an example of the law not catching up with technology: In 2009, a number of teens in Pennsylvania were initially threatened with felony child pornography charges after three teenage girls took nude photos of themselves and shared them with several male classmates (see Brunker, 2009). Many people felt that this was an inappropriate use of child pornography laws, however. In this case the teens and prosecutors reached an agreement on minor charges to avoid potential felony convictions, but this case still raised a lot of concerns about misuse of child pornography laws. Most states have since moved to enact newer, more targeted laws that treat sexting among minors as a juvenile "status" offense (a criminal offense, usually minor, applied to anyone under 18 years old) with minor penalties such as counseling, or to decriminalize sexting altogether.

Most studies find that sexting is a fairly common activity, particularly among the young. One early study by the National Campaign to Prevent Teen and Unplanned Pregnancy (2008) found that approximately 20% of teens and 33% of young adults (20–26) had sent or posted nude or seminude images of themselves to others. For sexy messages without photos, the numbers were closer to 39% of teens and 59% of young adults. A study by the University of New Hampshire (Mitchell, Finkelhor, Jones, & Wolak, 2012) found a much lower prevalence rate of 2.5%, although this may have been due to their sample including many youth as young as 10. Another survey that focused on older teens (14–18) again found the number to be closer to 20% (Strassberg, McKinnon, Sustaíta, & Rullo, 2013). In one of my own studies with young Hispanic women, I

246

also found a prevalence rate of sending nude images close to 20% (Ferguson, 2011). With the caveat that this is self-reported data, most of the numbers seem to suggest a prevalence rate for sexting, at least among youth and young adults, of near 20%.

Is sexting "bad"? Well, obviously there are risks of the photos being spread more widely than intended or used against the taker should a relationship turn sour (what is sometimes called *revenge porn*). And for underage individuals there may be some legal repercussions still, although child pornography charges seem to no longer be the norm. Some studies (e.g., Ybarra & Mitchell, 2014) find that sexting correlates with general risk taking and sexual behaviors, although this is probably not terribly surprising. In particular, sexting would be expected to correlate with all manner of sexual behaviors because sexting most typically takes place in the context of sexual relationships. But, if one wants to avoid nude images escaping into the public, sexting is probably not the wisest idea. As with many issues of digital privacy, it is one social media and Internet users will wish to consider carefully before they leap!

The Facebook Mood Study

Many Internet users have a sneaking suspicion (undoubtedly right) that they are being constantly manipulated by various online sites. Things like the news feed in Facebook may be manipulated to produce marketing results desirable to the company. This is something most of us accept; we understand that to get a basically free service such as Facebook, we'll be exposed to some forms of marketing. But what if Facebook manipulated the feed in order to change not just our purchasing behavior but our overall mood, to make us happier or sadder?

This is exactly what happened with one study (Kramer, Guillory, & Hancock, 2014). The study, using a whopping sample of over 600,000 Facebook users, randomly exposed participants to a higher proportion of either positive or negative comments in their news feed. Subsequent posts of these users were then examined for positive or negative words. People exposed to more

247

positive news feeds tended to write more positively in their own posts and vice versa for those exposed to negative words. The authors argued that this was evidence for "emotional contagion"; that by witnessing the moods of others, however subtle, our own moods change as well without our knowing it.

The first major problem of this study, and part of what gained it notoriety, was that the 600,000 participants were never informed they were participating in an experiment that could influence their mood. In their article, the authors (Kramer et al., 2014) note that all Facebook users sign onto a data-use policy that, they argue, effectively gives consent for research. However, most people probably don't read this policy and, if they did, would likely interpret it as Facebook using their general-use data, not subjecting them to mood altering psychological research. Ethically, it is usually incumbent upon the researcher to be sure that proper consent has been obtained, not the participant. However, as an independent company, Facebook is not necessarily required to follow government or professional group-mandated ethics, so long as no laws are broken. Nonetheless, this study tapped into people's preexisting concerns that social media outlets are manipulating them in cruel and unreasonable ways.

The second problem with the study, however, is that the results were never really as dramatic as the authors, and certainly the media hype that followed, would suggest. The study never actually measured people's moods, merely their keystrokes. People might mimic the news feed they were recently exposed to, not because their moods had been altered, but simply because they still remember words they had just read and may be more likely to repeat them.

More important, contrary to the hype, the study's results are so tiny as to have negligible real-world implications. Psychologist John Grohol of PsychCentral published an excellent analysis of this study (2014). Among other things, he notes that the "emotional contagion" claimed by the study amounted to the difference of one word typed differently out of thousands of words typed (for the statistically minded, the effect sizes in Cohen's *d* ranged from .001 to .02). As Grohol notes, for instance, decreasing negative news-feed messages altered people's typed posts by less than 1/15th of a percent. The authors (Kramer et al., 2014) use an old, fallacious argument that even tiny effects can be important when spread out over large populations. Readers should always be wary of this argument, as it is typically applied in defense of otherwise indefensibly small effects. But this interpretation of effect sizes is problematic for two reasons. First, this effect size reflects the change expected in any given individual, not the proportion of the people in a population effected. Second, small effects are highly subject to Type I or "false positive" effects due to researcher mistakes, researcher bias, statistical analyses choices, or even just random chance. When effects are very small, we can't have the same confidence that they are "real," or merely the product of a scholar's well-intentioned wishful thinking. This is one reason readers should always be cautioned that "statistical significance" does not always (or even often) translate into real-life significance.

DOES SOCIAL MEDIA INFLUENCE WELL-BEING?

The Kramer et al. (2014) "emotional contagion" study is particularly interesting as it bridges concerns about whether social media providers intrude on our privacy and whether social media can influence our moods and well-being. In my read of that study, they (inadvertently) provided good evidence of the former but only weak evidence for the latter. Although there is certainly some grumbling by older adults about things such as social media rewiring the brain or distracting people from talking via normal conversations, social media arguably hasn't seen the same kind of moral outrage as, say, violent video games or sex on television. The result is that there's somewhat less research on social media than on some of these other topics.

REFERENCES

Baek, Y. M., Kim, E., & Bae, Y. (2014). My privacy is okay, but theirs is endangered: Why comparative optimism matters in online privacy concerns. *Computers in Human Behavior, 31,* 48–56. doi:10.1016/j.chb.2013.10.010

Brunker, M. (2009). *Sexting surprise: Teens face child porn charges.* NBCNews.com. Retrieved from http://www.nbcnews.com/id/28679588/ns/technology_and_science-tech_and_gadgets/t/sexting-surprise-teens-face-child-porn-charges/#.VLZ9600tH3g

Chander, A. (2010). Youthful indiscretion in an Internet age. In S. Levmore & M. C. Nussbaum (Eds.), *The offensive Internet: Speech, privacy, and reputation* (pp. 124–139). Cambridge, MA: Harvard University Press.

Coldewey, D. (2013). *Young folks less concerned about privacy—But take more countermeasures.* NBCNews.com. Retrieved from http://www.nbcnews.com/tech/internet/young-folks-less-concerned-about-privacy-take-more-countermeasures-f8C11492998

Ferguson, C. J. (2011). Sexting behaviors among young Hispanic women: Incidence and association with other high-risk sexual behaviors. *Psychiatric Quarterly, 82*(3), 239–243.

Goldsmith, B. (2008). Porn passed over as web users become social. *Reuters.* Retrieved from http://www.reuters.com/article/2008/09/16/us-internet-book-life-idUSSP31943720080916

Grohol, J. (2014). Emotional contagion on Facebook? More like bad research methods. *PsychCentral.* Retrieved from http://psychcentral.com/blog/archives/2014/06/23/emotional-contagion-on-facebook-more-like-bad-research-methods

Ivory, J., & Kalyanaraman, S. (2009). Video games make people violent—Well, maybe not that game: Effects of content and person abstraction on perceptions of violent video games' effects and support of censorship. *Communication Reports, 22,* 1–12. doi:10.1080/08934210902798536

Kramer, A., Guillory, J., & Hancock, J. (2014). Experimental evidence of massive-scale emotional contagion through social networks. *Proceedings of the National Academy of Sciences, 111,* 8788–8790.

Leist, A. K. (2013). Social media use of older adults: A mini-review. *Gerontology, 59*(4), 378–384. doi:10.1159/000346818

Liu, C., Ang, R. P., & Lwin, M. O. (2013). Cognitive, personality, and social factors associated with adolescents' online personal information disclosure. *Journal of Adolescence, 36*(4), 629–638. doi:10.1016/j.adolescence.2013.03.016

Mitchell, K. J., Finkelhor, D., Jones, L. M., & Wolak, J. (2012). Prevalence and characteristics of youth sexting: A national study. *Pediatrics, 129*(1), 13–20. doi:10.1542/peds.2011-1730

Moscardelli, D. M., & Divine, R. (2007). Adolescents' concern for privacy when using the Internet: An empirical analysis of predictors and relationships with privacy-protecting behaviors. *Family and Consumer Sciences Research Journal, 35*(3), 232–252. doi:10.1177/1077727X06296622

National Campaign to Prevent Teen and Unplanned Pregnancy. (2008). *Sex and tech: Results from a survey of teens and young adults.* Retrieved from http://thenationalcampaign.org/sites/default/files/resource-primary-download/sex_and_tech_summary.pdf

Przybylski, A. K. (2014). Who believes electronic games cause real world aggression? *Cyberpsychology, Behavior, and Social Networking, 17*(4), 228–234. doi:10.1089/cyber.2013.0245

Savage, D. (2010). Supreme Court rules in favor of California police chief who read employee's texts. *Los Angeles Times.* Retrieved from http://articles.latimes.com/2010/jun/18/nation/la-na-court-worker-texting-20100618

Strassberg, D. S., McKinnon, R. K., Sustaíta, M. A., & Rullo, J. (2013). Sexting by high school students: An exploratory and descriptive study. *Archives of Sexual Behavior, 42*(1), 15–21. doi:10.1007/s10508-012-9969-8

Ybarra, M. L., & Mitchell, K. J. (2014). "Sexting" and its relation to sexual activity and sexual risk behavior in a national survey of adolescents. *Journal of Adolescent Health, 55*(6), 757–764. doi:10.1016/j.jadohealth.2014.07.012

Now What?

rom the preceding chapters we can see that the issue of media effects is complex. Discerning what effects media do or do not have on consumers is made difficult by the emotional investment, political intrusion, questionable researcher practices, and systematic cycles of moral panic that typically greet new media. This is particularly true for media with objectionable content such as sex or violence, although few sources of media are immune to a complex cloud of hyperbole that is often difficult to penetrate to get to the good data. Indeed, one study suggested that even reading the Bible causes aggression in a similar way as violent video games or television were alleged to (Bushman, Ridge, Das, Key, & Busath, 2007). Granted, this study uses much of the same problematic methods as we discussed for video games in Chapter 12. But the point is that there are few areas where politicization have not influenced media psychology.

Of course the same could be said for much of social science, given the sensitivity of many topics pertaining to our lives and behavior. Nonetheless, I view media psychology as being rather at a kind of crossroads. We can keep doing things the way that they have been done for the past 60 years, arguably with limited success, or we could embrace a kind of paradigm change and seek newer and different ways to do things (see Lang, 2013). At this point, I would argue that the data is making it difficult to support the types of "general effects" or "hypodermic needle" models, including most social cognitive models of media effects. Thus, with an eye to the future, I offer a few observations and warnings that may help us to frame media effects theory moving forward.

NEW MEDIA ARE MET WITH EXAGGERATED CLAIMS

By this point, it is clear that new media and new technology are met with historical cycles of exaggerated claims and moral panic. In the early years or even decades after new media or new technology is released, bad information proliferates. Unfortunately much of that bad information has historically come not only from politicians and advocates but also from scholars and professional advocacy groups such as the American Psychological Association and the American Academy of Pediatrics. Of course such claims can often go in both positive and negative directions. We certainly see considerable *warning bias* among scholars warning that new media or technology will create impending doom. But we can also find scholars advocating that new media (often the same new media) can have substantial benefits as well. Generally, both positive and negative effects tend to prove to be ephemeral, at least on a general scale.

Trying to cease this pattern in the future might be akin to stopping the passage of time. It's such an ingrained historical pattern that it would take a considerable cultural shift in social science and the way that social science is incentivized (through grants, news headlines, personal prestige for "saving the children," etc.) that disrupting this pattern may be difficult.

Understanding this pattern may be valuable, and it may be worth reminding the public about this pattern once concerns about new media begin to emerge. Society wants quick answers, of course, but research on new media tends to experience a "decline effect" (e.g., Coyne & de Voogd, 2012)in which societal fears appear to be initially supported by research, but such research proves difficult to replicate in future years. Thus scholars can caution against making extreme links in the early years of a new research field. Conservatism is key.

This also means that the rush to construct theories for why new media may be harmful or beneficial may experience a "wag the dog" effect, that is, be incentivized to support societal concerns (or excitement) particularly when grant money on the topic appears to be flush. Such theories may, in effect, feed on societal fears for their own prominence.

One way to address this would be to encourage research to examine *social science research* itself. In what ways do societal narratives incentivize certain types of theories and research results and disincentivize others? To what degree do researchers' expectations of effects influence research results? Are research results "true" or the product of researcher expectancies? For example, in a recent meta-analysis of video game studies on child and adolescent samples, the practice of citations bias (citing only studies that supported the author's personal views) was correlated with higher effect sizes, indicating that researcher expectancies do, indeed, influence results (Ferguson, in press). To what extent do politicians and advocacy groups meddle in the scientific process? Do research articles supporting societal beliefs about new media get more headlines than null studies?

A *sociology of media research* paradigm could be both rich and critical to our understanding of how media research itself is influenced by societal beliefs and incentives. This may aid us in efforts to promote greater objectivity and transparency in our field than

255

has been the case prior. As of yet, this approach to understanding media psychology has been virtually nonexistent. By and large, we have persisted with the myth that data in media psychology has been objective, despite considerable evidence to the contrary.

MEDIA EFFECTS ARE IDIOSYNCRATIC

Perhaps one of the greatest wrong turns in media psychology was the implicit assumption, implicit through most social cognitive and other "hypodermic" theories, that a given form of media will influence most viewers in more or less the same manner. Such theories may allow for the notion that some are influenced more than others, but there is a general impression that all or at least most users will be influenced, if to varying degrees in the same direction. Thus we get the simplistic notion that, for instance, violent television should increase aggression and nonviolent television should not. In the realm of media violence, for example, see Markey, Males, French, and Markey (2015) for numerous examples of scholars promoting an exaggerated version of "general effects" of media.

Putting it bluntly, far too much time, effort, and money has been spent in trying to force this idea to be true, and this has undoubtedly held back more sophisticated theory in media psychology. This has also resulted in a false dichotomy in which individuals are either characterized as supporting a "general effects" model or suggesting that media have no effects at all. Even "middle ground" might be mischaracterized as a belief in weaker "general effects" rather than stronger "general effects" (i.e., video games might not make mass murderers, but what about bullying?). This approach isn't a real, meaningful middle ground, however.

With a little bit of thought, the notion that all consumers react to media in exactly the same way (if to differing degrees) is remarkably simplistic. In this type of model, a stimulus-response model, the consumer is little more than a widget caught in the machine. Sure, some models may make a bit of noise about personological variables, but they rarely seem crucial to understanding media effects in a meaningful way. Does a particular form of media really influence everyone the same way?

Part of the difficulty in establishing media effects may be that most experiments or correlational studies look for general effects and assume they can be spread across most or all individuals. Thus, arguing against such an approach appears to argue against all media effects. But consider the possibility that null results are the product, not of the absence of media effects, but of the chance that a given form of media may influence different individuals very differently. Thus, the failure is less the concept of media effects but rather how it has been applied as a general effects approach, often in line with moral agendas.

We can see this with anecdotes, which are always poor science of course. But, for instance, some people say that playing violent video games relaxes them, whereas others say that such games agitate them. Traditional media effects theory would argue that the first group are simply wrong. But what if they're not? What if violent video games could increase aggression in some individuals, decrease aggression in others, and have no effect on the rest? In fact, the same could be true for nonviolent video games—which might increase, decrease, or have no effect on various users as well. I sometimes half-joke that shows like *Full House* (a 1990s family show that, in my mind, lacks any artistic value) make me angry because they are so terrible (I do, indeed, get irritated by such shows). In other words, morally valenced content such as violence or sex may be less important than the interaction between various forms of media and individual users. Indeed, even broad categories like "violent television" or "sexy movies" may be meaningless, as true effects may occur at the level of very specific interactions between specific shows, games, and so on, and specific individuals.

Some early work has supported this (Unsworth, Devilly, & Ward, 2007); however, studies of idiosyncratic effects remain few, and they are difficult to design well. This would be a promising avenue for pursuit for new research, and examining this potential might open up considerable new avenues for understanding. Granted, idiosyncratic effects likely make for poor headlines since they would be difficult to tie to moral agendas. But examining them may very well be informative for media psychology.

BROAD CATEGORIES OF MEDIA DON'T MAKE MUCH SENSE

As I alluded to in the previous section, we likely need to get away from the tendency to speak to broad categories of media like "thin-ideal television" or "violent video game," as if these terms have conceptual utility. For instance, the concept of "violent video game" is so broad that it actually includes almost all video games from *Pac Man* to *Grand Theft Auto 5* (see, for instance, Rushton, 2013). It is foolish to conceptualize *Gone with the Wind*, *Porkey's*, and *50 Shades of Grey* together as "sexy movies," yet this is effectively what we often do in media psychology. This has a kind of lazy simplicity that is likely effective in the context of moral panic but, I'd argue, means very little scientifically.

In other words, with what we've been thinking of as broad categories, such as "violent movie," different individual examples may, in fact, exhibit different traits. For instance, both the movies *Hostel* and *Schindler's List* are violent movies, but to suggest that these would have a similar impact on people emotionally is absurd. The problem, once again, is that within media psychology we have had a tendency to focus on broad categories of emotionally or morally laden media, such as "violent" or "sexy" media, in an incredibly simplistic way. Too often we forget that any one single example of media has multiple facets to it that interact with each other and have differing emotional influences on consumers. And, in keeping with the earlier point about idiosyncratic effects, differing individuals may respond to different facets of a given media source.

For instance, technically speaking, religious texts such as the Bible or the *Ramayana* are "violent literature." Yet no one would reasonably compare them to a Stephen King novel or *The Red Badge of Courage*, also examples of "violent media." But individuals also respond very differently to a text such as the Bible. Some focus more on the passages related to God's love, others on guidelines for improving oneself, still others passages that might be interpreted as condemnation of others who are different. No one could reasonably expect that the Bible can be meaningfully defined by belonging to a category "violent media," yet this is just what we do throughout media psychology at present. But a given form of media, like the Bible, is typically complex, having many facets, the interaction among which is undoubtedly more critical than a reductionist focus on any one.

EFFECTS ARE USER DRIVEN RATHER THAN CONTENT DRIVEN

As discussed in Chapter 2, a number of limited effects theories such as Uses and Gratifications Theory (UGT) and Self-Determination Theory (SDT) have been proposed to examine how individuals actively select media in order to attain certain outcomes or emotional states. Unfortunately, research emanating from these theories has traditionally been overshadowed by hypodermic needle models.

Many societal and scholarly discussions treat media as something that is *done to* consumers, with consumers as hapless victims. Thus we hear about children or adults being "bombarded" or "exposed to" sundry salacious media forms as if they were strapped to their chairs and helpless to involve themselves in the situation. But we know that individuals are active in selecting and processing their own media experiences (Rentfrow, Goldberg, & Levitin, 2011). How can we incorporate this into our understanding of media psychology?

As I noted earlier, most hypodermic needle approaches focus on a basic stimulus-response type model (or SR). They might sometimes include some window dressing of personological or situation variables, but these are rarely explained in detail, and the models generally remain SR (see Ferguson & Dyck, 2012, for discussion). When studies based on these models are then discussed in the public via news headlines, the public once again tends to hear about media effects as a "monkey see, monkey do" approach.

But I argue that the time has come to build the consumer into theoretical models both as selectors and processors of media. In effect, I argue for an organism-stimulus-organism-response model (OSOR). The consumer (the organism) selects media based on personality, preferences, mood, motivation, desired emotional impact, and so on, then is exposed to the media. After such exposure, different individuals will process this media differently, finally leading to a response behavior. All such response behaviors are, ultimately, the responsibility of the organism, not the media. The media may give consumers something to reflect on, certainly, but what they do with it is ultimately up to them.

OSOR models would obviously be much more complex than what we've had to date. They would require a new level of sophistication in study design and analysis. However, looking at things from a new perspective could also open up rich avenues for new research. Understanding better how the consumer fits into the media experience may give us a far more sophisticated understanding of media psychology than we have had previously.

THE DIFFERENCE BETWEEN FICTIONAL AND NONFICTIONAL MEDIA

One of the intriguing findings from the research we've looked at throughout the book is that nonfictional media appear to have more impact on consumers than fictional media. This is really interesting! For instance, advertising effects appear to be fairly robust, particularly for younger children. And Cultivation Theory seems to work best for news media as opposed to fictional shows. One interesting question regards how our brains process fictional and nonfictional media differently.

With false advertising, many advertisements might as well be fiction, but the information is presented to us as "true" (of course the same could be said about the dodgy way news media is presented to us as well). It is also clear that people emotionally process violence they know to be real differently from violence they know to be fictional (Ramos, Ferguson, Frailing, & Romero-Ramirez, 2013). Daring to use the language of evolutionary psychology (another controversial area of thought), it may be that humans develop a fiction-detection device of sorts in their minds, which helps them to evaluate the source of information and whether it is worth learning from or how to emotionally respond to it. This may help explain why the transfer of processing from fictional media to real life appears to be weak (Bennerstedt, Ivarsson, & Linderoth, 2012).

Detection of fiction or reality in childhood is obviously not something that turns on like a light switch, although evidence suggests that it begins remarkably early, by about age 3 to 4, and is largely complete by the onset of puberty, around age 10 to 12 (Woolley, Ma, & Lopez-Mobilia, 2011; Woolley & van Reet, 2006). It is not difficult to envision a fascinating line of research built around this premise, examining how children at different ages process information from media, not to mention examining how some forms of media, such as advertising, may try to worm their way around our fiction detectors!

WRAPPING IT ALL UP

As we can see, media psychology is an oftentimes contentious, confusing, hyperbolic, and morally infused field. Arguably, we have often made many more wrong turns than we have right turns. But

I hope that these discussions won't dissuade readers from being interested in or, if students, becoming involved in media psychology. Indeed, this means that there is still a lot of road to be traveled for the media psychologist and lots of room still for new theory and new data that may help us understand media psychology more than we currently do.

And, of course, media isn't going away soon—nor are people's concerns and excitements about it. Policymakers and the general public will continue to have questions about existing forms of media, and as new media continue to be produced, they will have questions about the new media as well (or in many cases, may skip the questions phase and simply come to predetermined conclusions!).

In many ways, media psychology historically has perhaps failed to present a careful and balanced perspective. Too often we have rushed to sound alarms when arguably a more cautious and nuanced discussion would have served everyone better. But it doesn't always have to be this way. Indeed, in my loftier moments, I hope that this book may serve to inspire at least a few people to be a part of the solution to a longstanding problem. It can be done with a change in our scientific culture, a return to objectivity and eschewing advocacy, commitment to open science, preregistering studies, an acceptance of null results when they come, a careful and conservative interpretation of effect sizes, and a willingness to say we don't know when we don't. To use cliché, change always starts with one person.

And, at the end of the day, studying media is fun! People are interested in it, students are interested in it. Media remains an important part of our society, our culture, and often our personal identities. As scientists, studying media psychology is what we do because we love the study of media. How many other people can say they have a job focused on video games or comic books (outside of the producers of media themselves of course!)? Not many people can have their boss walk in on them playing video games and defend it as an essential part of their work function. In fact, I think I'll do exactly that now. Time to wrap up this book and get back to some adventuring. Happy media!

REFERENCES

Bennerstedt, U., Ivarsson, J., & Linderoth, J. (2012). How gamers manage aggression: Situating skills in collaborative computer games. *Computer Supported Collaborative Learning, 7*, 43–61. doi:10.1007/s11412-011-9136-6

Bushman, B. J., Ridge, R. D., Das, E., Key, C. W., & Busath, G. L. (2007). When God sanctions killing: Effect of scriptural violence on aggression. *Psychological Science, 18*(3), 204–207. doi:10.1111/j.1467-9280.2007.01873.x

Coyne, J. C., & de Voogd, J. N. (2012). Are we witnessing the decline effect in the Type D personality literature? What can be learned? *Journal of Psychosomatic Research, 73*, 401–407.

Ferguson, C. J. (in press). Do angry birds make for angry children? A meta-analysis of video game Influences on children's and adolescents' aggression, mental health, prosocial behavior and academic performance. *Perspectives on Psychological Science.*

Ferguson, C. J., & Dyck, D. (2012). Paradigm change in aggression research: The time has come to retire the General Aggression Model. *Aggression and Violent Behavior, 17*(3), 220–228. doi:10.1016/j.avb.2012.02.007

Lang, A. (2013). Discipline in crisis? The shifting paradigm of mass communication research. *Communication Theory, 23*(1), 10–24. doi:10.1111/comt.12000

Markey, P. M., Males, M. A., French, J. E., & Markey, C. N. (2015). Lessons from Markey et al. (2015) and Bushman et al. (2015): Sensationalism and integrity in media research. *Human Communication Research, 41*(2), 184–203. doi:10.1111/hcre.12057

Ramos, R. A., Ferguson, C. J., Frailing, K., & Romero-Ramirez, M. (2013). Comfortably numb or just yet another movie? Media violence exposure does not reduce viewer empathy for victims of real violence among primarily Hispanic viewers. *Psychology of Popular Media Culture, 2*(1), 2–10.

Rentfrow, P. J., Goldberg, L. R., & Levitin, D. J. (2011). The structure of musical preferences: A five-factor model. *Journal of Personality and Social Psychology, 100*(6), 1139–1157. doi:10.1037/a0022406

Rushton, B. (2013). Backdooring it: Defense maneuvers around setback. *Illinois Times.* Retrieved August 20, 2013, from http://www.illinoistimes.com/Springfield/article-11440-backdooring-it.html

Unsworth, G., Devilly, G., & Ward, T. (2007). The effect of playing violent videogames on adolescents: Should parents be quaking in their boots? *Psychology, Crime and Law, 13,* 383–394.

Woolley, J. D., Ma, L., & Lopez-Mobilia, G. (2011). Development of the use of conversational cues to assess reality status. *Journal of Cognition and Development, 12*(4), 537–555. doi:10.1080/1524837 2.2011.554929

Woolley, J. D., & Van Reet, J. (2006). Effects of context on judgments concerning the reality status of novel entities. *Child Development, 77*(6), 1778–1793. doi:10.1111/j.1467-8624.2006.00973.x

Index